D1565279

THE U.S. PRESS
AND IRAN

THE U.S. PRESS AND IRAN

FOREIGN POLICY AND THE JOURNALISM OF DEFERENCE

William A. Dorman and Mansour Farhang

University of California Press

Berkeley   Los Angeles   London

University of California Press
Berkeley and Los Angeles, California
University of California Press, Ltd.
London, England

© 1987 by
The Regents of the University of California
First Paperback Printing 1988
Library of Congress Cataloging-in-Publication Data

Dorman, William A.
    The U.S. press and Iran.

Includes index.
    1. Iran—Foreign opinion, American. 2. Foreign news—
United States. 3. Press and politics—United States—His-
tory—20th century. 4. Iran—Politics and government—
1941–1979. 5. Public opinion—United States—History—
20th century. I. Farhang, Mansour. II. Title.
III. Title: US press and Iran.
E183.8.I7D67 1987   070.4′49955053   86-25032
ISBN 0-520-06472-0 (alk. paper)

Printed in the United States of America

1   2   3   4   5   6   7   8   9

To Pat, Kym, and Chris
                        W. A. D.

To the memory of my parents
                        M. F.

Contents

Contents

Acknowledgments

From our earliest work on this book, we were fortunate to have the intellectual encouragement of our friend and teacher Richard Falk. He has served as a model of compassion and scholarly inquiry for us, and as a model of commitment to a more humane world.

Similarly, from the beginning of this project, we have benefited greatly from the encouragement and thought of Eqbal Ahmad and Robert Karl Manoff. Their friendship has been equally valuable.

Our book in its final version simply would not have been possible without the sympathetic criticism and intellectual generosity of Nikki R. Keddie of the University of California at Los Angeles, our primary reader at the University of California Press. Drawing on a singularly impressive command of Iranian history, her stylistic and substantive comments were invariably on the mark. We are deeply grateful for corrections she offered as well. Naturally, all opinions and remaining errors are the responsibility of the authors alone.

For their part, Julian Colby and Jim Speakman read early drafts of the manuscript far more carefully than even friendship requires, and we were greatly helped by their comments on matters of style and argument.

Julie Kniseley and Thea Wares provided research assistance at a critical moment in the writing of the book. Their contribution was indispensable. Fergel Ringrose and John Hoffman also helped in this regard.

Our editor, Barbara Metcalf, and Jeanne Sugiyama and Gladys C.

Castor of U.C. Press guided us through the thickets of publishing with unfailing good cheer and useful advice. Grant Barnes, then with U.C. Press, gave us much needed encouragement during the early stages of the project.

We are also appreciative of the unstinting moral support of our families, and of many colleagues and friends, in particular Robert Curry, Ron Fox, Paul Goldstene, the late Jack Livingston, Ralph Talbert, and Betty Wolfman of California State University, Sacramento; Gail Russell of Bennington College; and Mohsen and Ghazal Farhang.

We owe a significant debt to Kennett Love, who generously shared with us a wealth of materials on his days as a correspondent in Tehran during the crucial early period of United States involvement in Iran. Throughout our association, his cooperation and patience were without limit.

Too, as the reader will discover, we make liberal use of the work of a wide range of talented scholars and writers, whose names appear in the text and notes. Without their work, ours could not have followed. We particularly want to thank Professors James Bill and Richard Cottam for sharing their insights in interviews.

Finally, we wish to gratefully acknowledge grants from California State University, Sacramento, and Bennington College, which made part of the research and writing of this book possible.

Introduction

    This is a book about how the United States press covered Iran from 1951 to 1978. During the quarter of a century spanned by our study the United States developed unprecedented bonds with Iran. Indeed, even though deep mutual estrangement followed the 1979 hostage crisis, most analysts believe that Iran will continue to have enormous strategic significance for American foreign policy. As Amos Perlmutter, editor of the *Journal of Strategic Studies,* has observed, "Iran, whether its ruler is the Shah or Khomeini or whoever follows him, *has been, is and will be the decisive power in the [Persian] gulf*" (emphasis ours).[1]

    How well did the news media inform the American people about "the decisive power" in the gulf region during its increasingly intimate twenty-five-year association with the United States? Did the press, as democratic theory supposes it should, critically examine the assumptions of policy makers about a country thought to be a major and reliable ally? Did American journalists exercise judgment independent of official Washington in reporting Iranian life under the shah? To what degree did journalism contribute to the "surprise" in the United States at the 1978 revolution? What is the role of the press in the foreign policy setting? In what ways may economics, journalistic practice, ideology, and ethnocentrism affect how the press performs in covering U.S. client states in the Third World? We believe that these questions and their possible answers, which are the substance of this book, should be of interest to students of Iran, the American foreign policy process, the press, the Middle East, U.S.

relations with developing nations, or any combination of these concerns.

While there have been many studies of the media's impact on domestic political affairs, few have concentrated on the role of the press in the foreign policy process, and we know of no study such as ours that examines how the press covered a client state over so long a period of time. Moreover, in our view, the relationship of the United States with Iran provides a particularly strong basis for a scholarly inquiry into the prestige, or elite, press and its bearing on foreign policy in that no other Third World country has figured so prominently in American fortunes since World War II as has Iran.

We should be clear from the beginning that we believe the link between press and policy is enormously complex and subtle. We certainly do not mean to suggest that there is a simple cause-and-effect relationship. But if the press does not *make* foreign or defense policy, in some important ways it helps set the boundaries within which policy can be made. In this respect, the press is usually *affective* in the policy process, rather than determining.

An understanding of how the press covers a United States ally in the Third World is essential to anyone who is concerned about the course of American foreign relations. And we believe our research and analysis have implications that go far beyond a case study of Iran, for there has been no apparent reduction in American involvement abroad in relationships quite similar to the one with the shah. Our treatment of the question of the press and the effects of ethnocentrism and ideology, for example, might apply in any number of situations in the Middle East, Africa, and Asia in which the United States now finds itself involved or is likely to in the future.

In brief, based on an extensive study of twenty-five years of press coverage of Iran by the prestige mainstream print media, our major findings are these: (1) The American news media more often than not followed the cues of foreign-policy makers rather than exercising independent judgment in reporting the social, economic, and political life of Iran under the shah; and (2) journalists proved easily susceptible to ethnocentrism, a condition that served the policy goals of official Washington remarkably well. From these conclusions we will argue that the case of Iran offers compelling new evidence for the contention that the press, far from fulfilling the watchdog role assigned it in democratic theory or popular imagination, is deferential rather than adversarial in the foreign policy arena.

The central failure of the press in the case of Iran, we contend, was to live up to its *own* professed values, not the failure to live up to some utopian set of ideals proposed by critics outside the profession. However, we are not suggesting that the press consciously set out to serve either the shah or U.S. policy makers. Moreover, we should make it clear that we have great respect for the ideal of a free press, and it is precisely because we consider the American press to be free of *external* constraints that we believe it has the potential to make a significant contribution to the formulation of a rational foreign policy. Our standard for criticism of the media throughout is relatively simple: Did the press report what was reasonably knowable about Iran?

Some observers, of course, may argue that what was reasonably knowable in Iran under the shah was not very much, given the closed nature of the society. Now that the shah's empire has collapsed in a heap, the prerevolution weaknesses in the regime are easy to see. But were these flaws discernible from the vantage point of the 1970s (to say nothing of the 1960s and 1950s)?

The contention that hindsight was necessary to recognize the fractured society that was Iran under Pahlavi rule simply does not square with the evidence. Throughout our book we make a point of including mention of observers and journalists—admittedly few in number for reasons we discuss—who as early as 1954 reported accurately on the nature of the shah's regime. We did this precisely to demonstrate what was "knowable" about Iran before the events of 1978.

We also discuss how journalism virtually ignored the voice of Iranian dissidents, unlike those, say, in the Soviet Union, who are listened to with great care. In this regard, Iran was no more difficult to cover as a closed society than the USSR. Moreover, as British journalist and author Martin Walker has observed, "other sources were available. Academics in the West who knew Iranian society and its history were not hard to find. . . . [Some of them] . . . were writing in English, about forces of religious and political opposition, yet remained untapped by the quality press."[2]

A major theme of this work is that throughout the association of the United States with the shah, the press tended to serve Washington's shortsighted policy goals by portraying political opposition to the regime in such a way as to suggest that the shah's critics were nothing more than benighted reactionaries. We argue that this was particularly the case during the 1978 revolution. Undoubtedly, some readers of our book will hold the opinion that, indeed, the outcome of the revolution, which has taken the form of a clergy-dominated state, proves that the press and policy makers were right: Muslims are fanatical and antimodern. They will have uppermost in mind the endless war with Iraq, the persecution of minorities and dissidents, and the repeated charge that the present Iranian government exports terrorism. In short, the stereotypes conveyed by the news media (and the U.S. government and the shah) may seem to some readers to have been confirmed by history.

There is no doubt that the tragic outcome of the revolution itself impedes a full understanding of the complexity of Iranian society by serving a half- or quarter-true stereotype. Yet no more inaccurate conclusion could be drawn by journalists or policy makers than that Iranians in revolt were not engaged in an authentic quest for freedom motivated by long-standing moral, political, and economic griev-ances. To dismiss the aspirations of Iranians as mere fanaticism is to prepare the way for future, equally serious, failures to understand forces at work in the Third World. Therefore, while the question of the revolution's outcome is not the focus of this study, some gener-alizations about what has happened seem necessary.

The revolution was probably one of the most popular in history. It united all classes and most political factions. During the first six months of 1978 the antigovernment demonstrations were composed largely of students and other middle-class opponents of the shah. However, as the vulnerability of the regime became more apparent, the urban poor began to join the demonstrations in ever-increasing number. By September 1978 the lower-class participants in the upris-ings constituted the dominant force of the movement. From this point on the religious leaders were able to direct the course of events be-cause they were much better equipped than their secular counter-parts, both ideologically and rhetorically, to address the grievances of the poor and appeal to their passion in order to sustain momentum. The clergymen of Iran have always been influential among the poor. Most of the people who regularly attend the mosques belong to the impoverished sectors of the population; also, mosques are used as headquarters for charitable activities to aid the poor.

During the second half of the revolution, this historic relationship between the poor and the Shi'i clergy was transformed into an un-precedented revolutionary alliance. On the one hand, the poor simply hoped to improve their marginal existence; on the other, the militant clergy gave priority to the moral objection of the religious traditionalists to the secular changes of the previous fifty years in sociocultural realms. Needless to say, the implications of the diverse motives in the revolutionary movement were not fully understood until the complete seizure of state power by the militant clergy in 1980. Indeed, the political, economic, and social abuses of the regime had caused such intense discontent that the vast majority of the participants in the anti-shah movement paid little attention to the question of what kind of political order could or should follow the collapse of the monarchy. It was assumed that the fall of the shah would necessarily lead to an improvement over the existing situation. Thus the kind or degree of this improvement was not treated as a serious question.

Certainly, by late 1978 the fundamentalist clergy under the surprisingly decisive leadership of Ayatollah Khomaini had come to overshadow all other participants, including the moderate and liberal religious elements, in the revolutionary movement. Yet even so, for about a year following the collapse of the monarchy, Iran witnessed a reasonably open political competition among the ideologically diverse forces that had taken part in the anti-shah movement. The fact that the fundamentalists won the battle and suppressed even the most accommodating of their critics should not lead one to deny the emergence of a short period of noncoercive struggle for power after the fall of the shah.[3]

Throughout the 1978 revolution, the U.S. press approached this complex situation by asserting that the revolt was motivated by antimodern sentiments. This perception led the journalists to conclude that fanaticism and reaction, instead of legitimate grievances, were the primary sources of the revolt. Thus many reporters and commentators can be said to have predicted the rise of clerical fascist or theocratic government in Iran should the shah fall. *Washington Star* columnist Carl T. Rowan expressed this view in the following manner:

> There is something a little eerie about the mass jubilation in Iran over the departure, and apparent defeat, of the Shah of Iran. . . . For all his arrogance and ruthlessness, the Shah used his power in many constructive ways—education of the masses, the emancipation of

women, making Iran an economic and military power. Khomeini's
contribution so far has been largely destructive.[4]

A similar appraisal in *Business Week* in February 1979 argued, "It
is not hard to posit a 'worst possible' scenario should Khomeini take
over. Khomeini's obscurantist religious pronouncements, his anti-
Americanism . . . all portend the kind of chaos that underground
Communist movements well know how to exploit."[5] And a *New York
Times* editorialist, on the shah's leave-taking, wrote of the "stern
Moslem zealot, the Ayatollah Khomeini . . .[who] raises the possi-
bility of a xenophobic government distant from, even hostile to, the
West."[6]

Our point here is that predictions based on prejudice that happen
to come true should not be confused with systematic and evidence-
oriented understanding of a subject, as the more sensible segment of
the horse-betting public is well aware. Furthermore, even though the
possibility of which journalists wrote became reality, it would be a
grave mistake to conclude that fanaticism and antimodernism were
the motive forces behind the Iranian revolution. Just as the rule of
Robespierre and Stalin was not the goal of French and Russian revolutionaries, the fundamentalist despotism of Khomaini was hardly
the objective of the anti-shah movement. Of course, Robespierrism,
Stalinism, and Khomainism must have had roots in the latent political culture of prerevolutionary France, Russia, and Iran, but such a
potential ought not to be confused with the reasons behind mass rebellion against the established regimes. Indeed, no one, journalist or
otherwise, should permit himself or herself to conclude that he or
she knew the outcome of a popular revolutionary movement in advance. For history shows that revolutions, like hurricanes, do not
follow predictable courses. Thus to search for the complex causes of
a successful revolt in the excesses of postrevolutionary developments
is abandonment of analytic curiosity and the desire to learn.

Finally, in this context, journalists and other observers would do
well to remember that the final chapter in Iran's postrevolutionary
history has hardly been written, any more than the excesses of the
Terror were the concluding moments of the struggle for participatory
politics in France.

To minimize the possibility of an impressionistic sampling as the
basis for our analysis, we examined, categorized, and analyzed

everything printed about Iran from 1951 to 1978 in the *New York Times,* more than 1,600 items in all. We used the *Times* as the foundation for our study for several reasons, some of which have theoretical significance, and others, practical. For those who make foreign policy and those who cover it the *Times* is probably the most widely read and influential newspaper in the United States.[7] Our study also revealed that the *Times* had devoted far more space to Iran than had any other periodical in the country, as might be expected of an institution that prides itself on being the national newspaper of record. Finally, the *Times* is the only daily newspaper completely indexed for the period of our study.

In addition to the *Times* we examined everything published from 1953 to 1978 about Iran in the *Christian Science Monitor, Newsweek,* and *Time,* and all articles that appeared for the twenty-five-year period in magazines indexed in *Readers' Guide to Periodical Literature.* In addition, using the dates of critical historic incidents or developments in Iran, we sampled various newspapers over the period of the study to provide a profile of coverage by the country's two major wire services, United Press International and Associated Press.[8] We also sampled the *Washington Post* and the *Wall Street Journal,* using the same critical-incident method. For 1953 and 1978, two particularly critical years in contemporary Iranian history, we sampled other major American daily newspapers as well, including the *Chicago Tribune* and the *Los Angeles Times.*

We do not include extensive discussion of television news, despite the arguable belief that people get most of their news from this medium,[9] or the more convincingly documented assertion that network television news programs devote *proportionally* more attention to foreign affairs than do the print media.[10] There is in the reporting of foreign affairs, we believe, a kind of "trickle-down" journalism at work, with the prestige print media, for the most part, providing the trickle. All the available evidence convinces us that in the area of foreign coverage, television news (and most daily newspaper journalism) tends to echo the themes, explanations, frames, and contexts established by the major print media and the two wire services.[11]

Subjective as our method of analysis may be, we are convinced that a useful examination of today's press performance in many important ways is dependent on an appreciation and a consideration of journalistic nuance, tone, emphasis, and context—none of which readily lends itself to quantification, and all of which we found to be significant dimensions of coverage during the period we undertook to study.

With one notable exception in chapter 2, we do not include the views of individual correspondents. This book does not intend to duplicate what has already been done. The conventional approach to an understanding of journalism in general and foreign correspondence in particular is to ask reporters and editors how they view their work, and chapter 8 is based largely on this literature. But our main contention is that _subjective_ factors are at work of which reporters are largely unaware, and therefore, formal interviews would have yielded little for our specific purposes.

Essentially, at one level, what we have done is to contrast coverage of Iran with scholarly evidence. At the second level, we have used a form of what has been called frame analysis.[12] As we use the term, frames are simply constructions of social reality that result from journalistic decision making about what information to include in a news story, what language to use, what authorities to cite, which nuance to emphasize, and so on. In short, frames are the contexts in which news occurrences are placed by reporters, and we believe that these frames are susceptible to textual analysis in much the same manner as literary texts.

Throughout the book we have tried to use examples that are representative of press performance rather than atypical, and we have concentrated on routine patterns of journalistic performance rather than on exceptions. We are confident that the sheer weight of our evidence will demonstrate that we have not taken the press out of context. Yet we do not claim that the result of our work is "the truth." Neither do we argue that we have avoided all pitfalls. Our effort is intended to produce a tenable and open explanation of the relevant issues through textual analysis.

This book should not be considered a comprehensive study of Iran since 1951. A learned examination of Iran's history, economic development, and religious orientation would be a much different kind of scholarly undertaking. Yet we do include some historical background on Iran and its association with the United States, perhaps even to the annoyance of the area studies or the Iran scholar who has no need for such a treatment. In writing this book, however, we felt it necessary to offer a general historical picture for the benefit of those readers who come from fields such as international relations or journalism. Without some historical orientation, our criticism of press performance in Iran would make little sense to those who do not have a specialist's knowledge of the region.

Finally, in our own writing we have used a more traditional academic scheme of spelling Persian words. However, where we quote or cite others, journalists and scholars alike, we have kept their spellings.

1

Iran, the Press, and Foreign Policy

Before 1978 and the Iranian revolution most Americans had only the vaguest perceptions of the Middle East. Certainly many Americans knew of the Arab-Israeli strife and had come to hold strong beliefs about oil-producing countries in the region following the 1973 embargo. But beyond these emotionally charged subjects there was little knowledge or broader sense of the area or its peoples. After all, the United States had never had direct colonial experience with the region, as had the British and the French. Beyond a small circle of scholars and State Department specialists, therefore, Americans had little interest in or understanding of the area. What most Americans knew of the Middle East came to them through such films as *Lawrence of Arabia* or *Exodus,* or novels such as James A. Michener's *Caravans,* or news coverage of periodic wars and guerrilla forays.

To be sure, sufficient attention had been paid the Middle East in the news media and popular arts, so that Americans hold many stereotypes about the region: harems, belly dancing, cruel punishments, lavish sheiks, oil, feudal governments, and so on for the Arab part, while the Israelis, generally, have come to be viewed as tough, gritty, beleaguered, heroic, outnumbered.[1] Non-Arab countries, like Iran, somehow got lost in the hazy middle distance.

It was unprecedented, therefore, that the attention of so many Americans should come to be riveted on erstwhile Persia almost con-

11

tinuously for so long a period of time: first as a result of the revolutionary drama; next during one of the most traumatic periods of U.S.
history, the hostage affair; then when Iraq invaded Iran; still later yet,
at the time of Iran's turnabout assault on Iraq in July 1982; and most
recently because of revelations in 1986–87 surrounding what has
become known as the Iran-Contra scandal.

The purpose of this book is to examine what the American public
was told about Iran by the press during a close association between
the two countries which lasted fully one-quarter of a century. We will
contrast the journalistic version of reality with what there was to be
known. Such an examination, we believe, combined with an analysis
of how and why the press operates as it does in the foreign policy
arena, has implications that go far beyond U.S.-Iranian relations,
insofar as development in the Third World, political as well as economic, may be the major foreign affairs story of our time.

Our standard for judging the media's performance in Iran is based
on a comparison of what the press said was going on with _what was_
reasonably knowable at the time. We believe that this standard is a
fair one in that (1) it transcends our particular political preferences,
and (2) it asks no more of journalists than they already say they
achieve, and, therefore, it cannot be thought "utopian." Throughout
this book, we attempt to ask, given the American media's vast resources, What is reasonable to be expected of journalists? Do they
open or close questions of political motive and action by using
loaded frames or biased language? What use do they make of available scholarly evidence, particularly evidence provided by anti-
status-quo scholars? Most important, do they remain independent in
their judgments from the foreign policy establishment?

There can be little doubt that the mass media have an educative
function, that they produce learning, whether distorted or not, particularly in foreign news situations about which little is previously
known. During the tumultuous period of the 1978 revolution, for
instance, Americans depended heavily on the mass media, as they
usually do for news of foreign affairs, and despite their cynical, time-
honored claim not to "believe what they read in the newspapers,"
most Americans probably did.

Our contention here will be that contrary to the expectations held
for a free press under American democratic theory, the U.S. news
media's coverage of Iran contributed little to the public's authentic

understanding of that country. Instead, as a result of generally uninformed and often highly ethnocentric, cold-war-oriented coverage of
Iran over the years and particularly in 1978, the American public
was taught many damaging lessons that may take years to unlearn.
We will argue that these lessons, instead of being unfortunate but
essentially harmless, helped make it possible for official Washington
to persist in policies that were contrary not only to the legitimate
national interests of the United States in the region, but to the policy
makers' own stated objectives as well.

It is not our intention here to suggest a conspiracy theory of the
media, in which we do not believe, nor is it our purpose to pursue
what might be termed a "running dog of imperialism" line of criticism. Rather, our view of contemporary press behavior is that it is
deeply rooted in a cold-war mentality that is highly internalized and
is more unconscious than willful. It is a form of spontaneity based
on conditioning—usually it is not conspiratorial.

Our thesis is this: The major shortcoming of American press coverage of Iran for twenty-five years was to ignore the *politics* of the
country. This failure was rooted in the assumption that the political
aspirations of Iranians did not really matter. This was an assumption
shaped and reinforced by the foreign policy establishment and was
given credence by highly West-centered preconceptions and an internalized cold-war-oriented ideology. Implicit in such an assumption
were the beliefs that the Iranian people were incapable of politics,
that they were incapable of self-rule, and that they were incapable of
an authentic desire for freedom. Given these beliefs, which were
held by policy makers and accepted uncritically by journalists, the
1978 revolution could only have come as a surprise to official Washington and the general public.

If the media are to produce undistorted information, within the
inherent range of their capabilities, the journalism profession must
recognize the existence and importance of political culture and the
importance of understanding sociohistorical context. We do not believe that every correspondent must be a cultural anthropologist to
understand politics or revolution in the Third World. We do believe,
however, that reporters must have a basic understanding of the differences between societies and of the inherently interpretive nature of
reporting, which is to say a healthy respect for the dangers of being
culture bound. The methods and information useful for understand-

ing other political cultures are readily available; they are neither mysterious nor particularly costly. Similarly, nothing we will say here is incompatible with the media's own professed values or goals.

In all of this, an argument can be made that the performance of the news media in the foreign policy setting is of little consequence and, therefore, does not deserve close study or understanding. For after all, isn't it true that, unlike domestic politics, foreign policy does not usually interest or excite the average citizen, whose knowledge of it is practically nonexistent? More significant, isn't foreign policy left almost entirely in the hands of elites? What does it matter, finally, whether the press misinformed the American public about U.S.-Iran relations if the press and public opinion are not significant factors in the making or carrying out of foreign policy?

The argument that the media and the public are of little importance in the making of foreign policy because the process is dominated by elites carries with it the peculiar strength of having been advanced at one time or another by those who believe themselves to be realists, idealists, conservatives, liberals, or cynics. Indirect evidence that it is the prevailing view, at least in the academy, can be found in the fact that only one general book-length study of the press and foreign policy has been brought out by a university press.[2] This lack of scholarship and serious attention has meant that consideration of the relationship of the press to foreign policy has routinely been superficial. The press as a factor in foreign policy usually rates only passing mention, and discussions are more often characterized by rhetoric, platitudes, clichés, and unsupported generalizations than by thoughtful analysis.

In sharp contrast to the slight attention paid the relationship of the news media to foreign policy, there is a rich literature concerned with the impact of media on domestic politics, which is based on extensive empirical research and speculative analysis. The critical impact of the media on domestic politics, in fact, is beyond dispute. This disparity in the attention paid domestic and foreign politics and the media is in some ways an extension of the tendency in the larger population to take far closer note of domestic than of foreign affairs, and generally to accept the state's judgment in the latter but not the former.

The arguments most often heard in mitigation against close study of foreign policy, the media, and public opinion are cloaked in the language of realism. Essentially, in its most thoughtful form, the view of a press lacking in critical importance is based on a mistaken interpretation of the inherent limitations of the press as a truth-seeking system and of the limitations of a mass citizenry. What we choose to call inherent limitations theory has been most clearly stated by Walter Lippmann in *Public Opinion*. Lippmann, who came to have little faith in the competence of either the press or public opinion, argued that because news and truth are not the same thing, and because of the average person's tendency to think in stereotypes and susceptibility to propaganda and prejudice, the conduct of political affairs can be left only to experts. According to Lippmann, "The function of news is to signalize an event, the function of truth is to bring to light the hidden facts."[3] The press, Lippmann wrote, plays at best a limited role, functioning like a searchlight that moves "restlessly about, bringing one episode and then another out of the darkness into vision."[4] His biographer, Ronald Steel, has pointed out what was equally important in Lippmann's view:

> Even if the press were capable of providing an accurate picture of the world, the average man had neither the time nor the ability to deal with a perplexing barrage of information. The Enlightenment conception of democracy—based on the assumption that every man had direct experience and understanding of the world around him—was totally inadequate to a mass society where men had contact with only a tiny part of the world on which they were being asked to make decisions.
>
> This ruthless analysis left Lippmann with the conclusion that democracy could work only if men escaped from the "intolerable and unworkable fiction that each of us must acquire a competent opinion about public affairs." The task of acquiring such competent opinions had to be left to those specially trained, who had access to accurate information, whose minds were unclouded by prejudice and stereotypes.[5]

Whether one agrees with Lippmann or not, the significant point to be made in this discussion is that he has often been misunderstood. His normative analysis frequently has been confused with a descriptive one, and his ideas have been used to support the contention that the media and the public are not important variables in the foreign policy process. A careful reading of Lippmann, we think, does not support the conclusion that he believed that the press had no effect or that public opinion did not matter. On the contrary, he was proposing a *normative* alternative to a flawed system that in his view was producing the *wrong* effects.

Indeed, Lippmann's plea was for the citizen to defer to specially trained elites. That such elites were often hampered by an imperfect press and a wrongheaded public was precisely his concern. Far from not intervening in the foreign policy arena, public opinion and the press too often were getting in the way of sensible men. The imperfection and imperfectibility of the press and the public, and not their lack of political effect, therefore, were at the core of Lippmann's argument.

In a variety of ways, the press and public opinion have assumed an even greater importance in the foreign policy process since Lippmann first wrote of his concerns about how competent they were to fulfill the roles assigned them in democratic theory. Following World War II, for instance, the frequently indifferent if occasionally intrusive public of the 1920s of which Lippmann wrote was transformed into a citizenry with far more of a sustained interest in what happens in the world. As historian Robert Dallek has noted:

> Whereas numerous Americans as late as World War II continued to share [William Jennings] Bryan's ignorance of the outside world, this changed rapidly after 1945. The return home of millions of Americans thrown into wartime contact with places as remote as Tunisia and New Guinea and postwar responsibilities as the world's premier power made them more aware of the foreign scene. . . . Burdened with the defense of the "free world," touched in countless ways by the rise of a "military-industrial complex," charged with securing U.S. interests abroad, Americans could no longer turn their backs on world affairs.[6]

Moreover, the rise of television, the country's only truly national medium, and its capacity to dramatize worldwide events visually, created an unprecedented immediacy for the postwar citizenry to foreign affairs, and for good or for ill, probably increased the size of the nominally interested audience for news from abroad of events that appear to affect American interests. The public has been made abundantly aware by television of the "American Century," in Henry Luce's phrase, and of all the privileges and perils such a century may provide. This development, of course, does not necessarily mean that Americans are better informed than they were in Lippmann's time (although they probably are); it means only that they may be paying closer attention.

Most important, as a result of the cold war, Americans acquired for the first time in their history what they perceived as a permanent and intractable enemy: the Soviets. At least psychologically, America embarked upon what seemed to be its own Hundred Years' War. Undergirding this unprecedented sense of perpetual crisis was the specter of nuclear Armageddon. In a sense, what exists now for many Americans, therefore, is a garrison state of the mind, and citizens living in a garrison state cannot help but be concerned about external events.

In a democracy, an aroused or frightened public, which in the final analysis must bear the material and human costs of foreign policy, cannot be ignored in the policy-making process. However, it is in electoral politics that public concern about foreign policy is more likely to make itself felt most directly. In this regard, it is the presidency rather than Congress upon which the public's attention most often comes to focus. Increasingly, it is the chief executive and his closest advisers who are *perceived* by the public as having the ultimate say in shaping foreign policy, instead of Congress or the bureaucracy. Whether the executive branch actually has absolute power is not the issue. Even if the power does not completely reside in the White House, every president since Roosevelt has behaved as if it did, and has done little to discourage the notion that it ought to.

As a result, presidential power and politics now are linked more than ever to foreign policy, and a president's electoral and legislative fortunes have come more and more to turn on foreign policy issues. This is not to say that foreign policy issues have replaced domestic ones or even eclipsed them in electoral politics; it is to argue that how voters perceive an incumbent president's foreign policy record can make an important difference. The nature of this vital difference is rooted in the willingness of Congress and the public throughout the cold war to defer on matters of foreign policy so long as a sitting chief executive stays within the bounds of the bipartisan cold-war consensus and *appears* to be firm in his commitment to seeking an American advantage in world politics (and, equally important, seems to be successful in his quest).

One reason for this deferential attitude may be the widely held assumption that living on the nuclear edge demands decision-making power be concentrated at the top. A second reason may be bipartisan agreement on the Soviet threat. A third reason may be that an activist foreign policy, which the United States has adopted since World War II in its open quest for global power and its confrontation with the Soviets, to be successful, similarly precludes shared decision making. Certainly, the goal of a dominant American liberal capitalism in the world has not bothered Congress, which has demonstrated no sustained willingness to seriously challenge the White House in the formulation of policy until well after a policy appears to be in serious trouble. Vietnam and the national debate which surrounded the United States' role is no exception, for popular concern about the war was aroused only after 1968, when the point of deep American involvement had long passed.

Whatever the explanation, the president usually is allowed to do things with foreign policy that he would never be permitted in the domestic realm. For example, since World War II, a president who is perceived as having a firm grasp on foreign policy has usually been permitted to define the *national interest* arbitrarily in ways in which he would rarely be allowed to define the *public interest* in domestic affairs. A citizenry that would engage in a great and howling debate should a president declare overnight that state-subsidized abortions are in the "public interest," for instance, has proven to be far more willing to accept uncritically a chief executive's judgment to send military aid or U.S. troops to some foreign land, in the "national interest."

Domestic politics, by comparison, is positively messy, and it is far more difficult for a president to establish a clear-cut image of himself as an effective and forceful leader in the domestic political realm. An administration's domestic programs can become bogged down in partisan politics, paralyzed by special-interest groups, or even blocked by the judiciary, and the president's reputation and chances for reelection suffer accordingly. If politics in the last quarter of the twentieth century has evolved toward little more than the art of getting elected (or reelected), as it apparently has, the general perception of the voting public becomes critical. And a positive image in the conduct of foreign policy can give the incumbent or the challenger a decided edge. This, of course, is where the ultimate power of the media resides, for the Lippmannesque pictures of events abroad which are in the heads of the typical voter are put there by the news media, which, after all, serve as the public's primary textbook on foreign affairs.

Where matters of foreign policy are concerned, it is press coverage of discrete events abroad and the media's portrayal of presidential response to those events that create a critically important general mood within the electorate about the competency of the chief executive and the effectiveness of the policy he advocates. In turn, in setting policy, a president ignores this mood at his peril. This mood consists of a vague, generalized set of beliefs and hazy understandings and produces a crude context into which even cruder stereotypes are often fit. Such a mood produces for those it affects, in sociologist Robert Park's terms, *acquaintance with,* rather than *knowledge of.* The difference between the two is critical: it is much easier to manipulate those with only a vague impression of events than those with a fair understanding.

For much of the public, then, the press frames on a day-to-day, situation-to-situation basis a highly generalized *sense of things:* of what is required and of what is not; of who is enemy and who is friend. The press sets the broad limits of our thinking about the "other." According to Prof. Doris A. Graber, a public-opinion and political-communication scholar, it is not necessary for readers to master the discrete detail of a news event for learning to occur. Facts presented in the media can be converted "into politically significant feelings and attitudes" even though the facts themselves are forgotten. Her studies indicate that this seems to happen routinely. Professor Graber has concluded that "general impressions, formed from media stories and other information, are likely to have a more profound impact on political thinking than the specific facts that are remembered only vaguely."[7]

If the frame provided the public by the media coincides with the interpretation of a foreign event offered by the White House, and if the president is portrayed as sure-handed and resolute, all is well and good for the chief executive. If the media come to provide a dramatically different version of events abroad, however, or if a president's actions are characterized as indecisive and ineffectual, the general mood can contribute significantly to political defeat: witness the Johnson and Carter administrations.

A close student of the presidency, James David Barber, has written that "journalism's role in Presidential politics has been significant—sometimes perhaps even decisive—at least since the turn of the century."[8] However, today's age of media politics has some important distinguishing characteristics. According to Barber:

> What is new is not mass communication as one of the major forces in politics, but rather its emergence to fill virtually the whole gap in the electoral process left by the default of other independent elites who used to help manage the choice [of a president]. Their power is all the stronger because it looks, to the casual observer, like no power at all. Much as the old party bosses used to pass themselves off as mere "coordinators" and powerless arrangers, so some modern-day titans of journalism want themselves thought of as mere scorekeepers and messenger boys. Yet the signs of journalists' key role as the major advancers and retarders of Presidential ambitions are all around us.[9]

To be certain, with the age of media politics has come a time in which image has more often than not come to dominate substance, and manipulation has come to replace persuasion. That people can be lied to or made to go along with bad policy, however, does not mean that their opinion does not count. The importance of public opinion, indeed, can be measured in direct proportion to the degree of effort taken to manipulate it, which, as recent history has demonstrated, has been considerable.

If there are some doubts in the academic community about the importance of the press in the foreign policy arena, key players in the U.S.-Iran drama did not share them. Clear evidence of this possibility is contained in the memoirs of the shah and of top officials in the Carter administration. Throughout Hamilton Jordan's account of the last year of the Carter presidency, for instance, the preoccupation of the administration with how the president's actions abroad were being perceived by the electorate is a major theme, particularly as they concerned the hostages. This concern is summed up in an exchange between Jordan, who was Carter's chief political adviser, and a French intermediary acting to end the crisis, who cautioned Jordan not to forget the political pressures in Iran in formulating a plan for the release of the hostages. "Don't forget the political pressures here," Jordan replied. "President Carter will have to be able to publicly explain and defend our actions to the American people. Khomeini doesn't have to run for re-election."[10]

The importance of the media and of public opinion in the making and execution of foreign policy is most pronounced in election years, whether presidential or congressional. Professor Laurence Radway of Dartmouth has argued convincingly that in an election year the public's view of how a president is conducting foreign policy can be a critical factor. Radway believes that the frenetic energy of the modern campaign temporarily enlarges the attentive public for foreign policy issues. Because the temporarily politicized citizen is far less well informed on foreign affairs than the typical member of the attentive foreign policy public, he or she is much more likely to be receptive to boldly nationalistic appeals and prone to "parochial nationalism."[11] To the extent that this is so, it does not seem unreasonable to assume from Radway's analysis that the temporarily politicized citizen is also far less forgiving of a president's perceived bungling away of American advantage, as Carter learned to his dismay.

Crisis situations, whether they occur during a political campaign or not, also temporarily increase the size of the attentive foreign policy audience. These crises can range from the manufactured (the early 1960s missile gap or the rediscovery of a Soviet brigade in Cuba in early 1980) to the very real (the invasion of Afghanistan or the invasion of Lebanon). How the press portrays these events and executive reaction to them can have much to do with establishing the boundaries of policy.

By late October 1980, Carter and Ronald Reagan were running neck and neck, according to polls taken by Pat Caddell of the White House staff. Yet, to the detriment of Carter's hopes for reelection, the anniversary of the hostage-taking fell on election eve. According to Jordan's recollection:

> All three networks concluded not with stories about the Presidential election the next day but with a commemoration of the anniversary of the captivity. . . . Rather than drawing the contrasts between the two men who wanted to be President, the news was a strong reminder of our inability over a long year to win an honorable release of the hostages or to avenge the wrong done us by the Iranians.[12]

Pollster Caddell conducted one final telephone survey following the evening news of 3 November, and then called Jordan early the next morning to tell him:

> The sky has fallen in. We are getting murdered. All the people that have been waiting and holding out for some reason to vote Democratic

have left us. I've never seen anything like it in polling. Here we are
neck and neck with Reagan up until the very end and everything
breaks against us. It's the hostage thing.[13]

In his analysis of the role of the news media in the defeat of Carter, Jordan believes that Carter underestimated the "aggressiveness
and hostility of the White House press" and that those around Carter
did not appreciate the "extent to which the Washington press corps
had changed in the past decade." Jordan believes that Watergate and
Vietnam "pushed the American media from wholesome skepticism
and doubt into out-and-out cynicism about the American political
process generally and the Presidency specifically. Both Vietnam and
Watergate had assumed the coloration of a struggle between the press
and the President."[14]

Yet Jordan's analysis, given the historical evidence, seriously mis-
interprets and overemphasizes the adversary nature of the press.
While there may be evidence that the press has grown more cynical
and less trusting toward the presidency in the past ten years, there
was no such evidence in its behavior toward Iran. The press did not
begin to question Carter's interpretation of events in Iran or his performance until *after* the revolution had succeeded.

Contrary to Jordan's argument, it is remarkable that it took so long
for the press to question official Washington's assessment of Iran.
The honeymoon between president and press, at least where foreign
policy is concerned, tends to last far longer than Jordan would have
us believe, an argument we will make at greater length in chapter 9.
It is enough to suggest here that what has confused Jordan, as it has
many press critics, is the reality that while the press is usually quies-
cent on *strategic* matters and is willing to go along with official
Washington's foreign policy consensus, the news media on occasion
can be exceedingly tough with a president on matters tactical and can
be relentless when (1) contradictions in policy become overwhelmingly apparent; (2) the policy consensus breaks down and elites begin
to defect, opening up public debate; (3) a president seems unsure in
his actions; or, finally, (4) there is evidence of a coverup of some
sort. The point to be made here is that the press does not usually
initiate these conditions; some other force does.

Carter's electoral misfortune, in fact, had deeper roots than the
hostility or aggressiveness of the press corps. For twenty-five years,

as we hope to demonstrate, the press had done little to question the official view of Iran. It was exactly for this reason that the political price extracted from Carter for simply following his predecessors' policies was so high. For a quarter of a century, Americans were told that the country was ruled by a vitally important and progressive ally, whose people were indeed happy and fortunate to have him. Carter happened to be the sitting president when a revolution revealed the myth for what it was. He was no more responsible for the Iranian revolution than Truman was for the Chinese, but it occurred, in one of Carter's favorite Navy phrases, during his watch. The hostage affair, however, is a different matter. His major mistake was to allow the deposed shah into the United States for medical treatment. This disastrous decision, taken despite the best advice, was compounded by Carter's often frenetic and inconsistent attempts to manipulate the crisis for domestic political benefit, his tendency to alternate between tough talk and conciliatory language and between threats and promises, the many plans that came to nothing, and the failed rescue attempt that ultimately proved his undoing.

The late and ill-fated shah, Mohammad Reza Pahlavi, who together with his father, Reza Shah, constituted the short line of the Pahlavi dynasty, had long been convinced of the influence of the American press in the shaping of relations between the United States and their country. Indeed, he saw the American press as his nemesis, despite considerable historical evidence to the contrary.

The first time the Pahlavis showed anger at the American press was in early 1937, when the *New York Mirror* printed an article about Iran in which it was claimed that "Reza Shah had once been employed as a stable boy at the British legation."[15] The Iranian embassy in Washington delivered a note to the State Department threatening to break diplomatic relations unless a correction and an apology were offered to Iran by the newspaper, which, of course, were never forthcoming. Total despot that he was, Reza Shah could not believe that the State Department was unable to order a newspaper to apologize to him.

Although Reza Shah's son, Mohammad Reza, never threatened to sever diplomatic relations with the United States, he was continually annoyed or angered by the Western press's coverage of his performance, even though such coverage was, in the main, exceedingly favorable by usual standards. In his memoirs, the shah repeatedly charged that the Western media practiced a "double standard for international morality: anything Marxist, no matter how bloody and base, is acceptable; the policies of a socialist, centrist, or right-wing government are not."[16] In describing his 1977 visit to the United States, the shah writes: "The friendship shown me by American citizens has always pleased and amazed me. It is in such stark contrast to media accounts, and, alas, government policy."[17]

What seemed to bewilder him even more was that over the years he had "enjoyed friendly contact with the media. Few correspondents of major media who spend any time in Tehran ever had much trouble obtaining an interview. Talks with foreign journalists, no matter how outrageous their questions, always gave me the opportunity to explain my views on major issues."[18] Yet, in spite of such a generous attitude toward the foreign journalists, "too often the media, especially American, came with set notions of what Iran ought to be, rather than what it really was and more importantly what it was becoming."[19]

The shah's three most important ambassadors during the crucial prerevolutionary years were Ardeshir Zahedi in Washington, Parviz Radji in London, and Fereydoun Hoveyda at the United Nations in New York. A major and continuous assignment of these men was to review Western press coverage of Iran and to do whatever they could to prevent or minimize negative publicity about Iran and its supreme leader.

Zahedi's approach to accomplishing his objective was to give gifts, sometimes expensive ones, to journalists, and to entertain at ostentatious parties at which many of America's most prominent journalists could be found.[20] A 135-page log kept by the embassy listed the names of journalists, editors, publishers, newscasters, broadcasting executives, and so on who had either attended embassy parties, been singled out for special courting, or been sent gifts ranging from Cartier silverware sets and tins of Beluga caviar to boxes of pistachio nuts and bottles of champagne. Among those whose names appeared on the list were Walter Cronkite, John Chancellor, David Brinkley, and Joseph Kraft.[21] When news of the gift-giving surfaced after the revolution,[22] some observers were quick to assume that somehow the bribe of a tin of Beluga caviar or a silver gravy bowl from Cartier might buy approval of the shah from a newscaster or reporter, and that the ambassador's largess explained the U.S. media's favorable coverage of the shah's regime.

Zahedi's intentions or hopes to the contrary, such an assumption of corruption is far too simplistic, particularly where journalists making salaries in six or seven figures are concerned. In the first place, some of the gifts were probably personal. The late Stan Swinton, vice-president of Associated Press and director of AP's World Service, said in 1980 that he first met Zahedi in 1948 while on assignment for AP in the Middle East. "He's a friend for a zillion years and I would expect to be on the list," Swinton has said, "and I sent him birthday gifts over the years, too." Swinton added that he stopped accepting the ambassador's gifts in 1976, and that he never received a Cartier salt-and-pepper set he is listed as having been sent in 1977.[23] Commentator David Brinkley has also been quoted as saying he had a close personal friendship with Zahedi.[24]

Another explanation is that Zahedi was merely making a routine public relations gesture to opinion leaders, a widespread practice among foreign embassies in Washington. Bill Moyers of CBS, for instance, who received gifts of caviar and champagne while in the Johnson White House and also when he joined the network, believes this may have been the case. According to Moyers, he did not know Zahedi personally, does not remember ever meeting him, and never covered or wrote about Iran.[25]

Beyond the possibility of personal friendship, which is interesting for reasons other than ethics, or of public relations routine, Zahedi's generosity is probably best explained as evidence of acknowledgment of what he regarded, the shah to the contrary, as a *generally* satisfactory relationship with the press as a whole.[26] In this respect, he had a far better understanding of the reality of press behavior than did the shah.

In sum, the relationship between Zahedi's "gifts" and journalists was far more subtle than the notion of bribery suggests. The gifts perhaps can best be understood as Zahedi's way of recognizing and consolidating what he considered to be a useful relationship. The gifts were not so much causes as they were effects. In this context, it does not matter whether journalists kept the gifts or returned them—as many of them evidently did. The important thing is that the gifts were offered in the first place, assuming, of course, that one does not give such tokens to authentic adversaries. Under this interpretation, it is useful to consider journalists whose names did *not* appear on the list, yet who had written about Iran. For example, the names of I. F. Stone, Fred J. Cook, Timothy Crouse, Frances FitzGerald, and

Gregory Rose, all of whom had written highly critically of the shah's regime, were not on the list.

The embassy's gift list, therefore, is not so much evidence of corruption as it is compelling testimony that the shah's representative perceived Iran's image in the mainstream media as acceptable if not ideal. The character of the relationship between the press and Iran of which Zahedi was protective is suggested by the comments of television's Barbara Walters, who received—among other things—a diamond watch but returned it:

> When Zahedi would come to New York he would have dinners for the empress (Farah) when she was in town. Everyone would be there: Chancellor, Cronkite, you know. As a kind of thank you gift for attending, I would get flowers or a pound of caviar the next day. . . . I think if somebody sends you a flower the next day I'm not going to send back a bouquet to the florist. That gets a little silly. You have to remember *at the time they were not our enemies* (emphasis ours).[27]

Ambassador Radji, for his part, wrote in his diary on 31 December 1976: "Iran's image in the Western press could not be worse; the one single factor most responsible for that image is the practice of torture which, for bureaucratic as much as for moral reasons, ought to be summarily stopped."[28] Mr. Radji once met with editors of the *New York Review of Books* to find out who "was responsible for the nasty things the *Review* had printed about Iran."[29]

To comprehend the shah's attitude toward the Western press, one must keep in mind that it is virtually impossible for dictators to understand or be content with even a mildly critical press. The shah expected always to be praised and under any circumstances. He genuinely believed his was an indispensable and perfect leadership in all aspects and thus regarded any criticism of his actions or intentions as uninformed at best or part of a plot at worst. He, not others, defined reality, and would not tolerate any challenge to his judgment. Like most dictators, therefore, he led a curiously naive life. William Sullivan, former U.S. ambassador to Iran, writes in *Mission to Iran* that when he went to Tehran in the spring of 1977, one of the first lessons he learned was that no Iranian official dared to be candid before the shah when reporting about the socioeconomic conditions of the country.[30]

The shah of Iran was not unique in this respect. Like-minded

holders of power throughout the Third World, whether allied with
the United States or not, similarly feel contemptuous and suspicious
of the Western press. Pinochet of Chile, for instance, and Marcos of
the Philippines both consider the Western press to be a principal
source of their negative international image. Marcos could even
claim that the image of Benigno Aquino, the opposition leader who
was assassinated in 1983 on his return from exile as a political hero,
was wholly a product of Western journalism. Dictators, in short,
resent being questioned about their failures, even though press criticism may not be substantive, sustained, or finally, authentically challenging. They cannot discriminate between a press that may criticize
certain apects of their regimes, but in the main poses no real, long-
term threat, and a press that is an authentic adversary. The point to
be made here is that the hypersensitivity of dictators about their image in the press should not be confused with evidence that the press
is performing as a genuine adversary.

It is some measure of how far the shah was removed from reality,
indeed, that he died believing that the Central Intelligence Agency,
the U.S. oil companies, and the Western press had conspired to overthrow his regime:

> Throughout the history of my country outside forces have contin-
> ually tried to [bring about] the disintegration of Iran. Time and again
> such attempts have been made—in 1907 and 1945–46 they did not
> succeed. Sadly, today they seem to be succeeding.
>
> In 1962, while at a ceremony in San Francisco, I saw a plane over-
> head with a streamer proclaiming "need a fix, see the Shah." Clearly,
> this was part of an organized effort to discredit me and my govern-
> ment. I cannot help but believe that the oil companies, and an orga-
> nization like the CIA were somehow involved in fomenting and fi-
> nancing this campaign against me. . . . For the next twenty years
> students and media echoed the same anti-Iran themes intermittently,
> whenever the West felt my wings needed clipping.[31]

The late shah's paranoia aside, we cannot agree with his assessment
that the American press was either an effective adversary to his conduct or a serious threat to his interests until far too late; we can agree
with his underlying assumption that the press is a major factor in
shaping perceptions about foreign policy, and an important factor to
be reckoned with in the formulation of policy.

To assert, as we have in this chapter, that the perceptions of the public, particularly because of their potential impact on electoral politics, set important limits on the formulation and execution of foreign policy, however, is not to argue for the notion that the people through pressure politics somehow *make* foreign policy, and are, therefore, ultimately and conveniently to blame if things go wrong. Rather, it is to reject the contrary notion that the people count for nothing at all, that foreign policy is wholly the product of elites. If public opinion does not count in the foreign policy process, indeed, then why has the state gone to such lengths to manipulate it? Why, for instance, was a secret history ("The Pentagon Papers") of the Vietnam War required? Why did a succession of U.S. presidents find it necessary to mislead the American public about U.S. involvement in Southeast Asia, in Iran in 1953, in Guatemala in 1954, and so on?

The very fact that there is a long history of concealment and manipulation on matters of foreign policy also points to another important dimension of public opinion: that the American general public may have a far higher moral standard than policy makers will usually admit or intellectuals and the popular press will give it credit for. While it may be true that most Americans are not well schooled in the details of foreign affairs, it may also be true that Americans at the same time expect those who act in their name to do so responsibly, which is to say in a manner that does not endanger the legitimate national interests of the country and in a way consonant with democratic values.

In brief, we are arguing that while public opinion may not be directly responsible for making foreign policy, in an open society it *allows* foreign policy to be made—and carried out. In this regard, it is not necessary in a democracy for public opinion to be vigorously supportive of a particular foreign policy; it is necessary for public opinion not to actively oppose it. For a policy to prevail, passivity is required, together with a willingness to provide the resources, human and material, to pursue it.

As for the press, there are three fundamentally important effects which journalists can have in today's foreign policy arena. The first has to do with the creation of a general mood in the larger public about what a foreign policy consists of and how effectively it is being pursued, an impact we have already discussed. The second effect of major significance which the news media can have on foreign policy derives from its capacity to provide an alternative source of infor-

mation for, and a reality check on, those elites that become directly
or indirectly involved in the policy process. These foreign policy
elites can be classified as (1) political elites, which include party
leaders, publicly elected officials, and high-level appointees; (2) administrative or bureaucratic elites, including the professional foreign
service; (3) interest elites, including the representatives of private
organizations and special-interest groups that are concerned with various aspects of foreign policy; and (4) communications elites themselves, most particularly decision makers in the mass media.[32]

As the foreign policy initiative has tended to concentrate more and
more in the executive branch since World War II, so has the power to
regulate, shape, even dictate intelligence information. Through executive powers of security classification,[33] and by gaining control
over or politicizing the usual intelligence apparatus, the presidency
often is able to control the information with which the foreign policy
community has to work.

If what is sought is a coherent, consistent, and effective policy
(measured by the elites' own standards), such policy can result only
from an undistorted view of the reality of a situation, as opposed to
partisan political need, ideological preference, wishful thinking, or
unbridled imagination. To the extent that journalists provide elites
with analysis and reportage that confirms (e.g., Iran) or challenges
(e.g., occasionally, El Salvador) an administration's version of reality, they make a significant contribution. The news media, if they are
independent in judgment and analysis, can serve as an important
corrective for all levels of the foreign policy community, formal or
informal. Operating outside the usual official information-gathering
system, the press can provide an alternative view that may serve as a
counterbalance to illegitimate or ill-conceived policy. Without such
an independent informational corrective, debate within and without
the official policy apparatus will inevitably be stunted, if not stilled.
Policy will be formulated on a one-dimensional basis, and "intelligence surprises," such as the Iranian revolution, will persist.

This reality suggests a third vitally important, if less obvious, way
in which the mass media may interact with the foreign policy process. Whether an ember of public dissent from official policy ever
becomes a threatening flame has much to do with how the dissent is
presented in the mainstream media. Is a criticism given legitimacy
by the media, or is it ignored, denigrated, or framed in such a way

that there is no opportunity to persuade decent opinion? Are dissenters, either here or abroad, portrayed as worthy of a fair hearing, perhaps even admiration? Or are they depicted as political outlaws whose complaints are as dangerous as they are unfounded? Certainly the behavior of the press during a time of national preoccupation with a foreign policy issue can have everything to do with how open and diverse any debate will be.

We will argue that the press, by deferring to rather than challenging the official policy consensus, played a significant part in stilling dissent against U.S. policy in Iran, particularly during the year of revolution. How the press portrayed Iranians in revolt cut the revolutionaries off, for the most part, from an important segment of American public opinion, created by the Vietnam experience, that might otherwise have been sympathetic to their struggle. The press also denied the attentive foreign policy public and opinion elites a much-needed corrective to the assumptions of a succession of administrations. The result was that neither the best interests of Iran nor those of the United States were served.

To make our case we have organized this book around what we see as the five major and distinct periods of American press coverage of Iran. The first period was from 1951 to 1953, during which the United States first became importantly involved in Iran by assisting in the overthrow of a popular, elected prime minister and helping to "restore" the Pahlavi regime. The second period lasted from 1954 to 1963, a time in which the shah consolidated his power and built the foundation of a police state while largely escaping the critical attention of the U.S. press. The third period, from 1963 to 1973, was the time of the shah's modernization program, which received largely favorable comment in the U.S. press. The fourth period, 1973 to 1977, was a time of quadrupled oil revenues as a result of Iran-led OPEC price increases, and the one period during which the shah was subjected to sustained criticisms of any sort in the U.S. media. The fifth period covers the year of revolution, 1978.

2

Mosaddeq and the U.S. Press: 1951–1953

Before World War II, the influence of great powers in the internal affairs of Iran was limited to Great Britain and Russia. Up to that time the American presence in Iran was insignificant. During the war, however, the United States played a decisive role in the British and Russian efforts in the country. The operation of the Lend-Lease Act in the region, for instance, led to participation by the United States in the Middle East Supply Center. And from 1942 to 1945 the United States Army was in charge of the Trans-Iranian Railway and controlled the southern parts of Iran to get urgently required materiel to the Russians at the Eastern Front. Too, during the war it became apparent that the importance of oil as a source of energy was going to increase beyond all expectations. This recognition would lead before long to competition between the United States and the British for Middle Eastern oil. At that time the British were in control of the petroleum resources of Iran and Iraq. The United States controlled only the deposits in Saudi Arabia.

The National Front movement in Iran after World War II, and the nationalization of the Iranian oil industry, set the scene for the first open competition between the British and the United States. A coalition of diverse liberal-left groups and progressive or anti-imperialist religious leaders, the National Front was led by the enormously pop-

31

ular Dr. Mohammad Mosaddeq. The National Front's unifying objective was to nationalize the Anglo-Iranian Oil Company and to end British interference in the internal affairs of the country.

During the war the Iranian army had been aided by United States advisers and later was provided with equipment and training. Once on the Iranian scene, the United States quietly encouraged the National Front in its challenge to the British, at the same time continuing to support the shah and the army. The strategy of the United States severely limited the British and Russian ability to influence this phase of Iranian national development.

The Truman Doctrine provided the ideological basis for the deepening military-political involvement of the United States in Iran. The doctrine had two interrelated objectives: (1) to contain the revolutionary or potentially revolutionary movements in the underdeveloped world; and (2) to maintain order and stability within the established framework. Where Iran was concerned, it meant suppressing those forces that challenged the existing structures of power; it meant, in effect, supporting a repressive and inequitable socioeconomic system. Thus from its inception U.S. policy in Iran perceived the forces challenging the status quo as hostile to American interests.

Mosaddeq won his immediate battle against the British and became prime minister in 1951, but his victory was only the beginning of a confrontation between the forces demanding reform and the shah as the personification of the traditional order. Mosaddeq was opposed by both the right wing (the landlords, the court, conservative religious leaders, and most of the high-ranking military officers) and the Tudeh party (Communist Party of Iran), which, following the Soviet line, regarded him as a front for U.S. imperialism. For the Soviet-controlled Tudeh, unconditional support for the Soviet Union came before everything else, and during this period the Soviet Union opposed nationalization of Iran's oil and demanded oil concessions in the northern part of the country as a price for withdrawing its troops from Azerbaijan.

For its part, the United States at the historically critical moment of 1953 took the lead against the Mosaddeq government and by so doing gave new life to the conveniently cynical view of its imperial predecessors that Iranians had no capacity for popular self-rule; the best the country could hope for was a stern ruler under the tutelage of a benevolent Western power.

The twenty-seven months of Dr. Mohammad Mosaddeq's premiership can be described as a highly passionate experiment in democratic politics, which was undermined by internal disunity and external pressure; conflicts within the country would once again leave it vulnerable to intrigue and interference from outside.

What the various factions and personalities of the National Front government had in common were sensitivity to foreign interference and opposition to domestic dictatorship. Mosaddeq was the personification of this oppositional unity. It was only through him that the diverse elements of the Front identified with one another.

The National Front coalition, however, suffered from serious organizational and ideological weaknesses. Equally important, Mosaddeq failed to appreciate the radical implications of his own goals. The Front had two objectives: nationalization of the oil industry, which was carried out in 1951 before Mosaddeq actually became premier, and the holding of free parliamentary elections throughout the country.

The efforts to bring about economic and political reforms were destined to create confrontations between Mosaddeq's government and the court. At the same time, the inability or unwillingness of the National Front to organize a popular base made the coalition vulnerable to the machinations of the courtiers and their foreign backers, first Britain and later the United States. The CIA-sponsored coup in 1953 obviously was a cruel act against a popular government, but the easy success of the conspirators was made possible by the Front's own weaknesses and divisiveness. The reasons for the political downfall of Mosaddeq aside, what is relevant to this study is an examination of how the press portrayed his tenure and shaped the views of the attentive foreign policy publics and elites in the United States.

It is the theme of this chapter that the American press, which had paid scant attention to Iran before U.S. involvement in the country, when confronted with the task of explaining the political complexity of the National Front years, adopted an approach that would presage coverage of Iran's revolution some twenty-five years later: Journalists followed the lead of official Washington and opted for simple themes that matched Western conceptions of Middle Eastern peoples and neatly fit within the context of the cold war. As a result, Mosaddeq at his political end appeared in the press as a highly irrational and discredited leader, a portrayal that could not help but serve the purpose of those who had planned the coup.

Mosaddeq had first attracted national attention in the early 1920s when as a young political leader he was one of the few members of the majles (parliament) to actively opppose Reza Khan's early moves to expand his power. A Western-educated liberal intellectual from the upper classes, Mosaddeq was forced into political silence when Reza Khan became shah, but reemerged as a political force during the early 1940s following the shah's forced abdication. By 1947, when the Iranian government entered into renegotiations of oil concessions with the British, Mosaddeq was the leading nationalist voice. Led by Mosaddeq, the National Front scored major gains in the parliamentary election of 1950, which turned largely on the question of oil, and the new majles voted in the spring of 1951 to nationalize Iran's oil. Mosaddcq became premier soon after.

A close examination of American press coverage for the period from 1951 to 1953 suggests that there were several distinct phases in press treatment of the postwar oil crisis. Each phase had an accompanying dominant news frame, and each shift in news frames followed, more or less, a change in official Washington's definition of the political situation in Iran.

The first frame was prevalent during early negotiations between Iran and the British over oil concessions. During this phase, U.S. officials saw an opportunity to gain a foothold for American companies at the expense of British interests and were generally supportive of Iranian demands, sufficiently so that Mosaddeq mistakenly assumed that the United States would remain neutral even after nationalization. The press during this period, by and large, portrayed Iran's position in relatively evenhanded terms.

Once nationalization occurred, however, U.S. policy makers became alarmed at such a radical action and reversed field to support the British in a variety of ways. At the same time, a new frame began to take shape in the press. Suspicion toward Mosaddeq verging on open hostility replaced a more moderate perspective.

Over about a two-year period, then, Mosaddeq's portrait would change from that of a quaint nationalist to that of near lunatic to one, finally, of Communist dupe. As historian Nikki Keddie has noted, "Mosaddeq was pictured increasingly but inaccurately as a dangerous fanatic, likely to deliver Iran to the Soviets. In fact he was an anti-imperialist nationalist who intended to keep Iran from being controlled by any foreign country or company."[1]

Major news-frame shifts on foreign policy issues in the American prestige press seem rarely to occur so clearly or quickly that they are immediately discernible at the time they are taking place. Such shifts are usually gradual and occur over transition periods characterized more by subtle changes in emphasis and tone than by stark evidence of reversal. For instance, nationalization was not so stridently denounced in the *New York Times* at the time it took place as it would come to be as time passed. Nonetheless, the *Times* greeted the move with stern disapproval, if not outright condemnation, in an editorial headlined "Recklessness in Iran."[2]*

And the *Times* man in Tehran at the time, Michael Clark, offered this interpretation in a Sunday news analysis:

> Moreover, Iran has this in common with the rest of Asia: A wave of nationalism has swept over it. An articulate minority thirsts for a victim through which a blow might be struck at that greater enemy, Western imperialism. Here the required victim was found ready made in the form of the [British] oil company. The process was greatly accelerated by fear derived from the activities and pronouncements of Moslem fanatics specializing in political assassination. An atmosphere of insecurity and perpetual menace pervaded the weak councils of the Government.[3]

Nowhere in this piece or in other prestige-press coverage of the 1951 nationalization was there a serious look taken at the specific grievances of Iran toward British oil interests, nor was Britain's historical role in Iran explored in any depth. The press was content to portray the British as relatively innocent bystanders, caught in a whirlwind of fanaticism and mindless nationalism.

The theme of rule by terror was also raised by the *Times*. Reporter Clark, in an article headlined "Terrorism Called Silent Ally in

---

*In our view, editorials can be important evidence in the study of the press and foreign policy. First, editorials often offer the first indication of a news-frame shift. Second, members of the attentive public who know little about a foreign situation may well take their cues on a given situation from editorials in authoritative publications. Third, members of the policy-making elites may be directly or indirectly influenced, intimidated, or reinforced by editorial expression in the prestige press. Finally, decision makers in other media, who may be uncertain themselves about a foreign news situation, may follow the editorial lead of the major national press, which can lead to the widespread acceptance of specific news frames.

Triumphs of Mossadegh," began his dispatch by asserting, "Premier Mohammed Mossadegh's remarkable 90-to-0 vote of confidence in the Majlis . . . last Sunday was not achieved without assistance from his stealthy, ever-present partner—incipient terrorism."[4]

The press for the most part readily came to accept the underlying assumptions of Washington, which were caught in a remarkable 1952 assessment of U.S. interests and objectives in Iran written as a briefing paper for the president, apparently without any appreciation of the contradictions it contained:

> (1) Our primary objective is the maintenance of Iran as an *independent country* aligned with the free world. A secondary objective is to assure access of the Western world to Iran's petroleum, and as a corollary to deny access to the Soviet bloc (emphasis ours).
>
> (2) In pursuance of our primary objective, it is the policy of the U.S. to extend to Iran, primarily through the Shah as the only present source of continuity of leadership, political support and military, economic, and technical assistance whenever this will help serve to: (a) increase stability and internal security, and strengthen the ability and desire of the Iranian people to resist communist subversion, (b) strengthen the leadership of the Shah and through him the central government, and (c) demonstrate the intention of the U.S. to help preserve Iranian independence.[5]

For the most part, the press went along with what would prove to be the U.S. State Department's self-fulfilling prophecy that the shah was the only source of political stability and continuity in Iran. Within the framework of Washington's analysis, Mosaddeq obviously was not such a source. *Time* magazine set the tone when it named Mosaddeq "Man of the Year" in 1952, a practice that many confuse with an honorific title. (To the contrary, *Time's* choice is merely based on its editors' estimate of what person or group has "done the most to change the news, for better or worse," as they had to explain to furious American readers during the hostage crisis when they picked another famous Iranian for the 1980 award: Ayatollah Khomaini.)[6] Indeed, *Time* captioned its cover picture of Iran's democratically elected premier with the assertion "He oiled the wheels of chaos," and wrote the introduction to its cover story as a fable, which began:

> Once upon a time, in a mountainous land between Baghdad and the Sea of Caviar, there lived a nobleman. This nobleman, after a lifetime

of carping at the way the kingdom was run, became Chief Minister of
the realm. In a few months he had the whole world hanging on his
words and deeds, his jokes, his tears, his tantrums. Behind his grotesque antics lay great issues of peace or war, progress or decline,
which would affect many lands far beyond his mountains.[7]

The article continued in this vein, and contended that the nobleman
(read Mosaddeq) had "increased the danger of a general war among
nations, impoverished his country and brought it and some neighboring lands to the very brink of disaster. Yet his people loved all
that he did, and cheered him to the echo whenever he appeared in the
streets." The article referred to him subsequently as a "dizzy old
wizard" who had put "Scheherazade in the petroleum business and
oiled the wheels of chaos," while his "acid tears had dissolved one
of the remaining pillars of a once great empire."

Consistently, throughout its coverage of the Mosaddeq era, the
mainstream American media made much of Mosaddeq's flamboyant
style, his penchant for the dramatic gesture, and portrayed him, in
Time's words, as "by Western standards an appalling caricature of a
statesman."[8] At one point in the oil crisis, *Newsweek* began an article, headlined "Mellow Mossy," with this description: "Premier
Mohammed Mossadegh did not faint once. He shed no tears. He
acted as a normal human being."[9] There was no attempt by the press
to place his "antics," including bouts of weeping, press conferences
conducted while he was wearing pajamas, and outbursts of temper,
in the context that such behavior was seen as acceptable in a culture
in which public display of emotions is perfectly normal and in a
society without democratic institutions, which is, therefore, given to
a highly personalistic form of politics. As Richard W. Cottam has
remarked, "Partly because of his histrionics, Mossadegh was able to
bring to Iranian nationalism a personal leadership that soon became
symbolic."[10] If Americans had known more of Iranian history, they
might have better appreciated why Iranians enjoyed so much the pos-
turing of Mosaddeq, in that his actions were interpreted as an expression of self-assertion in confronting the outside forces which for
years had interfered in the affairs of the country.

The version of history offered by *Time* deserves an extended analysis, insofar as it reflected the consensus media view of the period
that the toxin of nationalism had to be kept from spreading in the
Middle East. According to *Time*, in a passage only faintly critical of

Great Britain, "The Anglo-Iranian Oil Co. (AIOC), most of whose stock is owned by the British government, had been paying Iran much less than the British government took from the company in taxes. The U.S. State Department warned Britain that Iran might explode unless it got a better deal," but the British would not listen. Consequently, Mosaddeq nationalized the nation's oil, "much to the surprise of the British." As a result, in *Time's* estimate, (1) the West lost access to Iran's oil; (2) the Iranian government lost the oil payments; (3) this loss stopped all hope of economic progress for the country; and (4) in the ensuing chaos, the Tudeh party had made great gains.[11]

Time concluded its history lesson by listing "five grim conclusions" that constituted the "consensus" of U.S. correspondents in the region. Three of them are of particular interest in this discussion, in that they would appear to have a remarkable political shelf-life, which is to say that they were as prevalent in the popular press and Washington in 1978 as when first voiced in 1952. "If left to 'work out their own destiny' without help," wrote *Time,* "the countries of the Middle East will disintegrate. The living standard will drop and political life become even more chaotic." The second assumption was no less self-assured, paternalistic, and ominous: "Left to themselves, these countries will reach the point where they will welcome Communism." The third assertion is perhaps the most crucial one because of the historical record that has been written since it was published: "The United States . . . will have to make the West's policy in the Middle East, whether it wants to or not."[12]

The themes, then, that would permeate coverage of the 1978–79 revolution were clearly sounded by *Time* some twenty-five years earlier: Iran was portrayed as a country incapable of self-rule and in need of a Westernized guardian; Iran must be seen as particularly easy prey to the lurking Communist menace, and the United States, reluctantly or not, must fill the "power vacuum" created in the Middle East by the end of the colonial era.

Beyond any interest it may hold as an evidence of the historical continuity in press coverage of Iran, there is the question of what *Time's* history narrative left *out.* Errors of omission, then as well as now, are often more significant than errors of commission. For instance, *Time* and other news media in 1952 pictured Iran as a backward sort of place held under the sway of a petulant and decidedly odd old man, whose Anglophobia would prove to be the ruination of the country. Why Iranians might be predisposed against the British received only scant attention; in *Time*'s five-page "Man of the Year" cover story, for example, the question of British involvement in Iranian oil is given one short paragraph. There is indeed a reference to the "hatred of Britain" in the Middle East, and the assertion that "the British position in the whole area is hopeless," but in the specific context of Iran, these considered judgments were more than offset by the article's overall judgmental tone, denigration of Mosaddeq, and almost total lack of supporting detail on British involvement.

More to the point, American readers might have been able to understand the Mosaddeq phenomenon better if they had been told that (1) the Anglo-Iranian Oil Company (AIOC) had been paying Iran royalties fixed under a 1933 agreement, while oil prices and AIOC profits had tripled during that time; (2) Iran had no management say in the AIOC, not even the right to see the books; and (3) Iran was forced to pay an undiscounted rate for oil used for its own consumption.[13] According to one estimate, the AIOC had a net profit from 1945 to 1950 (after high British taxes had been deducted, along with royalties and "exaggerated depreciation figures") of £250 million. Royalties paid Iran for the same period amounted to £90 million.[14] According to another estimate, between 1913 and 1951 Anglo-Iranian grossed $3 billion, of which only $624 million went to Iran's government.[15] In our study of prestige-press coverage during this period, we could find not a single publication that spelled out these details for readers, let alone systematically reminded them of the facts. The so-called routine, or "drum-beat," coverage, with its formulistic phrases, background information, frames, and labels, was of a decidedly different, anti-Mosaddeq, nature.

The most glaring omission from *Time*'s account of events in Iran, however, dealt with its assessment of the "suicidal" effects of nationalization of the oil resource. From most media accounts and from *Time*'s treatment of the subject, readers could be forgiven if they received the clear impression that Iran's economic woes following nationalization were entirely of its own making. *Time*, it will be remembered, told its readers that because of nationalization, the West had lost access to Iran's oil, and Iran, in turn, had lost its oil revenues. (Actually, there was an oil glut at the time, and there is evidence that American companies were helped—not hurt—by the boycott of Iranian oil.) Such a simple equation represented a view that was incomplete at best and grossly distorted at worst, in that the deteriorated economic situation was, in large part, the result of an unofficial but highly effective worldwide boycott of Iranian oil organized by the AIOC after Mosaddeq's move to nationalize the oil fields. The boycott, which was unanimously joined by American oil companies and enforced by British gunboats, and which the the *New York Times* supported editorially,[16] was what deprived Iran of badly needed revenues.[17]

As a result of the boycott, Iranian oil production dropped from 243 million barrels in 1950 to 8 or 9 million barrels in 1952 and 1953; AIOC found substitute crude in Iraq, where production increased by 189 million barrels.[18] Moreover, in further retaliation, the British restricted Iranian trade in other areas and set unfavorable rates for converting Iranian bank deposits in England.[19] To compound problems, the U.S. government turned down a badly needed loan to Mosaddeq's government, which had previously been implicitly promised.[20] In short, Iran's desperate economic position was not simply the result of having lost British oil-field technicians or its lack of a petroleum-distribution system, as the popular press often made it sound, and the West had hardly been cut off from Iran's oil involuntarily.

Throughout the crisis brought on by nationalization, the press interpreted the American role as one of "honest broker,"[21] walking a righteous line of neutrality between an aggrieved Great Britain and an irrational Iran, despite the fact that the United States government was doing its best, deliberately or not, to undermine Mosaddeq's chances of survival. Only one such example of this journalistic approach was a 1952 *New York Times* editorial praising Secretary of State Dean Acheson's appeal to Mosaddeq and the majles to accept a joint proposal made by President Truman and Prime Minister Churchill for settlement of the oil dispute. Acheson's "unprecedented public appeal," the *Times* assured its readers, was an "effort to save Iran from national suicide,"[22] a much-favored term throughout the press. In making this appeal, according to the *Times,* Acheson was rejecting the "efforts of Mossadegh fanatics not only to exploit the conflict between the West and Soviet Russia for their own profit but also to play off the United States against Britain."[23] Yet in the judgment of at least one recognized Iran scholar, "The British and Americans involved were unwilling to allow Iranians really to control their own oil, while the Mosaddeq government would not settle for less."[24]

What the mainstream press left out in its analysis of the nationalization crisis was only a precursor of a much larger failure that would occur in its coverage of the 1953 CIA-planned and executed coup that overthrew Mohammad Mosaddeq in August of 1953. This failure centered on the willingness of the press to ignore, overlook, or dismiss the possibility of United States involvement in the affair.

Given the press's systematic denigration of Mosaddeq, his government, and his aspirations during the slightly more than two years of his rule, it might not have made much difference to Americans had they known of their government's involvement in the overthrow of the premier. The U.S. press was particularly hard on Mosaddeq during the six months preceding his overthrow. The two major focal points of press coverage throughout this period were Mosaddeq's personal political ambitions and what was perceived as the increasing vulnerability to communism of Iran under his rule.

In the first instance, the press repeatedly raised the specter of a Mosaddeq dictatorship in Iran, the last time American journalism would demonstrate much concern for consensus politics in Iran until after the revolution of 1978. The word "dictator" to describe Mosaddeq, for instance, was used routinely throughout 1953 by the *New York Times* and other elements of the prestige press. By contrast, that identification or its variation was used only on three occasions in the *Times* to describe the shah during the twenty-five years following the coup.

As early as August of 1952, the *Times* seemed to have made up its mind about Mosaddeq. An editorial dealing with the oil dispute began, "Having established himself as the nominal dictator of Iran, Premier Mossadegh has formally submitted to the British government another offer to negotiate a settlement of the oil dispute which brought him to power and his country to bankruptcy and mob rule."[25] The *Times* editorialist added this qualification to the nature of Mosaddeq's power: "First of all, he is a dictator only by proxy from a murderous mob."[26]

As the events of 1953 moved toward their eventual summer climax, and a beleaguered Mosaddeq, in the face of right-wing internal opposition and foreign economic and political intrigue, turned more and more to authoritarian methods to keep control of a rapidly deteriorating situation, the American press, led by the *Times*, sounded an increasingly shrill alarm. In early August, for instance, Mosaddeq called for a plebiscite to dissolve what by this time had become a largely chaotic and uncooperative majles. The plebiscite, admittedly a political ploy whose procedures were deeply flawed, nevertheless did not deserve the treatment the *Times* accorded it editorially: "A plebiscite more fantastic and farcical than any ever held under Hitler or Stalin is now being staged in Iran by Premier Mossadegh in an effort to make himself unchallenged dictator of the country."[27]

On the eve of the coup that overthrew Mosaddeq, a confused time in which the shah appeared vanquished and fled Iran—very temporarily, as it would turn out—and it looked as though Mosaddeq had prevailed, the *Times* began its editorial on the situation with this thought: "In a confused and so far bloodless revolt . . . Premier Mossadegh appears to have made himself the absolute dictator of Iran, who, in the Persian tradition, may be reaching for the throne itself."[28]

Among other major American newspapers echoing the *Times*'s concern about whither Iran were the *Washington Post* and the *Wall Street Journal*. In a lead editorial on the shah's seeming defeat, the *Post* told its readers:

> The Shah has been thrown out by a strong man whose fanaticism has led him into the embrace of the Communists. Precisely what will happen now no one can tell, but it is fairly certain that the only possible beneficiary of Dr. Mossadegh's grab of complete power will be the Communist Tudeh Party and its mentor—Russia.[29]

The *Journal*'s editorial on the supposedly successful ouster of the shah, headlined "Rise of a Dictator," told readers, "Dictators come in various sizes and shapes, but they all come the same way. They come like Mossadegh by emotional appeals to their countrymen and their designs are always the same: A search for complete power."[30] The editorial writer then goes on to compare Mosaddeq's rise to the careers of Mussolini, Hitler, Stalin, Perón, and Huey Long.

The issue of Mosaddeq's conduct during the final months of his government goes to the core of an important concern that runs throughout this study: the interpretive dimension of journalism in the foreign policy setting. In this regard, there seems little historical doubt that Mosaddeq turned to increasingly undemocratic means during the last hectic days of his political struggle. According to

Prof. Richard W. Cottam, who has written the standard study of nationalism in Iran, "[Mosaddeq] who had been devoted to liberal democracy now accepted dictatorial leadership and even staged a typically totalitarian plebiscite in which over 99 per cent of the people voted as he wished."[31] While we happen to disagree with Cottam's use of the word "totalitarian," the point to be made here is that Cottam made the claim only after carefully presenting the situation in which Mosaddeq found himself and his country in the summer of 1953. This the press utterly failed to do.

By the spring of 1953 Mosaddeq not only was faced with the enormous consequences of the oil and credit boycotts, but had to contend with a formidable internal opposition force consisting of big merchants, many landowners, most of the royal court, right-wing clerical leaders, and not least, general officers of the armed forces.[32] Moreover, the National Front was beginning to split under various pressures. In what proved a decisively disastrous tactic, in May 1953 Mosaddeq wrote a letter to President Eisenhower making a final plea for aid, which had been denied by both Truman and Eisenhower, in which he strongly hinted that Iran might be forced to go Communist should the United States fail to deliver. Eisenhower ignored the ploy and turned down the request in a June response. The president's letter was made public and, according to Cottam, broadcast to Iran over the Voice of America. "All Iran knew that Mossadegh had gambled and lost in his attempt to force the United States into active support."[33] It was at this low point that Mosaddeq began to move away from procedural democracy.

Ironically, as Cottam suggested elsewhere in his study, had Mosaddeq been less committed to democratic process earlier in the struggle and suppressed the Tudeh (Communist) party and the feudalistic right, he might have been in a far better position to deal with the oil crisis.[34]

Whatever the reasons for Mosaddeq's changed behavior late in the struggle, the point under discussion here is how his behavior itself was interpreted by the press. Aside from the plebiscite, his style of rule was far more democratic than anything Iran had known. He did not suppress the press during his term, nor did he order the arrests of opponents. He organized no secret police, and his tenure did not give rise to torture. Yet the American press was quick to label him a dictator, which it never did with the shah, whose regime for nearly a quarter of a century systematically engaged in all of the practices mentioned above.

What is at issue, therefore, are not facts themselves, but rather the interpretation that facts receive; what matters, at least in this discussion, is not the behavior itself, but rather the context in which it is placed. Context and emphasis in journalism are everything, for they transform literal truths into reassuring and legitimate acts in one instance, or threatening and illegitimate behavior in another. In this regard, it is no exaggeration to say that the *Times* demonstrated more concern for Iran's constitutional system during the single month of August 1953 than it would during the following quarter of a century.

One of two American journalists—the other was Don Schwind of the Associated Press—continuously in Tehran during Mosaddeq's final months was Kennett Love of the *New York Times*. Looking back on the turbulent summer of 1953, Love has said he always believed that Mosaddeq was a "reasonable man" acting under unreasonable pressures. He scoffs at the use of the term dictator to describe him.[35] Throughout his own reporting, Love did not use the term "dictator" himself, and his dispatches seem relatively evenhanded when compared with *Times* editorials at the time. According to Love, the *Times* editorial writers never consulted him for background on what was happening in Iran, and the shrill anti-Mosaddeq stance of the *Times* editorials was the result of the "ivory tower" judgment of an editorial board that, in Love's phrase, was "obtusely establishment."[36]

The other central interpretive failure of the press in 1953 was to put the Communist threat in perspective. Perhaps that was an impossible task for journalists working the early 1950s, given the mood of the United States and its leadership. Whatever the circumstances, the media during the last eight months of Mosaddeq's tenure seemed only too willing to share Washington's concern about the Communist role and the possibility of a Soviet takeover in Iran. Interestingly enough, much of the reporting from Iran during 1951 and 1952 had been relatively careful—compared with the reporting that would follow—to draw distinctions between the Tudeh and the National Front, to point out Tudeh contempt, suspicion, and hatred of Mosaddeq (which he returned), and to avoid broad generalizations about Communist influence. However, these distinctions came to be blurred in 1953 as the Tudeh, which had been outlawed in 1949, became more of a visible force in anti-U.S. demonstrations. According to Love, the new tack was due largely to the efforts of Loy Henderson, American ambassador to Iran at the time and a fervent cold warrior, who pressed his view of the Communist threat on every correspondent who came to Iran and whose reports to the State Department had the same effect. All perspective, particularly in editorials, seemed lost when Mosaddeq played his Communist-threat card in May of 1953.

Two analyses of the Communist influence and the Tudeh role in Iranian politics, written back-to-back in mid-January by Clifton Daniel of the *New York Times,* avoided stark predictions but still interjected dark hints. The beginning of the first piece, for instance, read: "Standing in the shadows, watching the present struggle between the rival leaders of the Iranian nationalist movement, there is a sinister and enigmatic force, Iran's Tudeh (Communist) party."[37] Neither piece dealt at all with the popular antipathy to communism in Iran, nor with traditional and virulent Iranian suspicion toward Russia, a common failure of American journalism throughout the period.

By early March a *Newsweek* headline announced that the "World's Eyes Are on Teheran; Moscow Holds Peace-War Key." The accompanying article, in a remarkably detailed anticipation of the domino theory, advised readers:

> The situation is such that the West may at any instant face the choice of occupying south Iran or watching the entire country go Communist by default. If Iran goes, then Pakistan—where the Reds have done a remarkable job of infiltration—would probably be next. This would isolate India, probably topple the rest of the Middle East within months, and would mean that the West would have to make the terrible decision whether to begin a fighting war or accept the loss of the cold war.[38]

There is little historical doubt that the Tudeh was well organized, financed, and disciplined and had become increasingly active as Mosaddeq's political situation worsened. But there is little evidence to support the contention that, had Mosaddeq prevailed in his struggle with the British and the United States, the Communists would have gained the upper hand. There simply was little chance that the Tudeh could have overcome the powerful combination of Mosaddeq's enormous personal popularity, historical Iranian distrust of Russia, and open contempt for the Tudeh, particularly given the party's willingness after World War II to sell out Iranian interests to Moscow. Kennett Love, the *Times* man in Tehran at the time, in a retrospective view, has said, "I don't think there was ever any likelihood of the Tudeh taking over Iran."[39] Indeed, it is important to note that the Tudeh made no attempt to resist the coup that restored the Pahlavis.

These realities became almost completely lost on journalists in mid-August 1953 and the final hectic days of Mosaddeq's rule when, first, the shah was forced to flee when an anti-Mosaddeq coup failed, and, six days later, when the successful counter-coup brought the shah to power. The press corps tended to stress the Communist threat throughout this confused period. On August 16, the day of the shah's departure, for instance, a United Press correspondent filed this dispatch:

> Young Shah Mohammed Reza Pahlevi fled Iran today after Communist-supported Premier Mohammed Mossadegh smashed a midnight attempt by the Shah's imperial guards to overthrow him. The wily old Premier was expected to be named President as soon as he could consolidate his victory.[40]

In a second-day dispatch, which the *Christian Science Monitor* headlined "Reds Bolster Mossadegh Grip," the United Press correspondent wrote, "Premier Mohammed Mossadegh took firm control of the nation August 17 with the support of the Communists after smashing an attempt by followers of the Shah to overthrow him."[41] On the third day of the crisis, UP cryptically began its story with the observation that "Communist mobs battled government troops today as the government widened its roundup of officers accused of loyalty to the Shah."[42] Associated Press began its account of the shah's ouster by telling of how "the young ruler and his beautiful Empress Soraya fled to neighboring Iraq and Communist mobs screamed for an end to the monarchy."[43]

By 19 August 1953, and the quick reversal of events that brought the shah back and ended Mosaddeq's political career, the rule of the aging premier had been thoroughly discredited by the U.S. press, and American public opinion had been amply prepared for the shah's assumption of power. The details of the coup need not be gone into here in great detail. Its salient points, however, were these: The British approached the United States for assistance in toppling the unpredictable and uncooperative Mosaddeq, insofar as all British nationals had been expelled from the country, and it had to be left to other than English nationals to mount a clandestine operation; the United States agreed and through the good offices of the CIA put together the successful coup that deposed Mosaddeq and "restored" the young shah to power. The coup set the scene for the shah's increasingly repressive reign and established the basis for a deeply rooted anti-American sentiment in the country, feelings that a quarter of a century later would be used to discredit Iranian opponents of the hostage taking. It was the first such "successful" operation in CIA history.[44]

Following the coup, whether by design or coincidence, Britain clearly was supplanted by the United States as the major foreign influence in Iran, and the oil concession was divided up among members of a consortium consisting of British Petroleum (40 percent); Royal Dutch Shell (14 percent); Compagnie Française des Pétroles (6 percent); Standard Oil of New Jersey, Standard Oil of California, Gulf Oil Corporation, Texas Oil Company, and Socony-Mobil (8 percent each). In other words, whereas before the coup American oil companies had controlled no Iranian oil, after the coup, whether by design or happy coincidence, they controlled about 40 percent.[45] A secret "participant agreement" signed by consortium members, which did not become known to the public or the Iranian government until some twenty years later, set forth terms under which member companies would buy oil and regulate production to avoid surplus production and lower profits for the companies, even though lower production levels meant less revenue for Iran.[46] In effect, the consortium assumed full control of Iran's oil industry.

For the mainstream American press, the coup was seen as a wholly internal matter brought about by widespread dissatisfaction with the ineptitude of Mosaddeq. Not a hint of suspicion appeared in the media about direct American involvement. *Newsweek* headlined its story: "Shah Returns in Triumph as Army Kicks Out Mossadegh."[47] In its account of the shah's "victory from exile," *Newsweek* told readers of the shah's return to Iran from Rome:

> As the Shah in a sky-blue air force uniform took the army's salute, his hand shook and he fought back tears welling in his bloodshot eyes. As he passed down the line of top-ranking officers who threw themselves in the dust to kiss his feet, a tear slowly rolled down his right cheek. He had returned to royal honors and royal duties. He greeted U.S. Ambassador Henderson warmly, then gave an icy stare to . . .

the Soviet emissary. Almost his first official act was a plea for quick
and heavy foreign aid. Washington indicated that the United States
might help.[48]

The only mention in the *Newsweek* piece about the CIA was in a
description of the confusion at Rome's Hotel Excelsior among the
shah's entourage when news of the successful coup arrived. In an
exceedingly cryptic paragraph, *Newsweek* advised readers, "Amid
the hubbub, Allen Dulles, director of the [CIA], arrived at the Excelsior. No one paid any attention to him."[49]

The patrons and hangers-on at the Excelsior were not the only
ones who paid little attention to Mr. Dulles. Mainstream journalists
were equally inattentive to the possibility that the United States or
the CIA might have been involved, or at least the total absence of
such speculation or analysis would indicate this to be the case. Instead, the press was content to quickly offer a warm welcome back
to the shah and to reach a consensus that Iran had been spared a
Communist takeover only by the narrowest of margins. For instance,
the *New York Times,* in a front-page article headlined "Shah Insti-
tuted Iranian Reforms," began by telling readers the young shah was
completely unlike his despot father and had begun widespread reforms before the crisis began.[50]

Editorial opinion throughout the prestige press about the turn of
events in Iran was unanimous: The country had been made safe at
the twelfth hour. In a view published just after the coup, for instance,
the *Washington Post* expressed cautious optimism: "If, indeed, the
Mossadegh regime now has been overturned, there will be cause to
rejoice."[51] According to a *Christian Science Monitor* editorial, headlined "Iran Rights Itself," "The sudden, dramatic events . . . are
probably the most hopeful that could have occurred."[52]

In its first editorial on the subject, the *New York Times* was ex-
tremely cautious, preferring to "let the dust settle before passing
judgment." However, the editorial did hint at the cause of Mosaddeq's overthrow: "There has always been a deep emotional attachment to the monarchy, which has a quasi-religious significance in
Iran," and the editorial concluded with the thought that "Mossadegh
will be an unlamented figure of the past."[53] The editorial writer apparently was oblivious to the contradiction between this assessment
and one his own newspaper had offered less than a month before in a
Sunday "News in Review" piece headlined "99.93% for Mossad-

egh," in itself a greatly inflated figure.[54] Evidently enough dust had
settled the following day for the *Times* to express "a deep sense of
relief in the West" at the political demise of Mosaddeq, who, in the
words of the *Times*, was a "rabid, self-seeking nationalist."[55] In a
passage that would richly presage the dominant attitude of the *Times*
toward Iran under the shah for the next quarter of a century, the
editorialist reassured readers: "The events of these last few days
bring him [the average Iranian] some reason to hope for better things.
They bring us hope, too."[56]

Gen. Fazlollah Zahedi, who replaced Mosaddeq, was greeted
warmly by the *Times*, which in several editorials called for immediate aid for Iran to help it through the transitional crisis,[57] and retrospective assessments of events surrounding the coup continued to
echo the tone suggested in this lead to a *Times* piece on Iran's economy by Robert C. Doty: "A political miracle on Aug. 19 jerked Iran
out from under the Iron Curtain as it was about to be lowered."[58]

As the inevitable arrests of Mosaddeq supporters began after the
shah's return, news reports generally tended to give the impression
that the major targets were only Tudeh members and supporters,
when in fact the sweeps were hardly so discriminating.[59] Within less
than a year, the suppression of political opposition to the ruling government in Iran would practically disappear as a news item, and a
clear pattern of uncritical reporting of the shah's policies would
emerge, a pattern that, by and large, would dominate until the 1978
revolution.

As for the possibility of American involvement in the overthrow
of Mosaddeq, nothing would appear until a year later when the story
was disclosed in a most unlikely periodical, the *Saturday Evening
Post*. In a 1954 piece, "The Mysterious Doings of the CIA,"[60] admittedly prepared with the assistance of the CIA, which was interested in improving its image for efficiency, the coup was gone into in
detail, some of which would later prove to be inaccurate. The general
thrust, however, was correct and was borne out in 1979 by a book by
Kermit Roosevelt, the self-professed mastermind of the operation.[61]
The story was never picked up and remained unremarked on in the
popular press, perhaps as an indication of the indifference of the
press toward, and general ideological acceptance of, U.S. interference in the internal affairs of Third World nations. Another possible
explanation for this silence will be explored later in this chapter.

Iranians who insisted on the CIA connection were dismissed as paranoid and naive. By the time of the 1978 revolution, or long after the capacity for public outrage about such a matter had been out-lived, as is so often the case, the press had finally come to accept the CIA's role. But by then, in President Jimmy Carter's memorable phrase used during the opening days of the hostage crisis, the coup had become "ancient history." When reporters thought to mention the fact at all in coverage of the 1978 revolution, it was usually relegated to a casual background clause to the effect that the shah had been "restored to his throne in 1953 by a CIA-engineered coup."

Kennett Love and the *New York Times:* A Case Study

The journalistic failure to uncover, let alone suspect, Amer-ican involvement in the events of August 1953 in Iran deserves ex-tended analysis. The case of Kennett Love of the *Times* provides the basis for such an examination. His experiences and observations of-fer a particularly rich and detailed view, not only of the press in Iran but of the complex and often subtle relationship between the press and the state throughout the cold war.

Kennett Love had been interested in a foreign assignment since joining the *Times* in 1948, following World War II service in the navy as a pilot. He worked as a general-assignment reporter for the news-paper in New York, and was on the night rewrite desk when he was assigned to the *Times* Middle East bureau in Cairo in January 1953. Twenty-eight at the time of his posting (he would turn twenty-nine in the midst of the coup), Love had no academic background in Middle East studies, nor did he speak a regional language. In Cairo he joined Robert C. Doty in the two-man bureau, which was responsible for coverage of parts of North Africa and most of the Middle East.

Love went from Egypt to Iran in April and filed his first pieces, including a Sunday news analysis, within the first week after his arrival.[62] According to Love, his preparation for this assignment had been to read several of the standard and scholarly works on Iran in the weeks preceding his arrival in the region. How then, with little or no background in Persian history, culture, or language, could Love file a lengthy, authoritative-sounding analysis of the turbulent

Iranian political scene in less than a week after his arrival in the country? At some thirty years distance, Love recalled:

> I introduced myself to Ambassador [Loy] Henderson as soon as possible, and I admit being charmed by him to the point of trusting him more than he deserved. However, full credit is due to my Iranian translator, assistant, and friend, Kazem Zarnegar, who was at the same time foreign news editor of *Kayhan* [a major Tehran newspaper.] His information and counsel balanced the malign paranoia of Henderson then and over my entire time in Iran.[63]

Reflecting in 1984 on his performance, Love cited his trusting nature toward Great Britain and the United States, signals from the home office, and the nature of his profession among the influences on how he reported Iran in crisis. "I accepted a world in which the British were our friends; I didn't realize what scoundrels they and we could be. I've learned a lot since then."[64]

In 1960 Love wrote a term paper while he was a Carnegie Press Fellow of the Council on Foreign Relations at Princeton University, where he would later continue as a part-time student in oriental studies, studying Arabic in preparation for a book he later wrote on the Suez and Sinai wars. Some six years later, he sent a copy of the 41-page paper, entitled "The American Role in the Pahlevi Restoration," to Allen W. Dulles, who had been head of the CIA at the time of the 1953 coup.[65] Love had mentioned the paper during an interview with Dulles for the Suez book, Dulles had asked to see it, and Love sent it to him as a courtesy. Love's recollections of his experiences during the coup as a *Times* reporter remained in the Dulles papers until 1980 when *CounterSpy,* an anti-CIA publication, obtained a copy of Love's work, published parts of it, and concluded that Love must have knowingly cooperated with the agency. A similar conclusion about Love's involvement was reached by journalist and author Jonathan Kwitny in his book *Endless Enemies.*[66]

Love began his analysis by asserting, "It is probable that the American role [in the coup] was decisive" and that the Iranians "who participated in the royalist coup could not have succeeded without American help. It is doubtful that the coup would have been attempted without American cooperation."[67] Love concluded his 1960 paper by arguing, "What is significant is that Americans restored the Pahlavi monarchy when it threatened to give way before a premier dependent on communist support and that Iranians are well aware of the American role *although the American public is not.*"[68]

In a passage that would later be cited by *CounterSpy* as an indication that Love had conscious knowledge of CIA involvement in the coup at the time it occurred, he went on to say, "According to my observations *at the time* (emphasis ours), operatives of the Central Intelligence Agency concerted plans for action with Maj. Gen. Fazlollah Zahedi, retired, who was to lead the coup and assume the premiership."[69]

What he meant by this, Love said some twenty years after the term paper had been written, was that putting together his observations in 1953 with what he learned *later,* it was his conclusion that the CIA had been involved. According to Love, at the time of the coup he had never heard of the CIA nor did he know what the initials stood for. He said he knew there would be trouble in July when the text of Eisenhower's letter to Mosaddeq refusing aid was made public and that some action to capitalize on the situation might be mounted from some quarter. However, he said he expected it to be a purely Iranian affair and that he never imagined that it would be the United States that would be the actor.[70]

In his paper Love wrote of gangs of "street toughs," "evidently" paid for with U.S. currency and directed by the CIA, who "played an essential part in controlling the streets when a resort to violence became necessary for the royalist cause on 19 August."[71] Love said he did not know at the time that anyone, Iranian or foreign, was paying for or giving orders to these roving gangs, but he noticed and reported four days after the coup that the value of the American dollar on the black market dropped drastically in favor of the rial. (By 1960 he had concluded that the drop was caused by the flood of dollars used to hire the gangs of street thugs.)

At the time of the coup, when he mentioned the drop in the dollar's value to *Time* magazine's correspondent, a veteran reporter in the Middle East, Love remembers being told, "You're on cloud nine." According to Love, a willing suspension of disbelief in the possibility of American involvement—and not a journalistic conspiracy—explains why the *Time* reporter scoffed at Love's information.[72]

Love also wrote in the paper that just after the coup, "members of the U.S. Embassy advised [the shah] and coordinated [his] course of action with the overall strategy of the movement. . . . At the same time, the CIA agents who had blue-printed the coup against Dr. Mossadegh continued to furnish technical assistance in quelling dissident movements that threatened the stability of the new regime."[73] Again, Love said the phrasing of this passage, written six years after the fact, reflected what he had since learned and obviously was not based on what he knew in August of 1953.

Yet another critical passage in the term paper could also be construed as meaning that Love knew more than what he told *Times* readers at the time of the coup. In his 1960 account, Love wrote that his "first observation of the association of the United States with the royalist cause began with a telephone call to me at the Park Hotel from Joe Goodwin, a CIA man attached to the embassy," on 16 August, three days before the coup.[74] According to a 1984 interview, however, Love said that in 1953 he knew Goodwin merely as a political officer attached to the embassy, and it was not until a year or more later that he learned that Goodwin was CIA. Moreover, Goodwin was a former Associated Press correspondent, which further served to establish his credibility in Love's eyes. At the time, Love said, "I knew the embassy had knowledge [of the coup], and was in touch with the coup-makers, but I saw nothing to indicate that [the link] was more than merely passively sympathetic and informational." Love said he neither saw nor heard of Kermit Roosevelt in Iran.[75]

Goodwin called with an offer to introduce Love to General Zahedi, who was in hiding at the time. According to Love, Goodwin invited Love and Don Schwind of the Associated Press, the only other American correspondent in Tehran at the time, to meet General Zahedi at, as it turned out, the residence of an American embassy official in Shemiran. Zahedi failed to turn up, but the reporters were met by his son, Ardeshir, who greeted Goodwin without need of introduction. Young Zahedi produced a decree, issued by the then-fleeing shah, which named the senior Zahedi as premier. Everyone present took "a handful" of photocopies of the decree. Love took his to the Park Hotel and left the stack with the manager at the front desk.[76] The idea was to make the text available to the rest of the press, and Love said he thought nothing of it at the time.[77] The incident has since been cited as evidence that he served as a propagandist for the CIA.[78]

In another passage of his paper, perhaps the most relevant to this particular discussion, Love wrote that

the American endeavors leading up to the coup have been largely ignored by Western accounts of the episode. Some versions treat the abrupt restoration of political power to the Shah as merely fortuitous for American policy, whereas, as we shall see, it was a consciously planned accomplishment creditable to American Federal employes.[79]

Love refers to the *Saturday Evening Post* article on the CIA in his paper and remarked that the *Post*'s revelation "appears not to have influenced subsequent accounts and if later writers have quoted the Harknesses [the co-authors] I am unaware of it." Yet, Love wrote, the "relevance of information on the American rescue of the Iranian throne to an understanding of American-Iranian relations would appear to be unarguable."[80]

Assuming for the moment that Love did not know of or suspect in 1953 the extent of American involvement in the overthrow of Mosaddeq, why did he not write of that involvement when he *did* learn of it? Love's answer to this crucial question says much about the relationship of the press to the national security state throughout the cold war.

Love's memory of the events of 1953 is aided by cables, dispatches, and letters that he saved from his tour in Iran (and he has made much of this material available to the authors of this study). Based on this evidence, we have concluded he did not learn of CIA involvement until some five months after the coup. To begin with, Love left Iran five days after the coup, when Robert C. Doty, the *Times* bureau chief, took over the story. If anyone from the *Times* knew in August 1953 of the American role in the coup, it most likely was Doty. Indeed, Love believes he first learned of this involvement from Doty in December of 1953 when he and Doty were home in Cairo for Christmas. Even at that point it is not clear whether Love understood that it was the CIA that had managed the coup. He does not use the initials in his correspondence until 1956, instead referring only to "U.S. agencies" or similar formulations. What is certain is that Love and Doty knew of the U.S. role by the summer of 1954, or before the *Saturday Evening Post* article, yet the *Times* published nothing.

Love says he failed to write of what he eventually learned for a combination of reasons that go to the heart of this study. First, he does not claim that the *Times* overtly told him not to, merely that the foreign news editor ignored his letters on the subject. Second, he does not remember making a *conscious* decision to keep what he knew a secret.[81]

In the first instance, according to Love, "[the *Times*] didn't encourage going back to things. You had to have hard news all the time . . . they didn't care for exposes of old stuff."[82] In Love's view, at that time the field reporter was expected to focus on topical or breaking news and was not encouraged to reflect back on events long past. What he described is an emphasis that even today actively defeats the development of historical memory for the public. News events become fragments of information floating in a contextless sea. In looking back, Love readily admits that the end result is a process that is always loaded in favor of the official version given at the time. According to Love, "The official version comes out right at the time. And the unofficial version is always something that drifts to the surface or that you dig out later, and that's what they [the *Times* foreign desk] didn't like. Bringing out things like this later was like sulking."[83]

Yet given the realities of cold-war politics and the processes and influences Love describes, it is not unreasonable to assume that the *Times* might define newsworthiness differently were an adversary state involved. For example, would the *Times* have regarded as "old stuff" information developed a year after the fact about Soviet involvement in a coup *contrary* to U.S. interests?

Looking back on his performance in 1953 and 1954, Love argues that the *Times* effectively, if indirectly, encouraged a reporter to favor the official version of events. He now believes that the reporter was operating under conditions that, in effect, exempted the official line from tests of evidence that are usually rigorously applied to any version that challenges it. "The *Times* in those days did not encourage . . . investigative journalism. It required that you answer all questions. In other words, if you couldn't prove it totally you couldn't say it. You couldn't often say there's something funny here, like the drop in the dollar, and then merely describe the evidence you had," Love said. "If you couldn't say why, you might as well pigeonhole it. And if you didn't, they did."[84]

For a young reporter hoping to do well, muckraking was not at the time the best way to proceed. According to Love, "The *Times* did not either appreciate, praise or encourage really going into it [the Iran story]. There was no praise for anti-establishment stories. Yet the embassy had a total vested interest in the Shah."[85] The whole system, in effect, conspired to get the reporter to go along with the frames established in Washington or the U.S. embassy in Iran.

As for the ideological dimension, which in the context of this study we have defined as the influence on a reporter of a particular world view, Love does not remember being at all conscious of being unduly influenced by a cold-war mentality or of being under pressure to follow a particular ideological line. However, he says, "it was the ambient element you lived and worked in. Is a fish aware of water?" According to Love, as a reporter, "you're not terribly aware of the atmosphere unless the wind is blowing hard. You just breathe it. There were certain types of conduct that simply weren't done," he said, in reference to challenging editorial positions from the field. "A constant, permanent factor," Love said, "was that the desk had the final say about what got printed and what stories got worked on. You couldn't waste time on what they weren't taking."[86]

The claim that Love was a conscious agent of the CIA is on the evidence unpersuasive. This is not to say that the press cannot be used as an instrument of foreign policy or that the consequences of Love's and the *Times*'s actions or inactions—whether the result of a conspiracy or a far more complex and subtle process—were not precisely the same. In this regard, press performance during the 1953 counter-coup—or since—has done little to allay the suspicions of those who believe that the press and the foreign policy and defense establishment are in a conspiratorial embrace.

In the matter of Love's performance, however, a number of aspects have been overlooked or left unexamined by his accusers in discussions of his behavior. First, he was assigned to Iran long after the story had been given a history by the mainstream press. He was subject to a body of fully developed received opinion. Moreover, he was caught in a fast-moving crisis on unfamiliar social terrain without benefit of language skills, adequate knowledge of the situation, or other, more experienced reporters to turn to for advice. Even so, a systematic review of his reporting during the crisis and during much of 1954 indicates that his work usually was more careful than that of his competitors, despite a general tendency to accept cold-war frames. Indeed, scholar Richard Cottam, who in the early 1950s was a young Iran-desk officer in the State Department with serious doubts about the official U.S. reading of events in Iran, remembers that he and some of his colleagues considered Love a "courageous hero" for providing a view contrary to the one provided by Ambassador Henderson.[87]

A second consideration in Love's case is that the existence of the CIA was not a subject of common knowledge or the topic of widespread discussion in 1953. Only five articles on the subject appeared in the press before 1953. The first *New York Times* piece of any length appeared in the Sunday Magazine in March of 1953 after Love had left for the Middle East,[88] and the first major media treatment was a *Time* cover study on Dulles and the organization published in June of 1953, four months *after* Love had arrived in Iran.[89] He says he neither saw nor heard of the article. Moreover, all of the published accounts dealt only with the intelligence-gathering mission of the agency; no mention was made of clandestine operations. Finally, in this regard, the overthrow of Mosaddeq was the first major clandestine operation undertaken by the CIA. In short, there is no reason to disbelieve Love when he says he knew nothing of the organization at the time of his first trip to Iran, not even so much as what the initials CIA stood for.

A third piece of evidence is a July 1956 letter from Doty to Love, the phrasing of which makes it clear that Doty had first told Love of U.S. involvement in the coup, not the other way around. Doty was replying to a request by Love for more information about Americans involved in the coup, and while Doty provided it, he did so on the basis that it be held confidential until the two could talk the matter over.

The final and most significant point to be made here concerns Love's reporting when he returned to Iran in early 1954 after a six months' absence. Love's dispatches generally demonstrated a willingness to report on less favorable aspects of the new regime, far more so, for example, than had the work of Robert Doty, who had succeeded him in Tehran following the August coup. Though hardly a crusade, Love's work sufficiently offended the shah that he twice ordered the reporter's visa lifted, and an Iranian official visited the *Times* foreign editor in New York to complain. Ambassador Henderson, for his part, worked to undercut Love in New York and intimidate him in Tehran.

The high-level charges that Love was undermining Iranian and

U.S. policy with his reporting led to a series of letters and cables dating from February to October of 1954 between Love and foreign editor Emanuel R. Freedman, which provide a compelling view of the pressures that can affect a journalist in the field. Throughout the correspondence is an undercurrent of tension that builds as Iranian complaints about Love's work became more shrill. Not surprisingly, Love became increasingly concerned about how he was being perceived by the *Times*. His letters were carefully considered briefs for the defense, in which he set forth persuasive arguments and evidence that the real issue was not the quality of his reporting, but rather attempts at censorship by Iran and the American embassy in Tehran.

In practically all of his letters to Freedman during 1954, there was an implicit plea for reassurances that his situation was clearly understood and that his superiors were firmly behind him. Yet the response from New York was far from all that it might have been. For example, a two-page, single-spaced letter from Love in February explaining that he had been threatened with expulsion by the Iranians for his coverage of Senate elections and explaining his side of things was answered only with a cable to the effect that the letter had been received.[90]

Love did not hear further from New York on the subject until four months later when Freedman wrote to tell him that a minister, acting on the instruction of Iran's ambassador to the United States, had come to see him to complain about Love's performance and ask that Love not be posted back to Iran.[91] Freedman assured Love that he had backed him up fully on the matter. However, the editor's letter contained a reference to Israeli complaints about Love's earlier work in covering strife with the Arabs, a reference that Love considered to be both gratuitous and obliquely threatening. Too, in closing, Freedman's letter cautioned Love about a tendency to editorialize.[92]

Responding to Freedman's letter, Love defended himself against the charge of editorializing by arguing that his use of the word "crookedness" in a story about the Senate elections and of the word "blackmail" in an earlier story about Iran's trade practices came only after long deliberation on the weight of evidence. Love wrote, "These words, as I recall, were respectively changed to 'irregularities' and 'pressure,' which got the ideas across in milder form more in keeping with our style. In general, I watch for words that might seem loaded and try to avoid even using strong words where the

situation seems to demand calling a spade a spade unless I have time
to reflect at some length on their accuracy and appropriateness."[93]

The months of harassment appear to have begun to have some
effect on Love's approach to the Iran assignment. In several letters to
New York, he speaks of consciously seeking out "positive" stories
about the regime to compensate for the negative ones. In one instance, Love, apparently bending over backwards, accepted the version of the breakup of a Communist spy ring offered by U.S. embassy officials.[94] For his troubles, paradoxically, he received a letter
from Freedman in New York chastising him for overstating the case
for Soviet involvement without sufficient evidence.[95]

In another instance, Love filed a lengthy eyewitness report on the
execution of ten army officers alleged to be Communists. He wrote
in some detail because he "believed that the conduct of the condemned proved effectively that at least that part of the organization
[Communist cabal] were dedicated and even fanatical communists
and that they were a formidable factor in Iran if merely because of
the extremity of their beliefs."[96] This story resulted in a cable from
Freedman questioning the necessity for "urgenting" his story, which
was the most expensive way to file it, and for "overwriting" the
piece, which the Times decided to use only as a three-paragraph
"short" in the late editions.[97]

As for the regime, Love found himself in continuing trouble with
stories such as one on the Qashqai tribe in which he mentioned that
the shah's father had poisoned the tribe's late chief.[98] In retrospect, it
appears that Love's disfavor had as much to do with the shah's hypersensitivity to adverse coverage, which we discussed in chapter 1,
as it had with hard-nosed reporting. For instance, Love found himself having to account to an outraged palace press officer for a Times
story (which Love had not even written) that used the word "fled" to
describe the shah's behavior just before he was returned to power the
previous summer.[99] What is certain is that Love's work continued to
antagonize Ambassador Henderson, who Prof. Richard Cottam has
said came to view Love as an "enemy, an unpatriotic American," for
failing to toe the embassy line.[100]

It was during his attempts to defend himself in July of 1954 that
Love first told New York of the American role in the coup almost a
year before. In a rejoinder to an Iranian official's claim that his reporting had been damaging to Iranian and U.S. policy, Love wrote

Freedman, "As a matter of fact, the only instance since I joined the *Times* in which I have allowed policy to influence a strict news approach was in failing to report the role our own agents played in the overthrow of Mossadegh. Perhaps I was wrong in this avoidance but I felt that the evidence I had was too good grist for the Russian propaganda mill."[101]

The second time Love mentioned U.S. involvement was in a letter to Freedman in early September when he recounted what he had said in a meeting with a top member of the regime over yet another press flap:

> I explained to him that if either the correspondents or editors allowed any particular policy to influence their news judgement they would be in serious trouble with the paper. . . . I said that the only story I had avoided because of policy reasons was the role U.S. agencies, including the Embassy, had in the overthrow of Mossadegh and the establishment of the Zahedi regime. I explained that despite the historical importance of these events and the U.S. role, the thing had been done and could not be reassessed to anybody's advantage but Russia's. He said he appreciated this and that he hoped everything would be all right in my case, which he said he would report in detail to the Shah.[102]

The final time that Love brought the matter to the attention of Freedman was in a 9 September letter, in which Love told of an "extraordinary" meeting he had had with Ambassador Henderson:

> But Henderson still seemed to think it was inconsistent to insist on free coverage here regardless of the dangers involved. Then I brought up the refusal of both [Robert] Doty and myself to report the U.S. role in the overthrow of Mossadegh and the establishment of Zahedi. I said we were responsible and fully aware of the weight of what we wrote and that we had avoid [*sic*] this large aspect of Iranian events voluntarily. Henderson said "My God, I should hope so," and we turned to other aspects of the case.[103]

In a retrospective assessment, Love said that he wrote these letters specifically to draw attention to U.S. involvement in the coup, but that he had to do so in a way that would not compromise Doty, his immediate superior, who had first learned of U.S. involvement but for whatever reasons had decided not to file the story. By slipping the "admissions" of his failure to report on U.S. involvement in the coup once he eventually learned of it into an overall defense of his conduct in Iran, Love said he hoped his editors in New York would immediately seize on the implications of this new revelation and order Love to follow up on the story.[104] Be that as it may, the phrasing of these passages and the context in which they were used could suggest that Love may have been at least as interested in convincing Freedman that he was not an antiregime partisan as in bringing the U.S. role in the coup to the attention of the foreign editor of the *New York Times*.

Love's motives aside, what is significant is that the *Times* was *told* three separate times of direct American involvement in the affair beginning five months before the story was revealed in the *Saturday Evening Post* in November 1954. Yet according to Love, Freedman totally ignored the references, never once mentioning the subject or asking for clarification or further detail. The first major American clandestine intervention of the cold war, therefore, went completely unnoted in the newspaper of record. Equally crucial, the *Times* failed to correct the historical record in the twenty or so years that followed. Although the story came to be treated as accepted fact in a number of books, it was never told in detail in the press until after 1978 and the revolution.

According to Love, from the perspective of some thirty years distance, "More and more, it seems to me that the importance now of what happened was the impact of silence on history; the impact of silence by eminent journals and journalists whose very essence and creed list wrongful and knowing and deliberate silence as the chief sin."[105]

It seems reasonable that any judgment of Love's work in Iran should be tempered by the realization of the forces at work on the man. Caught as he was in the riptide of the cold war, eager to establish a reputation as a reliable foreign correspondent, faced with open official hostility, left only with tepid encouragement and ambiguous support from his superiors, it is a wonder that his reporting from Iran in 1954 was as tough-minded as it was. As for his knowledge of the coup, he was confronted with his superior's complete lack of interest in the tale he had to tell, and so he let drop the matter of U.S. involvement in the events of August 1953. Whatever may be said of his individual decision, the harshest judgment must be reserved for the *New York Times*.

The important point to be made here is that a CIA conspiracy was not required to insure the silence of either Kennett Love or the *New York Times*. The forces at work on Love in 1953 were perfectly in keeping with a wide body of anecdotal evidence in the memoirs of journalists, working both abroad and at home, and in more systematic studies of the journalistic process, which clearly indicate that ideo-professional osmosis can be as effective as conspiracy in producing an uncritical press. In this regard, if adequate remedies for failures of the press in the foreign policy setting are to be found, careful distinctions between causes must be made. To focus on supposed individual culpability, particularly based on highly ambiguous evidence, is to divert attention away from the reality of how the *system* of journalism in the foreign policy setting actually functions.

Whatever the explanations for press behavior, the consequences seem plain, particularly in considering how the press covered Iran in 1953. As careful an observer of the contemporary Iranian scene as Richard W. Cottam, a political officer in the U.S. embassy in Tehran from 1956 to 1958 and distinguished Iran scholar, concluded in his 1964 study of the period, "The distortions of the Mossadegh era, both in the press and in academic studies, border on the grotesque, and until that era is seen in truer perspective there can be little hope for a sophisticated United States foreign policy concerning Iran."[106]

According to Cottam, seriously flawed situational analysis will inevitably lead to serious foreign policy errors, which has been the case in the Middle East. In a judgment that would prove prophetic, given the events of 1978 and the subsequent hostage crisis, Cottam wrote, "Future foreign policy will suffer, because the most fundamental prerequisite for a successful foreign policy is an accurate situational analysis. In Iran the original error was made in regard to Dr. Mohammad Mossadegh and Mohammad Reza Shah."[107] For its part, American journalism did little in 1953 to provide a situational analysis independent of official policy. This failure would be repeated over the ensuing twenty-five years.

3

The Consolidation of Power: 1954–1962

The course of Iranian history following the overthrow of Mosaddeq was marked by two central trends. The first was the transformation of Mohammad Reza Shah Pahlavi from an uncertain figurehead into a dictatorial monarch. The second was the gradually increasing involvement of the United States in Iranian affairs, a relationship that over time would come close to constituting an American raj.

During the early stages of such a new alliance is precisely when the press can play its most significant role in the foreign policy setting. In this regard, the literature of media impact has long held that one of the most potent effects mass communication can have involves the *establishment* of opinion where none existed before. Therefore, the general public and even attentive policy elites—if they have little specific knowledge about a country or a region—are particularly susceptible to the initial assumptions and frames given currency by journalism. Should the context of the new alliance provided by the media be congruent with declared policy, the immediate benefits to advocates of the alliance are obvious. Too, these early assumptions, both in the press and in the popular mind, tend to be lasting ones, unless they are overcome by the weight of events, as was the case in Vietnam, or there is a major shift in declared policy, as was the case with China in the mid-1970s.

During the eight years from the shah's ascendency to power until the beginning of the White Revolution—the name for the Pahlavi modernization program—the press helped establish many of the root assumptions about Iran that would prevail until the 1978 revolution. Perhaps what is most interesting about this period, however, is the evidence it offers for the contention that the press often follows official Washington's cues in the foreign policy setting. During much of the early part of this period, when Washington's concern about the shah's style of rule was muted, the press was content to portray the new regime as one authentically committed to modernization and consensus politics. Yet by the end of this period, even though the shah's methods and intentions had been clear for some time, mainstream journalism, following Washington's lead, became far more critical as the Kennedy administration increasingly voiced open concern about the direction Iran was taking. In the following chapter we shall discuss how, as the shah began his so-called modernization program and a mollified Washington decided once again to embrace the ruler uncritically, the press followed suit.

The critical transitional year of 1954 was one in which the shah and his prime minister, Fazlollah Zahedi, moved quickly to prevent a resurgence of the nationalist movement represented by Mosaddeq, and to restore ties with the West and the United States. The earliest press reaction was uniformly favorable, with only occasional hints at the methods the new regime might be using to achieve its goals. During this period the dominant themes were Iran's allegedly narrow escape from a Soviet takeover and the country's growing rapprochement with the West.

In the first instance, mainstream journalism had no doubts that the overthrow of Mosaddeq had averted a disaster for the free world. According to the lead paragraph of a news analysis by the *Christian Science Monitor*'s Washington bureau chief, William H. Stringer, "The oil of Iran was snatched from Soviet hands, and Iran itself was snatched from bankruptcy and chaos, in the nick of time." In Stringer's analysis, which carried the headline "Iran Oil Pact Foils Soviet," "The history of the oil settlement . . . ended a titanic three-year-old dispute between Iran and the Anglo-Iranian Oil Company in which were intermixed the gyrations of former Premier Mohammed Mossadegh, the Communist Tudeh Party, and grim Soviet Intrigue." Should his readers still miss the point, Stringer wrote two paragraphs later:

It is now the estimate of responsible officials that Premier Mossadegh's regime was so infiltrated with Communists at the time it was overthrown by Gen. Fazullah Zahedi, that if it had lasted two weeks more the Communists would have seized control of the Government of Iran. It was a close shave.[1]

In a similar vein, the United Press filed a story from Washington to the effect that "Russian agents were revealed to have been on the verge of gaining control of Iran a year ago. Secret information, made known for the first time, showed that Red conspirators were planning to seize power when they were check-mated by a revolution."[2] The wire service never made clear its sources, nor were there follow-up stories dealing with the charge.

In a story dealing with U.S. aid, Kennett Love of the *New York Times* wrote of a grant made to "the anti-Communist Zahedi Government" which was "swept into office to replace the administration of Premier Mohammed Mossadegh which was being swallowed by the Tudeh Party."[3]

As might be expected, journalism warmly greeted settlement of the oil dispute in August and the generous new position for American companies provided for in the agreement. No questions about its equity were raised in the mainstream press, and it was generally portrayed as a boon for all. According to a *New York Times* news dispatch from Tehran, "There is even a measure of gratitude [in Iran] toward the United States and British governments for persuading the major oil companies to form a consortium to sell Iranians oil at a time when the world market is glutted."[4] Given the lucrative terms of the secret consortium accord, in retrospect there must be some doubt about precisely how much persuasion was required.

A single dissenting view from the journalistic good tidings was offered in the *Nation,* a journal of opinion hardly in the mainstream, by an Iranian engineer and former employee of the Anglo-Iranian Oil Company, who was a research assistant at the University of Chicago at the time his article was published one month after the settlement. Using impressive statistics, he convincingly argued that widespread optimism over the agreement and the renewal it promised for Iran was based on a number of misconceptions, chief of which centered on the size of the oil industry's contributions to the national budget, national income, employment, and finally, in the "life of the Iranian people." The author went on to wonder about the disadvantages the new agreement might pose for Iran, not the least of which was how the "entrance of six powerful American oil companies into the Iranian domestic scene [would] affect the freedom of operation of the Iranian government."[5]

Whatever the merits of the oil agreement, there was little serious debate allowed within Iran about its ratification, which ought not to be surprising, given the new regime's vigorous campaign to crush the remnants of opposition. The campaign was carried out in the name of anticommunism, but it swept up any and all opponents as well. Too, the regime moved quickly to override the intent of the 1906–7 constitution, which provided for a freely elected majles, a figurehead monarch, and, significantly, freedom of speech and the press. In short, the shah began to establish what one Iran scholar has termed a "Royal Dictatorship."[6]

Although occasional dispatches in the *Times* did indicate that the 1954 elections for the senate and the majles were given to "irregularities," conspicuously missing was the drum-beat alarm sounded in 1953 about Mosaddeq's alleged trampling of electoral procedure.

In March, during the majles elections, the *Times* did publish three pieces by Kennett Love that were hardly flattering to the regime's conduct.[7] Indeed, in a lengthy analysis of unrest in the Middle East that was filed from Beirut, Love wrote, "in Teheran [where] the military dictatorship of Gen. Fazlollah Zahedi is barring undoubtedly the strongest faction in the country, the partisans of the jailed former Premier Mohammed Mossadegh, from any political role whatsoever."[8] This was the only time the term "dictatorship" was used by a *Times* reporter to refer to a shah-backed regime in 1954 or for the next quarter of a century. Love continued:

> It [suppression of political opponents] is being done fairly crudely. A combination of Army, police, elections boards and self-appointed vigilantes . . . is running the elections so thoroughly that not a single opposition candidate is expected to be elected either in the Senate or the Majlis (lower house).[9]

Three days later, Love wrote another article, which began, "Scores of persons were wounded, many critically, today as gangs of armed toughs toured polling places attacking persons suspected of being opposition voters and Communists."[10]

These three relatively candid accounts to the contrary, on balance the *Times* glossed over the regime's behavior, according the corruption neither the space nor the condemnation that Mosaddeq had received. Indeed, throughout 1954, by contrast with the Mosaddeq era, the *Times* published not a single editorial expressing concern over the course of the elections. Too, while coverage of Mosaddeq tended to erase the distinction between him and his supporters, the shah was portrayed as far removed from the fray in 1954.

Beyond the decided tilt implicit in the newspaper's performance is the question of how much the *Times* actually knew about the Zahedi regime. Again, correspondence between Love and the *Times* foreign editor provides a compelling indication. As with information about the CIA's role in the 1953 coup, this correspondence—together with a comparison of Love's dispatches and the stories as they were actually published—indicates that for whatever reason and despite the *Times*'s professed goal of publishing the news without fear or favor, the newspaper of record failed to publish what it knew.

Beginning in February of 1954, Love privately informed his superior, foreign editor Emanuel R. Freedman, of his growing concerns about the excesses of the new regime. Love had returned from Cairo to Iran in January after a six month's absence and had come to have serious doubts about Zahedi. His letters to Freedman, in addition to providing further persuasive evidence that Love was not serving the interests of the CIA, formally or informally, make it plain that the *Times* had been amply warned about the developing situation in Iran.

In the first letter to Freedman that dealt with the subject, Love still demonstrated a cold-war orientation: "Regarding the Government itself, the best thing I can say about it is that it is anti-Communist and that it may be the best thing available so far as our side is concerned." But the reporter then added:

> I am not, however, convinced about the latter point. The Government would not last a minute but for U.S. aid and I am not sure it will last anyway. Mossadegh is more popular than ever, far more so than he was last August. The elections are being run with an iron hand with a view to creating the weakest possible Majlis, and are regarded as the crookedest in recent history.[11]

He went on to relate a cautionary anecdote dealing with the extent of electoral corruption and to make some observations about the elections, based on his first-hand experience:

I myself saw how the polling was conducted, everybody writing their ballots in full view óf the election officials (see my delayed dispatch of Feb. 1). And a daily check of total votes at the most important polling centers indicated that the final official figure of 34,000 votes cast was at least double the highest possible actual number.[12]

As Love observed in this letter, "The worst of the situation is that we, the U.S., are getting a worse name among the rank and file than ever before." To bolster his position, Love cited the judgments of two of his fellow *Times* reporters:

I am not alone in these observations. [Robert] Doty had misgivings about this government and [Welles] Hangen frankly described it to me as a bunch of "bargain-basement Fascists." Before I returned [to Iran], I was, if anything, partial to this Government, having been in on its fortunate triumph and because it prevented Iran from going Communist. But I wonder if we are not giving too much faith and support to something that has such visible signs of weakness.[13]

In his continuing correspondence with Freedman about Iranian efforts to revoke his visa (discussed in chapter 2), Love again brought up the elections:

With regard to the elections, I think it is significant that the Government won 100 per cent, with results in some areas approximating Mossadegh's notorious plebiscite. Since my copy is all in Teheran, I am at a slight disadvantage. It might be interesting, however, if [Welles] Hangen has an hour or so to spare, to check against the actual election results *my advance list of Teheran Majlis winners and the votes they would get*. These items were filed the first and second days of the election, respectively, Mar. 9 and 10. The results were announced after I left. The list of winners was obtained from a young, pistol-packing member of the top, city-wide elections board (emphasis ours).[14]

The stories to which Love referred told of how he had received—*in advance* of the election—a list of the expected winners and the votes they would receive. Love was clearly led to believe by his source that the list was not merely a prediction, but rather a blueprint. (Mention of the list and the expected totals was edited out of the dispatches as published.) A comparison of the sort suggested by Love was never published by the *Times*.

What is clear from a careful reading of Love's correspondence and his dispatches filed during this period is that the *Times* was made abundantly aware of the nature of the Zahedi regime and its methods. For whatever reasons, the newspaper chose to look the other way, in the phrase of Iran scholar Richard Cottam, as "Iran moved steadily from a loose authoritarianism in the direction of totalitarianism."[15]

The critically important transitional year of 1954 ended with a visit from the shah to the United States. Nowhere was the *Times*'s benign view of the new regime and selective interpretation of history made more plain than in its editorial welcome, which read in part:

> Only a year ago last summer Iran was a bankrupt country, ruled by the fantastic and fanatical demagogue, Dr. Mossadegh, a nation full of xenophobia and disorder with a powerful Communist movement in the Tudeh party, and with the vast oil industry at a standstill. Today Mossadegh is where he belongs—in jail. Oil is flowing again into the free markets of the world. A strong and able Premier, Major General Zahedi, supports the Shah, and his Government is leading Iran toward new and auspicious horizons.[16]

For the most part, this view would prevail for the next six years in American mainstream news media, with only occasional news stories or analyses that seriously examined the question of the shah's legitimacy, style of rule, or social progress.

Aside from a sharp drop in press attention paid Iran after 1953–54, several patterns emerge from a close study of the journalistic view of the country until the early 1960s. Most prominent of these patterns was a curious cycle of stories that usually began with enthusiastic appraisals of the shah's ambitious plans for Iran and the country's stability, only to be eventually followed by less encouraging reports of government corruption, then by indignant Iranian denials at first, followed by grudging admission that the charges might be true, earnest promises of reform, announcement of the shah's appointment of a new prime minister, and expressions of American editorial approval and high hopes for the new government.[17] At this point, the cycle would begin again.

Press criticism, particularly of high-level *corruption*, occasionally appeared during this period, although it was hardly sustained and was slight compared with the attention paid the Mosaddeq government. What was completely missing were serious analyses of political repression. For example, the establishment in 1957 of a state security apparatus, SAVAK, an acronym for the Persian equivalent of the Organization of Information and Security of the Country, went completely unnoticed at the time and virtually unremarked upon until the 1970s. SAVAK, which has been aptly described as the "Iranian equivalent of the Gestapo,"[18] was trained in large part by the CIA and the Mossad, Israel's secret police.[19] True, throughout this period there were routine reports of Communist plots uncovered, of conspirators tried and executed. But the government's version of these incidents was rarely questioned, and nothing in coverage hinted at these actions being anything more than necessary housecleaning.

Another significant omission in press accounts and editorials dealt with the extent of the shah's power. For the most part, the shah was routinely portrayed more as an interested and concerned onlooker rather than the central actor on the political stage. The dominant journalistic frame was of a principled ruler whose good intentions were, to his dismay, too often being thwarted by venal underlings. The result was that the shah was largely absolved of responsibility for the course of Iranian affairs, and there was a total absence in the mainstream press of editorial concern for his methods of rule. As a result, his unwavering drift toward absolute control went virtually unnoticed. Until the early 1960s, to the extent that concern was expressed at all, it dealt with the shah's spending habits.

The shah's regime was well served by the idea of reverence for the monarchy by the Iranian masses, a facile assumption on the part of the press, which took root early and lasted until the 1978 revolution rendered it unsupportable. According to a 1954 news account in the *Times,* for instance, Iranians regarded the shah with "a semi-religious veneration."[20] Similarly, some six years later, a *Christian Science Monitor* writer observed, "The great mass of the Iranian people, with an age-old tradition of royalty behind it, is believed to be in favor of the Shah himself."[21]

On balance, then, assessments of Iran and the shah during the mid to late 1950s, as we have indicated, were generally favorable. A 1955 report on Iran's prospects in the *Atlantic,* for instance, informed readers that "it was not until 1945 that the young ruler [the shah] emerged as an articulate and positive force in his country."[22] The article singled the shah out among Middle Eastern rulers for his commitment to progress, praising him for initiating a Seven-Year Plan. According to the *Atlantic:* "In promoting this far-reaching

plan, the young Shah began to display for the first time the characteristics of moderation and good sense which have come to distinguish him. He made it clear that he hoped to transform Iran into
a modern and healthy state by democratic means rather than by
force."[23]

The magazine's rosy assumption that the plan had somehow been
accomplished is difficult to understand, in that its failure was generally recognized by this time, and the Zahedi regime had already announced yet another, a Five-Year, plan. As for Iran and democracy,
Atlantic told its readers, "Given the continuation of the improved
political climate in Iran, it can be expected that there will be real
economic progress on a wide front,"[24] and dismissed complaints
about Zahedi's military dictatorship with this judgment:

> There are protests, of course, and it must be assumed that there is a
> good deal of ferment behind the orderly facade. But it is also clear
> that the state of near anarchy reached during the Mossadegh regime
> frightened the more responsible elements and the memory of this
> makes them willing now to tolerate military domination. This gives
> the present government time to concentrate on economic revival.[25]

This assessment of Iran's prospects and others like it tended to
routinely ignore the possibility that the shah and many of his foreign
advisers "preferred large, impressive projects to those that would
increase the output of the intensive labor of peasants, nomads, and
small-scale workers."[26] The shah's preference for inappropriate technology and development schemes, although apparent from the beginning, was uniformly overlooked by American journalism throughout
this period. One explanation for this myopia is that the models to
which the shah was devoted were Western and clearly increased
Iran's dependency on the West. The highly ethnocentric tendency to
confuse modernization with Westernization would be a constant in
journalism for the next twenty-five years in its coverage of Iran.

The view of the shah as a strategic asset also may have led to the
media's nearsightedness. Journalism uniformly agreed early on that
he was a bulwark against communism in the Middle East, an assumption that would eventually obtain greater credence during the
Nixon-Kissinger years in the White House. By 1956 the *New York
Times* offered reassurance to its readers with a news analysis that
began:

> Iran is the calmest country in the troubled Middle East today. Partly responsible for this is a highly successful campaign against subversive elements. The pro-Soviet Tudeh party was a real menace a few years ago, even after it had been officially banned and driven underground. It is considered now to have been completely liquidated.[27]

The writer, who asserted that "extreme nationalists" had been almost as "subversive" as the Communists, stressed that Iran's new stability had been accomplished with U.S. aid.[28]

Occasionally, it is true, a discordant note could be heard in the press. One such instance involved a *New York Times* analysis written by correspondent Sam Pope Brewer. Brewer had covered Iran on and off for several years, and his previous reporting, as published, did not deviate much from the uncritical norm. His early-1958 profile of Iran, however, was a different matter. He began the piece, which in retrospect appears rather cautious but for the time represented a marked departure, by offering an unusually dark assessment: "Iran is in a state of discontent that is dangerous to her internal security and to the stability of the Middle East."

Basing his observations on a week of talks with persons of varying political persuasions in Tehran, Brewer examined charges of corruption and political repression. He told readers that he had found it "striking to see the precautions that must be taken by any Iranian who wants to complain about anything done by his government," and he concluded his article with this observation: "The Shah has been increasingly authoritarian. The fear is that this may drive the non-Communist Opposition into the arms of the Soviet Union."[29]

The Brewer piece touched off a storm of protest from Iranian officials, and he was permanently barred from Iran.[30] Nearly a month later, the *Times* published a four-paragraph account of the arrest of twenty-five persons on charges of subversive activity. The arrests were linked to the Brewer article.[31] What is perhaps most remarkable about the whole affair was the apparent indifference of the *Times* toward (1) Brewer's findings and major premise; (2) his expulsion; and (3) the arrest of his suspected sources. Completely absent were editorial expressions of concern about freedom of information or political rights in Iran.

Moreover, whatever questions Brewer's single piece may have raised in the minds of his readers most likely were overshadowed by the coverage accorded Iran and the shah later in 1958. For instance, full attention was paid the shah's fortieth birthday and yet another announced round of reforms.[32] Other major stories on Iran's development plans and progress published in October and November had nothing to say about internal unrest and, on balance, more than offset Brewer's earlier concerns.[33]

Aside from Brewer's modestly dissenting view, the only other discouraging words throughout much of this period were heard in predictable places: the liberal-left opinion press. For instance, a reporter for the St. Louis *Post-Dispatch* published a scathing indictment in the *New Republic* of American policy makers for their unstinting support of the shah.[34]

For its part, *Time* magazine in late 1958 could confidently tell its readers that there was little organized opposition in Iran, although the magazine did refer to "police-state" tactics. According to the newsmagazine, "The Shah's reforms have one thing in their favor: Iran has already been through [a] violent upheaval" that had had a "cathartic effect on many young people."[35] Five months later, in April 1959, *Time* sounded gloomier. In an assessment of a Soviet propaganda campaign aimed at its neighbor, the magazine wrote:

> In a land where millions are illiterate and hard pressed, where autocratic rule suppresses opposition and corruption is widespread, and where the long-term benefits of invested oil royalties are insufficiently visible, Communist lies and half truths so powerfully spread were bound to have an unsettling effect.[36]

Although occasional storm clouds might be seen in the media by 1959, the rain began falling the following year. Certainly, by this time the major news frames regarding Iran had been well established, and these frames in one form or another would persist until the revolution. But for a brief period from 1960 to 1963, for the first time since the counter-coup, to varying degrees Iran—if not the shah—underwent critical scrutiny from the press.

Some background is necessary to understand the news-frame shifts that occurred toward Iran in the early 1960s. Journalism's generally warm embrace of the shah from 1954 to 1960 to the contrary, there are at least two schools of thought regarding official Washington's relations with the shah following his restoration to the throne, and there is evidence to support both perspectives.

The first case has it that American policy makers, who harbored *private* doubts about the shah's ability to survive with a narrow base of popular support, proceeded cautiously in developing relations with his regime and gave him no more in the way of economic or military aid than was absolutely necessary to keep Iran solvent and out of the Soviet camp.[37] In this view, a kind of gradualism marked U.S. assistance and involvement in internal planning and affairs. Secretary of State John Foster Dulles, for instance, according to one account, had serious doubts about Iran's immediately joining the new Baghdad Pact in 1955.[38] Too, a bilateral U.S.-Iranian defense pact was not signed until 1959,[39] and the shah complained in his 1960 memoirs that since World War II, "the U.S. government has actually given more direct non-military aid to *the Soviet Union* than she has to Iran" (emphasis in original).[40] He petulantly added, "In the same period Communist Yugoslavia has received more than twice as much military and non-military aid from the Americans as we have," and expressed similar dismay at greater amounts of American aid given to Spain, Turkey, and Taiwan.[41]

The second school of thought argues for an earlier and more unstinting American role, one based on a rapidly emerging "dependence relationship."[42] According to this line of thought,

[following the coup] the internal opposition and the perceived external threats in the face of the disturbed state of the Iranian economy and the weakness of the country's armed forces . . . meant that the Shah was left with little choice but to persevere with his original reliance on the United States for his survival. As a matter of conscious policy, therefore, he pressed for further American help. Washington responded with a full commitment to ensure the continuation of the Shah's regime.[43]

What is not in dispute is that the Eisenhower administration immediately extended to the shah the financial assistance that had been denied to Mosaddeq: $23.5 million under the U.S. technical assistance program, together with a $45 million emergency grant-in-aid.[44] From 1953 to 1957, under various programs ranging from the Export-Import Bank to the Agency for International Development, Iran received $366.8 million in economic assistance, and such aid continued at the rate of $45 million a year for the next three years. In 1961, because of Iran's domestic economic woes, the United States increased the aid to $107.2 million. By 1960 Iran had become one of the largest non-NATO recipients of American foreign aid, and some nine hundred American economic and technical experts were at work in Iran. Similarly, Iran by the early 1960s had become the largest non-NATO recipient of military aid, having received $535.4 million from 1953 to 1963.[45]

The early 1960s marked a turning point of sorts for the shah's regime, both domestically and in its relations with Washington. In the crisis of 1960–62, the shah faced his first serious domestic challenge since being returned to power. Too, the Kennedy administration was demonstrating a marked coolness toward the shah's preoccupation with accumulating military power and his increasingly harsh human rights policy.

Widespread and varied protests were triggered by an obviously rigged 1960 parliamentary election. The protests continued into the next two years, fueled by an increased awareness of corruption, severe inflation, and the deaths of two striking Tehran schoolteachers killed in a demonstration in 1961. In January of 1962 students at the University of Tehran staged a major anti-regime demonstration calling for the resignation of the prime minister and for free elections. The students were dealt with brutally by the authorities, prompting the university's chancellor to publicly issue a much-celebrated (within Iran) letter of resignation, in which he denounced the unheard-of "cruelty, sadism, atrocity, and vandalism" that occurred when troops literally invaded the campus.[46]

In an attempt to defuse the rapidly deteriorating situation, the shah had appointed a "reform" prime minister, Dr. Ali Amini, in May of 1961. Some analysts, both Iranian and American, have speculated that the shah took this move as much as anything because Amini was a favorite of the new American president, John F. Kennedy, who had met him when Amini was ambassador to the United States.[47] Amini, during his fourteen-month term, proved to be a favorite of the American press as well. Certainly, Kennedy's administration was concerned about continued strife, political instability, and economic difficulty in Iran, and had made it clear to the shah that Iran's economic progress, not a continued military buildup, was what Washington considered most important. Toward this end, and later under President Lyndon Johnson, the shah was kept on a short military-assistance tether. Indeed, Kennedy was so worried about the need for socioeconomic reform that he set up a special task force to deal with the problem.[48]

It was under these circumstances, then, that news frames shifted

and not because of a fundamental change in the independent judgment of the journalistic establishment. As Washington grew concerned, so did the press, much to the chagrin and displeasure of the
shah, ever conscious of public relations.

Even so, although by 1960 the extent of the challenge facing the
shah's regime was clear both to Washington and to the mainstream
press, there was no evidence that the press either fully appreciated or
cared that Iran was well on its way to dictatorship or that the shah
had become increasingly dependent on his security forces to preserve
his position, which had alienated his erstwhile and natural allies,
ranging from landowners to large merchants and religious leaders.[49]
Indeed, the great majority of stories about Iran continued to present
a generally favorable view, and the journalistic criticism that did surface should not be confused with open condemnation. Despite harsh
criticism of various aspects of the Iranian scene, the press persisted
in its high opinion of the shah and gave the impression that he stood
well above the political chicanery.

How this worked can be seen in accounts of the corruption surrounding the 1960 elections. Not a single mainstream news account
or analysis assayed the possibility that the electoral corruption might
have been the result of officials trying to advance the *shah's* perceived
best interests, particularly insofar as both parties allowed to partici-
pate in the election were wholly creatures of the shah's regime.[50] The
tenor of coverage is caught in the beginning of this *Times* dispatch:
"[The shah] said today that he was not fully satisfied with the current
national elections, which he had promised would be 'free and fair.'
Responding to charges that the elections had been rigged, he said at
a news conference that Iran's fifty-four-year-old electoral system was
faulty and would have to be improved by legislation."[51] According
to the opening of a *Newsweek* article, "Fed up with the patent dis-
honesty of Iran's first party elections to Parliament, [the shah] last
week called the whole thing off and set about cleaning house in preparation for another try later."[52]

In its issue of the same week, *Time* magazine ran a cover story on
the shah, in which the newsmagazine told readers that "trouble is
nothing new in Iran." *Time* regarded corrupt elections as "standard
through Iran's modern history" but warned that the unrest caused by
the most recent ones might foretell a "new discontent among the
swelling city masses." As did much of the media, though, *Time* did

not look closely for internal causes, but rather throughout the piece argued that the Soviet Union was largely behind the shah's troubles. According to *Time:* "Should the Shah lose his fight for his dynasty and his nation, the Soviets would at last be free to dominate the Middle East."[53] The article was accompanied by a picture of the shah at a banquet for orphans, with the caption: "A benevolent autocrat with classic problems."[54] After praising the shah as a monarch determined to "convert Iran into a healthy and stable modern nation," the cover story concluded with a view widely held throughout the mainstream media, a view that neatly separated the shah from his absolutist policies:

> He has committed himself not just to a holding action for feudalism but to the evolution of a modern state. Sooner or later, the Shah must find *trustworthy and independent subordinates to whom he can delegate authority* and must create responsible institutions to close the gap between the court and the people (emphasis ours).[55]

In what by this time had become a predictable move to deal with public outrage, Premier Manouchehr Eqbal tendered his resignation, and Jafar Sharif-Emami was named to replace him. Emami, in turn, would last less than a year. In a farewell profile of Eqbal, the *Times* offered the astonishing judgment, given the historical record, that he had compiled a "long record of success in defeating subversion *without suppressing democracy*" (emphasis ours).[56] Seemingly ever on the lookout for external explanations for internal problems, a Sunday *Times* analysis published a week later went so far as to link Eqbal's fall to the winds of nationalism fanned by Egypt's Nasser.[57]

As turmoil continued into 1961 and Washington's concern mounted, mainstream media similarly continued to pay increasing attention to the problems of Iran. The *Christian Science Monitor,* for instance, ran a long and unusually perceptive analysis by Geoffrey Godsell under the headline "Iran: Is It Really Reform at Last?" Employing a candor absent in the *Times,* Godsell told his readers that "during more than four years in the Middle East, this writer saw more disturbing signs of poverty and malnutrition in Iran than any other country." Still, Godsell judged the shah to be a man fully aware of the country's problems and "anxious to do something about them—but perhaps oversensitive to criticism of his person and hitherto lacking the bold resolution needed to overcome the forces of reaction and conservatism so resistant to change." And Godsell accepted uncritically the assumption that Iranians have a deep attachment to the monarchy.[58] The rest of the press as well persisted in ignoring the logic and implications of the shah's absolutist path, instead emphasizing the obstructionist role of the traditional upper classes.

In its editorial salute to Amini and his push for reform, the *New York Times* argued, "The old ruling classes, with a few notable exceptions that include [the shah], are balking. They do not want to make the necessary sacrifices."[59] An editorial several months earlier, which called for more aid for Iran, presented a similar viewpoint: "The United States is preparing to send some more money into Iran. The authorities in Washington must wonder: is it worth while after all these years, after so much money and so little, apparently, to show for it? The answer . . . is, yes." The editorialist continued with the opinion that the shah, unlike his father, was not a strong ruler, but he "is earnest [and] well-intentioned."[60]

Resistance to the regime throughout 1961, while widely reported, was usually cast in terms suggested by these headlines over an antigovernment demonstration story in the *Times:* "Foes of Iranian Regime Routed As Police Smash Demonstration." The second deck read: "Pro-Western Premier Scores a Victory Over Reds and Mossadegh Backers—Teheran Weighs Protest to Soviet."[61]

Despite the shah's continuing and growing troubles, his visit to the United States in 1962 was greeted with a hopeful note by the press. According to a *Times* editorialist, for example, the outlook for the shah's kingdom "has recently much improved." In the judgment of the *Times,* Premier Amini had "halted economic deterioration, checked governmental corruption and launched a sweeping distribution of land to the oppressed peasantry." The *Times* told its readers that his opposition consisted of "the wealthy Right and the Communist-leaning Left" and that the shah and Amini had continued to ignore "rioters' demands for new elections on the sound ground that further stabilization under the present program for progress and a change in the electoral system are both necessary if a return to former chaotic parliamentary situations is to be avoided."[62] Aside from a monumental double standard in the editorial, suggested by a comparison of the newspaper's earlier treatment of similar actions taken by Mosaddeq for similar reasons, perhaps what is most interesting about the *Times*'s optimistic paean to Amini is that it was published just three months before Amini felt compelled to resign over a split with the shah on military spending.

As for the *Washington Post,* its major treatment of the event was Maxine Cheshire's overwrought piece on the occasion of the shah's and Empress Farah's meeting with the equally glamorous Kennedys, a piece filled with superlatives.[63]

As we have indicated, there was a distinct change in the tenor of reporting about Iran from 1960 until 1963. The two best examples of the new criticism can be found in the work of the *Times*'s Harrison E. Salisbury in 1961 and 1962, and in news accounts and analyses of the *Christian Science Monitor* from 1960 on. (The *Monitor*'s changed perspective proved to be enduring, and the newspaper's *generally* more critical perspective toward Iran under the shah lasted until the 1978 revolution.) Salisbury's dispatches included the first major interview with an opposition leader, Karim Sanjabi,[64] since the 1953 counter-coup, and one of the earliest *Times* news pieces on the depth of despair of the Iranian poor.[65] In late 1961 he also produced the lengthiest and most thoughtful assessment of Iranian development (or lack of it) to appear in the American press.[66]

Salisbury's work was not without its flaws. For example, much of it was informed by a distinct cold-war perspective, as is evidenced by this caution (contained in the long article referred to above) to readers that Iran's struggle for modernity was being carried out under "a menacing shadow from the Soviet Union to the north."[67] It is difficult to understand, moreover, how Salisbury could be impervious to the contradiction contained in his assessment of the political climate in Iran under the shah:

> Nothing is further from the mark than complaints that Iran has been turned with United States aid into a "police state." Nowhere in the world, in all probability, is so much free swinging comment and criticism hurled at the Government and chief of state. However, there is steel under the suede gloves of Savak and if any oppositionist was really feared he would quickly find himself behind bars.[68]

On balance, however, particularly when compared with coverage in the *Times* up to that point, Salisbury's work represented a major improvement, short-lived as it might prove to be. Of course, Salisbury was a highly prestigious journalist visiting Iran for a comparatively short time, which may have protected him from the wrath of the shah and given him some latitude with his editors. Perhaps one way of dealing with the problems of reporting from a client dictatorship, therefore, may be to send similarly talented and credentialed reporters. Obviously, to be effective, such trips would have to be scheduled more frequently than once every decade, as was the case with the *Times*.

As for the *Christian Science Monitor*, a distinct—if gradual—difference in coverage can be detected as the extent of the crisis of the early 1960s became plain. Although displaying the same cold-war worries as the *Times,* the *Monitor* nonetheless reported on the exploitation of Iranian workers,[69] restrictions against unions,[70] and student opposition.[71] Another dispatch, although it began by conceding the need to be on guard against communism, gave a fairly even-handed and measured picture of communism in Iran. More important, the report raised questions about the work of the SAVAK and its suppression of dissent.[72]

Despite the press's tougher stand toward Iran during the early 1960s, the reality of the shah's regime was never made clear to the American public—either by the Kennedy administration or by journalists. Evidence that became available in 1984 revealed that several prominent members of the Senate Foreign Relations Committee in 1961 had warned the administration in closed sessions that the shah was in far deeper trouble than was ever publicly acknowledged. For instance, Democratic Sen. Frank Church of Idaho said of the shah, "All I know about history says he is not long for this world, nor his system. And when he goes down, boom, we go with him." Sen. Hubert H. Humphrey of Minnesota added, "I don't care what revolution it is, somebody is going to get these fellows. . . . It is just a matter of time. . . . It is inevitable."[73] There is no reason to believe that journalists could not have reached similar conclusions on the available evidence.

The Senate committee ended up by deferring to the administration and keeping its deeply serious doubts private, as such committees routinely have tended to do throughout the cold war. For precisely this reason, a press less under the thrall of official Washington might have made a dramatic difference at a critical time in the development of U.S. policy toward Iran—just as the *New York Times* might have made a difference had it prominently reported what it knew of the planned Bay of Pigs invasion.

But a period that began with the *Times*'s indifference to the U.S. role in the 1953 coup ended with only marginally improved coverage, and the general perception of Iran remained largely unchanged. To be sure, the adverse publicity that he did receive bothered the shah greatly. An astute student of his American policy audience, he realized that a dramatic gesture was needed to offset his tarnished image. The conciliatory course of reform under Amini, combined with the use of coercion to suppress dissent, was judged to be insufficient to the task, and Amini's resignation was accepted in July of 1962 as the economy continued in decline.

It was at this point that the shah and his advisers decided to mount their own reform substitute, the White Revolution. In theory, the program had only advantages: It would modernize Iran; it would defuse the challenge of the growing middle class; and it would assuage the peasantry. In brief, it would meet most of the concerns about Iranian social policy at home and abroad and preserve for the shah his image as a progressive monarch. Most important, it would serve to further concentrate and centralize the shah's power while undercutting the political ground of his opponents. To an amazing degree, at least the public relations goals of the shah were realized, as we shall discuss in the next chapter.

4

Modernization, Myth, and Media: 1963–1973

The central myth of the Pahlavi regime on which American press coverage largely rested was the shah's White Revolution, the modernization program that began in 1963. At its core, when myth, public relations hyperbole, and the shah's own self-delusion are stripped away, the White Revolution was an effort to blunt challenges to the shah's move toward absolute power through a program of pseudodevelopment. The plan was intended to seduce at once the Iranian people, American policy makers, and world opinion; it proved exceedingly successful at its latter two tasks, if not the former one.

By the early 1960s, as we discussed in the previous chapter, the Kennedy administration and therefore the American press had begun to take a far more critical view of the shah's progress (or lack of it) in social if not political reform. His spending priorities had raised serious questions as well. Even the *New York Times,* among the shah's most eager supporters, by 1962 had become concerned. According to a *Times* editorial, "The Washington view, which we believe is the correct one, is that Iran's military forces are bigger than they need to be and that they absorb funds that would be better spent on desperately needed economic development." The editorial closed with the thought that what "is essential is better utilization of the potential resources of oil-rich Iran for its own development needs."[1]

Clearly, the shah realized by 1963 that this time domestic unrest and the concerns of official Washington could not be met by the usual tactic of condemning corruption, changing prime ministers, and announcing yet another five-year plan. In many respects, his response to the challenge proved brilliant in its public relations aspects. First, the shah within only one year virtually silenced public criticism of his regime in Washington. Second, the American mainstream press with only occasional exception reverted to a pattern of enthusiastic support for the Pahlavi regime. Third, the shah was able to successfully identify political dissent from his absolutist regime with the forces of reaction to modernism, thus isolating such dissent from decent opinion.

In short, the root motives of the White Revolution were political, not social or developmental. Yet its cosmetic qualities proved overwhelmingly attractive to the nominally liberal American press, which historically in its coverage of the Third World has often confused aggregate economic growth with progress, superficial reforms with substantive change, the trappings of the electoral process with democracy. It is not unreasonable to argue, in our view, that the largely uncritical support by the American mainstream press for the shah's pseudodevelopment program was a critical factor in shaping and sustaining the relationship between the United States and the shah from 1953 through 1978.

The mainstream press, willfully or not, ignored a century of struggle for social justice in Iran when it portrayed Iranian resistance to the shah as an unreasoning reaction to the Pahlavi regime's efforts at modernization. As we have argued, the sources of a people's discontent must be understood before the press's indictment of the results they have produced can be properly evaluated. This chapter will sketch out the broad historical background of the Pahlavis' scheme of modernization and will examine in some detail the White Revolution. The lessons to be learned about modernization from the Iranian experience go far beyond that country's borders. The press and American foreign-policy makers are likely to face similar situations in the future, and while the particular conditions may differ, the dynamics could be similar.

As a traditional society moves toward a modern political order, people often find themselves in new and unexpected situations. However, individuals or groups do not always respond to the challenges of the new situation in uniform ways. There is a mediating or intervening mechanism, a prism through which possibilities are seen and refracted. As Barrington Moore, Jr., has explained:

> The intervening variable, which it is convenient to call culture, screens out certain parts of the objective situation and emphasizes other parts. There are limits to the amount of variations in perception and human behavior that can come from this source. Still the residue of truth in the cultural explanation is that what looks like an opportunity or a temptation to one group of people will not necessarily seem so to another group with a different historical experience and living in a different form of society.[2]

It should not be surprising, therefore, that modernization as a concept and as a policy can be seen as either a hope or a curse, depending on a people's cultural perspective and concrete historical experience. The term "modernization" refers to the relationship between economic growth and the social structure. The interrelated processes frequently accompanying modernization include mechanization and commercialization of agriculture, industrialization, expansion of public education, and urbanization.

Furthermore, modernization historically has involved a change *from* conservative *toward* liberal values in the realm of culture. These developments, which usually but not necessarily occur simultaneously in the process of modernization, produce social disturbances because they dramatically affect or threaten the habits, customs, living conditions, and values of individuals and social classes. Generalizations about the nature of such social disturbances cannot be made about all societies or cultures, simply because there are variations in premodern conditions, impetus to change, and the content of dramatic events during the transition. Different experiences, past and present, may produce different results. Thus each society produces its own distinct national response to the challenge or demand of modernization.

The processes of modernization are frequently disruptive of the sociopolitical order because, besides the inevitable traditional resistance to structural change, the distribution of the fruits and sacrifices of modernization, no matter how well coordinated, is often uneven. The degree and kind of this unevenness, however, determine the character of the modernization process and whether it will have a positive or negative impact on the lives of people.

When the unevenness is hopelessly wide, as it was in Iran under the Pahlavis, it creates anomie in the classical sense, which often results in the growth of anxiety, hostility, and fantasy. Historically, such development in the process of social change has produced a variety of mass sociopolitical movements. For when the fruits and sacrifices of modernization are so unbalanced that large and diverse sectors of the population feel oppressed by the resulting sociopolitical situation, then the society becomes susceptible to radicalization and polarization. It is also at this point that the appeal of religiocultural resistance to social change gains in popularity and intensity.

Ideally, modernization is supposed to improve the material conditions of life in the society as a whole. Historically, however, the process often produces inequities and disaffection for large sectors of the population. There are also some cases in which in the name of modernization the life situation for the vast majority of a nation becomes more insecure, more inequitable, and more dissatisfying. Iran under the shah was such a case.

Professor Farhad Kazemi, who did a study of urban poverty in Iran during the 1970s, has observed:

> My daily travels in a private vehicle from opulent North Teheran to the poor migrant and squatter areas of South Teheran was a consciousness-raising experience of the first magnitude. Few individuals could remain unaffected after observing such fundamental and drastic differences in life styles of two groups in the same city.[3]

Kazemi's statistics, largely derived from official publications, show that the demise of agriculture under the shah's style of modernization caused the "increasing impoverishment of the poor peasantry."[4] Furthermore, "agricultural mechanization, which was designed to increase labor productivity, had the inevitable side effect of reducing the number of villagers needed for farmwork."[5] These conditions produced "widespread social alienation among the agricultural proletariat."[6] According to Kazemi, a survey of three villages in Fars province in 1967 found that

> 66 per cent of agricultural workers in the sample expressed extensive alienation as compared with 27.9 per cent of the new landowning farmers. Moreover, only 11.5 per cent of the agricultural workers were satisfied with their jobs. Ismail Ajami [the sociologist who conducted the study] attributes the alienation and job dissatisfaction of

the agricultural proletariat to the fact that land reform programs did
not distribute any land among them.[7]

It was largely because of dislocation and alienation in the countryside that during the 1960s and 1970s millions of peasants moved to
the cities in the hope of improving their lives; instead they ended up
joining a new class of urban squatters and slum dwellers. Kazemi's
work shows that the Iranian peasants, like their counterparts in Mexico and Brazil, have a tendency to migrate with the family.[8] Therefore, one would expect modernization planners to anticipate the need
for low-income housing for the migrant poor, but in Iran such a provision defied the royally determined priorities. As Kazemi writes:

> Considering the vast oil wealth of the country, the official performance
> in low-income housing has been abysmal. Those portions of oil reve-
> nues earmarked for housing were generally used to construct massive
> modern housing complexes that could be afforded only by the upper-
> middle and upper-income groups; the same applied to the housing
> projects built by the private sector. These ultramodern apartments
> have been purchased by the well-to-do, not migrant poor.[9]

As the marginal existence of the squatters and slum dwellers worsened, so did their sociopolitical alienation increase. For, contrary to
what the advocates of dual economic development suggest, increased
urbanization in Iran did not lead to meaningful political participation.

The shah's modernization drive produced drastic changes in the
structure of the Iranian economy. It also enabled the upper, and some
elements of the middle and lower-middle, classes to accumulate tremendous wealth. But for the majority of the population, modernization was simply a curse and a source of anger. More important, even
those who benefited from the oil income and the state-sponsored development projects did not gain any political power. There is much
evidence that during the 1970s wealthy Iranians were plagued with
an unprecedented degree of political insecurity and uncertainty. It
seems that in the midst of modernization the despotic character of
the Iranian monarchy became more rigid than ever before.

Furthermore, to understand the contemporary dialectic between
traditional and modern forces at work in the Third World, there must
be consideration of the international political impact on local conditions. Specifically, a useful analysis of the clash between tradition

and modernity must account for the influence, manipulation, and sometimes direct intervention of the developed powers. The degree and significance of this variable cannot be overemphasized. What complicates the matter is the absence of a general theory to explain the influence of the advanced industrial states, particularly the superpowers, on the course of events in developing nations. As a result, the influence of developed powers is often overlooked. Because of the country's oil deposits and its geopolitical significance, Iran's internal affairs have long been the target of, and vulnerable to, the designs of powerful international actors. This fact is crucial to an understanding of how modernization came to be carried out in Iran.

Perhaps the single most significant contradiction that the press missed in the shah's program of development is the incompatibility of genuine modernization with feudal politics, for the politics of modernization requires a degree of collective and rational decision making. Feudal politics, on the other hand, involves only a single person at the head of the polity as a proprietor responsible to no one. The shah definitely was such a ruler. Furthermore, he literally considered himself an expert on all areas of public affairs. No one among his elite could question the wisdom or the feasibility of his decisions.

The shah's assumption of this position was not typical of the history of the Iranian monarchy. For even though Iran's political system has always been despotic, with the king as the ultimate despot, the actual exercise of power was rarely confined to the domain of the court. For instance, during most of the 128 years of the Qajar dynasty the office of the Sadr-e Azam, or chief minister, was regarded as a significant and independent source of initiatives and judgments on matters of public concern. Even Reza Shah chose independent-minded men as his prime ministers during the first half of his kingship. Thus by ousting Ali Amini in 1963 the shah did more than simply change premiers; he practically abolished the institution of premiership as it had functioned historically. Amini was the last prime minister to the shah with any degree of independence in making important policy decisions.

It seems to be the case that a feudal ruler in pursuit of modernization must increasingly rely on repression and daily perpetuation of fear in dealings with both the political elite and the public at large in order to maintain control over the state. Various postrevolutionary writings on the shah's regime by both his close associates and foreign observers all testify to the reality that even the highest-echelon technocrats did not dare to take initiative on their own or to raise critical questions about the shah's favorite projects. Such docile behavior, induced as it was by coercion, does not signify stability.

Yet American policy makers and the press routinely characterized Iran under the shah as a stable country. Official Washington failed to realize that feudal politics in the contemporary world is inherently unstable and persisted in propping up the shah's regime for short-range gain. The mainstream press, virtually without exception, echoed the official view of life and politics in Iran for almost thirty years.

There is an argument that the shah had a curious ambivalence about him, as Prof. Richard W. Cottam has suggested. On the one hand, he exhibited a clear willingness "to utilize the instruments of terror to remain in power," while on the other, he seemed genuinely "sincere about wishing to bring economic, social, and political reform to his country."[10] We would argue that the contradiction between his intentions, however good they may have been, and his desire for absolute rule was too great. True modernity simply cannot be achieved through feudal politics.

The major aspects of the White Revolution, later renamed the "Shah-People Revolution," were (1) a land reform program, which had actually begun a year earlier than the January 1963 announcement date of the White Revolution; (2) sale of state-owned factories to finance land reform; (3) a plan whereby workers would be given 20 percent of net profits from the remaining government-owned factories; (4) a revised election law that would prevent the rigging of elections; (5) the nationalization of forests; and (6) the formation of several national service corps, including one for rural education.[11] Women's suffrage also came to be identified with the reform package.

Coverage in the mid-1960s of the shah's program of modernization was remarkably similar to coverage of the 1978–79 revolutionary period, which we will survey in chapter 7. The themes in both instances were almost identical, the frames given readers were basically the same, and the labels assigned various groups and elements remained virtually unchanged from 1963 to 1978. Most important to note in both periods was the tendency of journalists to assert claims about the shah and his development program *without* citing sources, which was a curious lapse indeed, given the journalistic command-ment to always include attribution in cases where the reporter is not personally expert. On balance, the intervening years between 1963 and 1978 evidenced not even modest change in journalistic percep-tions of the shah: he remained for the most part a modernizer of striking if unappreciated vision.

The prevailing journalistic assumptions about the shah's White Revolution, around which coverage of a decidedly more bloody one would revolve some fifteen years later, were transformed almost im-mediately into hardened stereotypes after the shah's program was officially introduced on 26 January 1963. Mass protests against the White Revolution, which reached their apex in the spring, were in-terpreted and portrayed by the press merely as unreasoning cultural reaction to progress, and journalists made little attempt to differen-tiate between the diverse motives, groups, and forces that were at work. News accounts of the mass uprisings triggered by the sup-posed reform measures tended to focus only on the agendas and com-plaints, real and imagined, of religious factions opposing the shah and his program, or of narrowly self-interested economic elites; the larger political dimension of the dispute went largely unexamined and unnoticed, as it would in 1978. As a result, the American public remained ignorant of the deliberate political aims of the shah and the determined political response they provoked. In the main, journalists and their public came to confuse a political program, and one depen-dent on force, at that, with a social program of development.

For the shah, having suppressed all nationalist political activity, the White Revolution was a way of moving in a different direction. The plan was intended to enlist the support for his regime of the previously politically inarticulate, indifferent, or uninvolved masses, particularly the landless peasantry, and to isolate potential opposi-tion, while at the same time reassuring his benefactor, the United States, and world opinion about his intentions. The program, not incidentally, also served to nurture the shah's self-image as a modern-izer.

From the beginning, mainstream American journalism was enthu-siastic about the shah's so-called revolution. The first *New York Times* account of the program appeared on the front page under the headline "Reforms of Shah Transform Iran." The account, filed from Washington by Max Frankel just before the program was officially announced, began with the assertion that "the Shah of Iran is rapidly altering his country's political and economic life with a reform program of revolutionary proportions."[12] The article said the revolution centered on the "distribution of nearly all Iranian farmlands and abolition of peasant-serf contracts." Moreover, according to Frankel, the plan would also include "major political reforms" and a "sweeping" literacy campaign.[13]

Less than one month later, in an editorial headlined "Iran's Royal Reforms," the *Times* was of the opinion that "after years of criticism that reforms in Iran were at best superficial and at worst nonexistent, the Shah today is personally pushing through social and economic change as drastic as any attempted by a nonrevolutionary regime anywhere in Asia."[14]

For its part, the *Christian Science Monitor* greeted the program editorially with this thought:

> It is hard for people in an economically advanced country to comprehend the changes that are taking place in Iran. There probably is some bungling and some harshness in certain phases of the transformation that is going on under [the shah], but on the whole the effect is one of progress for most of the 21,000,000 people in the land that history knew as Persia.[15]

The editorialist concluded with the hope that "the glories of a new Iran be shared by all its people."[16] *Life* magazine was similarly impressed and ran a pictorial entitled "Future to Outshine Ancient Glories."[17]

Occasionally, more considered judgments were published. One such example of a more judicious approach was a *New York Times* Sunday Magazine piece by Jay Walz published in the fall of 1963. Walz, whose coverage of Iran over the years for the *New York Times* usually exhibited a blind spot on political repression together with undue optimism about development programs, nonetheless showed at least modest reservations about the White Revolution in his Sunday Magazine assessment.[18] But on the whole, any such caution clearly seems to have been lost in the literally thousands of words published praising various aspects of the shah's program.

The prevailing view of the shah for the next several years, indeed, is caught in this *Times* profile published in 1964 on the occasion of a visit by the shah to the United States to, among other things, receive an honorary degree—one of several received from American universities during his rule—from New York University in recognition of his "'farsighted vision and personal courage' in forwarding the 'progress of social reform based on social justice.'"[19] According to the *Times*, "With the institution of land reform, the enfranchisement of women and the *granting of political freedom on a broad base*, the shah demonstrated his concern for the masses" (emphasis ours).[20]

The only early dissent from the general high praise accorded the White Revolution was found in the *Christian Science Monitor*, which will be taken up in the following discussion of land reform, and in the *Nation*. How much effect such criticism in a single, small-circulation, left-liberal journal of opinion can have compared with the near unanimity of the mainstream press remains doubtful. Nevertheless, in the summer of 1964, the *Nation* greeted the shah's visit to the United States with this observation: "The truth is, that among all the dictatorial regimes shored up by the United States the Shah's is among the most vicious." The *Nation* editorial continued in this vein:

> His public relations men project an image of the Shah as a progressive, "Western" monarch. His progressivism is shown by a typical Iranian budget which allows nearly 12 billion rials for the armed forces, 1 billion for the Ministry of Health, and 0.6 billion for the universities. As a clincher, the Shah's land reforms are cited. The fact is that after all the reforming, 60 per cent of the farmers own no land at all.[21]

Such dark views of the shah's motives and actions to the contrary, the mainstream press was only too willing to suspend disbelief in the White Revolution. This accommodating nature is particularly evident in how the press covered the national plebiscite called just after announcement of the reform plan to legitimize (and publicize) the shah's modernization program.

Admiring press coverage to the contrary, the shah's plebiscite was nothing more than a public relations ploy aimed at demonstrating public acceptance of his program and was hardly an indication of democracy at work. Yet the American press gave widespread and approving coverage of the vote, with "hardly a suggestion that the vote had been staged,"[22] and thought nothing untoward about a final tally of *99 percent* in favor of the reforms. Too, there was scant mention of the shah's having effectively suppressed *all* political opposition.

The Associated Press, for instance, described the vote as a "triumph for the Shah and his 'revolution from the throne,'" telling readers that the revolution was one in "which Iran's ruler has aligned himself directly with workers and peasants against conservatives and traditionalists."[23] *U.S. News & World Report* reported that "peasants, workers and women turned out in droves to endorse the shah's program of 'legal revolution'" and ended its account with the conclusion that "the referendum clearly has given the Shah new authority. Reforms may come faster in Iran from now on."[24]

Richard Cottam, the political scientist and former diplomat who served in Tehran as the American embassy's political officer from 1956 to 1958, has pointed out a double standard on the part of journalism in its coverage of the plebiscite, which was conducted under far more questionable circumstances than those surrounding the Mosaddeq referendum ten years earlier:

> Compare for example the remarks of *The New York Times* editorial after the Mossadeq plebiscite with one referring to the Shah's plebiscite. In August 15, 1953, the *Times* wrote: "We thought of [Dr. Mosaddeq] as a sincere, well-meaning, patriotic Iranian who had a different point of view. We now know that he is a power-hungry, personally ambitious, ruthless demagogue who is trampling upon the liberties of his own people." On June 10, 1963, the *Times* wrote: "The great mass of the Iranian people are doubtless behind the Shah in his bold new reform efforts. The national plebiscite he called early this year gave emphatic evidence of this. . . ." The vote in 1953 was 2,043,389 to 1,207. The vote in 1963 was 5,598,711 to 4,115.[25]

In September of 1963 the shah followed up the dubious success of his plebiscite with elections for the majles, and the press proved generally every bit as uncritical of the process and enthusiastic toward the results. A dominant theme of coverage was the right of women to vote for the first time in Iranian history, although journalists completely missed the point that the vast majority of Iranian women could not effectively exercise the franchise, given their high rate of illiteracy and low political consciousness, and that there was no authentic diversity of candidates in any event.

An Associated Press dispatch, however, did raise some concerns about the election in advance. After favorably commenting on the "revolutionary" nature of the election, the article spoke of "shortcomings" that included a ban against campaigns by opposition factions, the jailing of opposition leaders, and a boycott by some opposition organizations. "Many Iranians appear indifferent to Tuesday's election," the article concluded, "or fear it will be the same old story of corruption."[26]

Whatever the reservations of the Associated Press, they were completely overshadowed by the dominant tone of coverage of the election itself. The *Times* observed editorially in what can only be considered a classic example of colonial thought:

> The Shah of Iran and his Government have won an overwhelming and well-deserved victory in the national elections for a Majlis, or Parliament. This time the election was carefully prepared, and while it would not qualify as free and democratic by United States standards, it was doubtless the fairest and most representative election Iran has ever had.[27]

As we indicated at the beginning of this chapter, the White Revolution provided several significant benefits to the shah, not the least of which was the opportunity to discredit his political opposition in the eyes of the liberal West in general and the United States in particular. Demonstrations against the shah's program actually began before the White Revolution was officially announced, when several of the ulama (Islamic religious leaders) organized their followers around the issue of land reform legislation that was passed in 1962. (According to Nikki R. Keddie among others, the word *ulama* is "inadequately rendered by 'clergy,' as their role is not to intercede between people and God, but to carry out Muslim law, education, charity, and so forth—a broader role than that of the Western clergy.")[28] Other factions joined in for different reasons, and the protests escalated in October and December 1962, culminating in three days of antigovernment demonstrations in June of 1963.

Throughout mainstream coverage of these events, those opposing the shah's modernization program were uniformly portrayed in one-dimensional terms as the forces of reaction. No major journalistic effort was made to go beyond the convenient explanations offered by the regime that the shah's opponents represented either benighted fanaticism or narrow feudal self-interest. The assertions of the mainstream American press to the contrary, opposition to the White Revolution was grounded in rejection of the regime's claim to legitimacy—not in opposition to progress.

The journalistic distortion resulted in large part from the failure to understand that what the shah was engaged in was not progressive reform but instead an attempt to graft bits and pieces of advanced industrial capitalism onto a preindustrial society while at the same time preserving his royal dictatorship. Basic structural change was neither desired nor sought. To be sure, various elements of the society, including parts of the clergy, had narrow vested interests, which appeared to be threatened by the shah's moves. This dimension, however, was irrelevant to the dramatic underlying currents of political protest that depended on a growing awareness that the shah's program of modernization was nothing of the sort; that the program's costs and benefits would be unjustly distributed; and that, most important, the price to be paid for the modernization program was intensification of political repression. In short, journalists came to confuse a political program, and one dependent on force, at that, with a project of social development.

Typical of the treatment given demonstrations against the shah's program early in 1963 was a Reuters dispatch in the *Christian Science Monitor* which told of government moves against "National Front supporters of former Premier Mohammed Mossadegh [who] had called for a demonstration against land reform." The story added that students opposing the shah's program were forced to flee from the university when pursued by some two thousand workers and peasants shouting "Long live the Shah, death to the traitors."[29] Nowhere in the story is there a hint of an explanation for why the National Front, an organization made up largely of middle-class liberals, should be against land reform, nor does the story offer any sort of explanation for why university students might be similarly inclined.

In their rush to portray the shah's initiatives in the best possible light, journalists ignored or overlooked his simultaneous move to suppress his major political opposition, the remnants of the National Front, by ordering the arrest of the Front's central council and most of its second-level leadership. As Richard Cottam has explained, it was a clever ploy by the shah in that his liberal reform measures distracted the American press from the political repression.[30] Much to its credit, the *Christian Science Monitor* was the only prestige daily newspaper during this period to publish an editorial raising serious questions about human rights violations in Iran or, for that matter, even to mention the mass arrests that had taken place.[31]

Furthermore, the shah's direct move against the Front placed it in a curiously awkward position. While the Front philosophically agreed with many of the provisions of the shah's program, it could hardly appear to be supporting him following the mass arrests. Therefore, angered at the shah's repressive tactics and personal dictatorship, the Front opposed a national plebiscite on the reform measures, arguing that a democratically elected majles should decide any reform measures. This position in turn made it possible for the shah's propagandists to paint the Front as being anti progress and anti liberal reform.[32]

By the early summer of 1963 religious elements had moved to the fore of the anti-shah movement for a number of reasons, not the least of which was the successful suppression of major secular opposition. Even though the religious opposition could not provide an adequate analysis of the sociopolitical problems facing the country, Shi'i symbolism and doctrines lent themselves to the expression of generalized alienation and discontent. Lacking any understanding of or sympathy for the Islamic content of the protests and seemingly unaware of the political nature of the reform program, reporters were easy prey for the stereotypes offered by the Pahlavi regime.

An account of the June uprising by *Time,* headlined "Iran: Progress at a Price," captured the general tone of American press coverage. The article began, "For three days last week, Teheran was a battleground; crowds shrieked, machine guns chattered and smoke from smoldering rubble mixed with clouds of tear gas. Ironically, it was a battle against progress." *Time*'s editors described the shah as "that most unusual, reform-minded monarch," and wrote of his "long struggle" to turn his feudal nation into a modern state. The "formidable opposition" to the shah, according to *Time,* ranged from "corrupt bureaucrats" and "big landlords" to mollahs who "condemn as heretical his plan to give women the vote" and to lease out "shrine villages" to peasants.[33]

The wire services echoed these explanations. United Press International, for instance, began one account, "Thousands of fanatical Moslems stormed through the heart of Tehran,"[34] and in another explained that the demonstrations were the result of religious figures who opposed "the Shah's reforms because the reforms cut into their income from lands now being given to the peasants."[35]

Even publications usually more suspicious of the behavior of American clients proved susceptible to the easy stereotypes applied to the shah's opponents. Without their own correspondents in the field and in the absence of a strong political analysis of the situation, smaller publications, including those with a nominally left-of-center perspective, in some cases deferred to the news frames of the larger news organizations. Too, American liberal journalism has never felt completely comfortable with political rebellion in the Islamic world and frequently has fallen prey to the facile explanation of such rebellion as being nothing more than the meddling in the affairs of state by a reactionary and benighted religion.

In any event, the denigration of the 1963 revolt was not limited to the more conservative reaches of journalism. For instance, an editorial essay in the *New Republic* headlined "Iran Rioting for Islam" cited the bitter opposition of religious leaders to land distribution and women's suffrage. In what can only be described as an absurd judgment, given the facts of history, the author argued that the government's reforms had radically altered the balance of power away from "the landlords—old allies of the clergy—*to the working peasant classes*" (emphasis ours).[36]

A view of events in Iran not too dissimilar to that of the *New Republic* was offered readers of *Harper's* magazine. John Fischer in an "Editor's Easy Chair" column entitled "The Shah and His Exasperating Subjects" presented a series of unequivocal assertions, including the contention that the "Moslem religious leaders hate him because the Shah is trying to modernize the country—and Islam cannot thrive in a modern atmosphere."[37]

The heart of Fischer's argument in the piece, which was the second of two installments and was based on a personal interview with the shah, is contained in the writer's view that "undemocratic the government certainly is . . . but any conceivable alternative government would be equally undemocratic, or worse, simply because Iran has never known any other kind of regime."[38]

Given the assumptions of the mainstream press, the regime's brutal treatment of the thousands involved in the 1963 uprising became a matter of necessity in the eyes of journalists. Those opposing the shah were almost completely cut off from the sympathy or under-standing of the outside world. Nowhere was this attitude more appar-ent than on the editorial pages of the *New York Times*. When it be-came clear that the shah had prevailed during the June uprising, the *Times* offered these editorial congratulations:

> The Shah appears to have surmounted another crisis in his drive to reform and develop the semi-feudal kingdom of Iran. Violent rioting and a plot to overthrow his Government have been suppressed. Back of the new troubles are reactionary Moslem mullahs and landlords, angered at the prospective loss of their lands as a result of the Shah's new land-redistribution program. The military forces, however, have remained loyal to the Shah and have effectively smashed outbreaks in Teheran, Shiraz and other cities.[39]

The *Times* editorial spoke admiringly of these developments as "new evidence" of the shah's "courage and determination in personally directing the suppression of this latest upsurge of opposition." Ac-cording to the *Times*, "He will have continuing need of these quali-ties."[40]

Perhaps the most effective way of coming to understand what the vast majority of Iranians found objectionable in the White Revolu-tion is to judge the shah's professed goals and claimed successes, at least the most significant ones, against what is known and argued in the scholarly literature. At the same time, this version of reality can be compared with what was asserted in the popular press, particu-larly its treatment of land reform, a comparison that should provide at least one bench mark for measuring journalistic performance.

The major shortcomings of the press in 1963, as we argued in chapter 1, were grounded in the unwillingness or inability of the press to appreciate or comprehend the political culture of Iran. This flaw is manifest, most significantly and most clearly, in how the me-dia portrayed, first, the nature of the opposition and, second, its motives, but it was also evident in the news media's failure to place the revolt against the White Revolution in historical context. The press consistently failed to point out that the June riots followed three years of high unemployment, economic decline, the closure of the majles by the shah, suppression of political opposition, and general public anger with the continued rigging of elections. Moreover, the events of 1953 had hardly faded from the national memory, nor had resentment diminished toward ever-increasing American involvement on the Iranian scene. Long-standing grievances, in short, formed the wave on which anger at the White Revolution became merely the crest.

In terms of how the press portrayed the opposition, it is true that American journalists often included in their accounts of the 1963 turmoil at least mention of the varied groups opposed to the shah. (It is also true, as the above excerpts from *Time* and *Harper's* indicate, that this mention was hardly favorable.) On balance, however, the press tended to focus on the religious dimension of the protest without explaining its context and tended to avoid mention of those groups whose motives were political rather than religious. The role of the members of the National Front, for instance, or the critical part played by university students, including the Iranian students in the United States and Europe, rarely received attention.[41]

Evidence of yet another form of selective reporting by the press during this period was reflected in descriptions of the tactics and behavior of the opposing forces. *Time,* for instance, in its first article on the events of June told of a mob that had yanked an unveiled woman from her automobile, forced her to undress, and then pummeled her to death. No attribution for the isolated incident was included.[42] Yet many major incidents that in large part gave rise to popular outrage against the shah went unreported. These involved protests on the eve of the shah's plebiscite in Tabriz, Qum, Tehran, and Shiraz, all of which were brutally put down. In March hundreds were killed in Tabriz and Qum. The latter occurrence involved an invasion by paratroopers and SAVAK of a *madrasa,* or religious school. In some instances, troops hurled students to their death from the roof of the school. Similarly, the press usually went along with the government's estimate of the number of deaths among opposition elements (between sixty and ninety, in most accounts), while scholars put the number between hundreds and thousands.[43]

However, it was not selective reporting but the general tendency of the press to identify opposition to tyranny with antimodernity which should be regarded as the major failing of media performance in the mid-1960s. Nowhere was this more apparent than in the uncritical acceptance of the regime's contentions about the linchpin of its program: land reform. Throughout its contemporary coverage of troubled Iran, the American press has persisted in (1) the belief that significant land reform occurred in Iran and (2) the belief that religious opposition to land reform was a chief cause of the uprisings in 1963 and the revolution of 1978. These two contentions, more than any other, came to be used to support the view that the shah was serious about improving the lot of his people in the face of religious reaction and was therefore a worthy and deserving American ally.

Furthermore, by presenting over the years as truthful the shah's claims about his modernization plans, as well as the nature of the opposition, the press played the principal role in creating the general sense of unease among liberal constituencies in the United States toward the Iranian revolution. The result was a noticeable lack of *active* support for the 1978 revolution in much of the left-liberal community in the United States, which usually, at least after Vietnam, can be expected to voice sustained criticism of American support for antidemocratic regimes locked in struggles with their people.

To the extent that this is so, it is instructive to compare both press treatment of and the liberal public's reaction to the revolution against Anastasio Somoza in Nicaragua with that accorded the revolt against the shah. Both rebellions, of course, occurred at roughly the same time. It is not difficult to discredit resistance to oppression in a client state, at least for Americans, if it can also be made to appear resistant to progress. In this regard, at no time had the press seriously argued that Somoza's rule brought anything resembling progress to his country, nor did the press exhibit an unwillingness to use the term "dictatorship" to describe Somoza's tenure.

Yet throughout our study of elite-press treatment of the shah over a twenty-five-year period we could find only four uses in the *mainstream* news columns of the word "dictator" to describe the shah, and rare use of the term in editorials. How the shah emerged as merely "autocratic" and Somoza as a "dictator" is, in our view, at the heart of the matter. Both were put in power by the United States, both were facing concurrent internal crises of legitimacy, both used similar methods to crush dissent, and both intended to stay in power at whatever human cost. It can be argued, of course, that the press treated Somoza differently from the shah simply because Nicaragua's star in the constellation of U.S. interests hardly had the sparkle of Iran's. Certainly this was a contributing factor. But the explanation for U.S. press coverage of Iran as opposed to its coverage of Nicaragua in revolt is probably more complicated than a straight national-interest argument suggests and, more likely, revolves around the notion of modernization, a concept inextricably linked in the minds of journalists to land reform.

Land reform, of course, was only one piece of evidence offered in the court of public opinion to support the image of the shah as a benevolent modernizer. Women's rights, election reform, educational and literacy gains, and the industrialization of the country were also much pointed to in the press as results of the White Revolution, and will be discussed. But on balance, land reform received the most attention and seemed to the press to be the best solid evidence of modernization at hand. As we have suggested, there are two significant dimensions to American press coverage of this aspect of reform in Iran: the first deals with land reform as a policy, and the second deals with land reform as an organizing issue around which protest centered.

In the area of policy concerns, the chief shortcoming of the press was to *confuse land redistribution with land reform.* Specifically, the media, in the main, (1) assumed the purity of the shah's motives and failed to look for hidden agendas or alternative explanations for his policies, (2) overlooked the contradictions inherent in the theory and practice of Iran's version of land reform, and (3) failed to examine systematically the results of the program independent of the regime's claims for success.

An editorial in the *Christian Science Monitor* during the early stages of the land-redistribution program is typical of the uncritical enthusiasm and range of arguments with which the press greeted the plan, although the *Monitor,* alone among the prestige media, would later come to express serious doubts about the shah's efforts. The editorial began by arguing that landowning aristocracies in Latin America and Southeast Asia as well as the Middle East would do well to follow the shah's example. According to the *Monitor,* "To resist successfully the specious appeal of communism, land reform is gravely needed in many parts of the world as well as in Iran."[44]

Another *Monitor* editorial the following year, headlined "Iran's Social Revolution," noted that the shah recently had completed distribution of the last of the crown lands, some 3,500,000 acres, immediately before the plebiscite that gave him sweeping powers to run the country. "Such powers are always suspect," the *Monitor* cautiously observed, "[and] they may be abused. But the indications are that the Shah intends elections for a new Majlis . . . and that literacy programs and profit-sharing in government factories will follow." The *Monitor*'s editorial concluded: "May the glories of a new Iran be shared by all its people."[45]

The first appearance of something resembling land reform in Iran occurred in 1951 when the shah, in a much-publicized move, issued a royal decree putting up for sale to peasants his holdings of 2,000 villages. (The nonmigratory rural population lives in about 67,000 villages.) The shah had become convinced that there were more long-range political and economic advantages in the move than disadvantages and hoped that by his example other large landlords would engage in similar redistribution without government intervention. (They failed to cooperate.) Through this act, the shah became identified with the pro-land-reform movement, particularly in the American press. For example, according to an *Atlantic* assessment published in 1954, the shah in 1945 "emerged as an articulate and positive force in his country," evidence of which was his willingness to break up the royal estates acquired by his father and sell them to peasants on "easy terms."[46] This view persisted and became part of journalistic received opinion as demonstrated by a *Los Angeles Times* correspondent who wrote in 1975 that the Shah-People Revolution centered on "land redistribution in which the shah himself set the example by giving away much of the royal holdings."[47]

No questions were raised about how the royal family had accumulated its vast land holdings. After all, the founder of the dynasty, Reza Khan, was a man of humble origin who owned no land at the time of crowning himself shah in 1925. It is indeed strange that American reporters covering the story were not curious enough to ask how the royal family in less than twenty years had come to possess so much land that it could sell 2,000 villages in 1951 and yet remain the biggest landlord in the country.

The failure of the press to investigate fully this early "reform" established an unfortunate precedent for the media's uncritical coverage of more formal reform measures ten years later, which, in turn, meant that assertions about land reform by the time of the 1978 revolution had taken on the hue of undisputed historical truth. Had the press looked more closely at the shah's early seeming generosity, indeed, the attentive and elite foreign-policy public in the United

States might have been better able to judge the 1962–1971 program. And for those who would argue that what is known of land reform today is largely the product of hindsight, an examination of the footnotes and the dating of the sources cited by the scholars who have written on the subject is probably the best evidence to the contrary.

As it was, we could find no mention in our survey of the mainstream press from the early 1950s of several critical facts germane to the action taken by the shah in breaking up the Pahlavi estates. First, most of the lands distributed had been acquired by the shah's father, in the words of one scholar, "mostly by dubious means,"[48] making him the largest absentee landowner in the country.[49] After Reza Shah's abdication, there was a clamor for their return to former owners. Second, in reality the shah's distribution of the royal estates was largely symbolic, had little practical effect, and took ten years to complete.[50] Moreover, fully a third of the lands were sold not to peasants but to wealthy favorites of the shah, and the money raised by the sales remained in the royal coffers.[51]

There are two lines of thought, besides the commonly held view in the press of a beneficent, liberal-minded monarch committed to social change, on why the shah pushed for land redistribution in the early 1960s. The first school interprets the shah's motives as largely *political*. First, redistribution was a move to break the power of his once and future competitors, the large feudal absentee landlords, in the villages. There would be other important benefits to the regime as well. Reform would create a new class of landowners loyal to the regime; head off rural instability as a threat to the crown; insinuate Tehran's power in rural areas, which contained more than half the country's population and which, effectively, had been beyond the central government's influence; and provide evidence to concerned American foreign-policy makers of the shah's commitment to liberalization.[52]

Proponents of the second school of thought, which is not at all mutually exclusive of the first but instead places a different emphasis on things, argue that the shah's major motive was economic. Under the heavy influence of his American advisers, the shah's was a development scheme to create agricultural surplus, which in turn could be used for the purposes of capital accumulation to finance industrialization. Furthermore, the old landlord class would be forced to shift its capital into the industrial sector; also, excess labor created by fragmentation of the old estates would then be "freed" for use in the emerging industrial sector. All this could be accomplished without basic structural change in the authoritarian nature of the society. If what had once been self-sustaining economies were ruined in the process, so be it; the reforms were a necessary precondition for state capitalism.[53]

Whatever his motives, the execution and results of the three-phase program that the shah launched in 1962 and officially ended in 1971 were susceptible to a clear-cut evaluation, which to our knowledge the mainstream press failed, with the exception of the *Christian Science Monitor*, ever to engage in. While the press may be excused during the early years of the reform for failing to assess its outcome simply because the results were slow to come in, no such excuse existed in the 1970s.

On the surface, which is where the press appeared content to remain, the raw figures for redistribution provided by the regime clearly must have seemed impressive: Nearly one-half of village families acquired at least limited landownership. In the ten years of the land reform program, about 92 percent of former *sharecroppers* had become peasant proprietors. More land was redistributed under the program than under any similar program in the Middle East since land reform had been introduced as a government policy in Egypt in 1952.

Mere redistribution of land, however, as we have suggested, does not mean that reform has taken place—and this is a possibility the press completely failed to consider. The most recent and careful scholarship on the subject of Iranian land reform has been done by Dr. Eric Hooglund. In his 1982 book, *Land and Revolution in Iran,* Hooglund posed the critical questions the press failed to ask:

> In order to evaluate the effects of any particular land reform, it is necessary to examine the details of the program with the objective of determining which groups benefited; how much land was acquired per family and at what cost; which groups were excluded and upon what rationale; and what new class alignments, if any, resulted. Such information is a virtual prerequisite for understanding the economic developments—both positive and negative—which are the consequence of land redistribution.[54]

It is not necessary to answer Hooglund's questions in great detail to arrive at some sense of whether the shah's program proved to be more chimerical than modernizing. From the outset, the Iranian program had some important limitations. Under the first phase, which proved to be the most ambitious of the three, for instance, affected landowners could choose which of their holdings to keep and invariably chose the most profitable; and several types of lands were exempt from the program entirely: fruit orchards, tea plantations, woodlands, mechanized fields, and religiously endowed properties called *vaqfs*.[55]

More significant, under the terms of the Land Reform Law of 1962 only those peasants with existing customary rights of cultivation, called *nasaq* holders, were eligible to receive land. In effect a sharecropper, the peasant who held a *nasaq* could buy from the government the plots which he had most recently farmed. A major drawback of the scheme, therefore, was that it *excluded* those individuals who did not possess *nasaq*. These people were called *khwushnishin*s and in 1960 constituted 40 percent of the rural households.[56] How the Associated Press could conclude that 75 percent of Iran's *entire* population ended up owning land must remain a mystery.[57] Besides depriving a significant portion of the rural population of a chance to own land, the exclusion of the *khwushnishin*s would have other disastrous effects as well, which will be discussed presently. Moreover, when the dust settled, not all that much land had been redistributed, because of exemptions, loopholes, and the like: more than half of all villages ended up not being covered by the law.

The result was devastating: Even after excluding the 40 percent of the rural population represented by the *khwushnishin*s, there were far too few parcels to go around for the eligible peasantry holding *nasaq*. Consequently, according to Hooglund, the *average* figure for land obtained by the typical five-member family turned out to be about 4 hectares (or 9.9 acres), and this figure did not reflect "tremendous disparities" in the actual distribution.[58] In 1976, final reform figures showed, less than 10 percent of all peasants received more than 10 hectares of land, the majority of these holdings in the 10–20 range. Thirty-five percent, or four times as many peasants, had holdings of only 1 hectare (2.4 acres) or less. This meant that overall, *72 percent,* or nearly three-fourths of all peasants, received less than 6 hectares of land, whereas most authorities agree that the bare minimum for *subsistence* farming in Iran is 7 hectares.[59]

Another authority estimated that in the final analysis "between 40 and 50 percent of those engaged in agriculture" ended up landless, and noted that "as incongruous as it may seem, land reform [in Iran] may *lower* the proportion of the agricultural labor force that has land rights."[60] This odd state of affairs resulted from the reality that the allotted plots were so small and therefore uneconomic that the indebted farmer was forced to sell out, often to speculators, which led once again to the consolidation of lands.

Compounding the problems was the undercapitalization of the new landowners. In theory, government-sponsored cooperatives would provide capital to work the land (indeed, to receive land the peasant had to join a cooperative), but in practice the cooperatives became more vehicles for government control in the villages than friendly, low-interest lenders. The cooperatives were never adequately funded by the central government, even after 1974 and the massive influx of oil revenues. From 1962 to 1974, for instance, the average per capita cooperative loan was about 6,000 rials, or a sum equivalent to the amount needed to produce "a single hectare of dry farmed winter wheat!"[61]

The situation, then, following land redistribution, was this: Far too many peasants were sharing far too little land (the vast majority ended with less than enough for subsistence) and were left with practically no capital to pay for (the land was not given away) or work the parcels they had received. Too, nearly half the rural population, the *khwushnishin*s, who were mostly agricultural laborers, received no land at all. According to the consensus view of most scholars, voiced by Hooglund:

> Thus, by 1971, when land reform was declared officially completed, the overwhelming majority of villagers were in no better economic situation than they had been prior to implementation of the program. Indeed, the evidence suggests that the relative economic position of thousands of rural families *actually worsened* during the "revolutionary" decades of land reform (emphasis ours).[62]

The land reform had consequences far beyond the countryside. For instance, it intensified rural-to-urban migration. Perhaps as many as two million villagers migrated to the cities between 1966 and 1976,[63] the vast majority of them young men. Slums burgeoned not only in the major cities of Tehran, Mashhad, and Isfahan, as a result, but in smaller cities as well; equally destructive of forced migration was the robbing of the rural areas of essential workers.

But most important of all, the adverse effects of land reform on agricultural production were felt by the whole country. Considered self-sufficient before "modernization" and "land reform," Iran became a food-deficit country in the 1970s, and by 1977 was importing $2.6 billion in food; that figure was expected to rise to $4 billion by 1980.[64] The abject failure of land reform, certainly, cannot be blamed entirely for this situation: increased food consumption played a role, and the regime's emphasis on agribusiness and corporate farming, both of which achieved a "miserable record,"[65] played an even greater one.

The point to be made here is that the land reform program in Iran was, in fact, a failure by all rational standards. Perhaps the ultimate proof of this is that the rural areas, which supposedly had benefited from the reform, proved to be either utterly indifferent or actively hostile to the regime when the revolution, which was primarily an urban-based revolt, occurred in 1978. The general peasantry by that time was well aware of what had occurred—or what had not—under land reform.[66]

In no way did the shah's program earn or deserve the image it enjoyed in the American news media. What mention of land reform that did appear in the media, to be sure, was routinely brief and never consisted of more than a sentence or a paragraph. Nonetheless, the alleged success of the shah's land reform program was asserted often enough during coverage of the revolution to constitute an important theme and to raise serious questions about the media's performance, questions that we will deal with in a later chapter.

The single exception to the journalistic ardor for the shah's land reform program was the *Christian Science Monitor,* which after its initial enthusiasm had diminished, ran several articles over the years that raised some disturbing possibilities left unexamined in the rest of the press and cast at least a shadow over the regime's claims. An early August 1963 article by Arnold Beichman, headlined "Iran Land Reform Doubts," was remarkable (1) because it was published so early on and (2) because its perspective offered such a stark contrast to the ready acceptance of the rest of the mainstream press. The tone of the article is conveyed in Beichman's opening:

> Deepening concern is being expressed by knowledgeable Iranians that the much-touted land reform program, decreed by [the shah] in

January, 1962, is all "public relations" sound and expropriated land-lord fury with little prospective benefit for Iran's 16-million peasants. These criticisms come from Iranian liberals, whose identification would jeopardize their freedom in this authoritarian land.[67]

Beichman was careful to identify his sources as longtime opponents of the feudal land-tenure system, and described their concerns along the lines that much later would be suggested by Hooglund. Perhaps most important, Beichman's analysis offers evidence that criticism of the shah's program did not require hindsight.

In a piece filed several days later from Tehran, Beichman asked some tough questions of Premier Asadollah Alam about the White Revolution, perhaps the toughest questions—at least to appear in print—to be asked by an American reporter. The questions centered on issues of freedom and human rights in Iran. For instance, Beich-man asked why the leader of the National Front had been jailed with neither charges filed nor a trial scheduled. Beichman also asked the premier for the number of political prisoners being held in Iranian jails, and told his readers of how some seventy-five newspapers and magazines had been curtailed, which had led to "strong criticism that there is no freedom of the press in Iran."[68]

A column one year later by Geoffrey Godsell, commenting on the replacement of Alam as premier by Hasan Ali Mansur, asserted that Alam's downfall might have been because "the much-heralded land reform was less impressive than claimed" and because Alam was remembered by the public for his government, which had "given the shoot to kill orders at the time of last June's riots." Godsell also wrote of a majles whose members "are virtually handpicked by the Shah."[69]

A 1965 news analysis by Godsell, headlined "Iran's Land-Reform Program: Has the Shah Gone Far Enough," argued that the benefi-ciaries of land reform "have not been those Iranian peasants who were most land hungry." In a particularly perceptive insight, Godsell said that what land had been distributed had created a new "rural bourgeoisie" which only served to sharpen the resentment of peas-ants denied the fruits of land redistribution. In short, Godsell found that "land reform had not touched the poverty of the poorest Iranian peasant."[70] He also was the only American journalist to point out that the number of cooperatives brought into being was woefully in-adequate. The *Monitor* published a similar analysis by Iran scholar

James A. Bill in 1968.[71] Professor Bill recalls sending the article, based on two years of research in Iran in the mid-1960s, to a number of publications, including the *New York Times* and *Foreign Affairs*. According to Bill, who still remembers the affair with some irritation, "nobody would touch the piece except the *Monitor,*" a publication for which he has high praise.[72]

Land reform may have been one of the more spectacular myths of the shah's regime, which the press accepted uncritically, but there were others as well, and the press accepted them almost as uncritically. Most stories about the White Revolution shared certain things in common: A bewildering array of statistics, a "gee-whiz" attitude toward Iran's oil wealth, a litany of examples of economic waste, and a view of the shah as a man with a dream. The gold-rush aspects of the shah's supposed push toward modernity tended to overshadow the elements of doubt raised in news accounts.

The flavor of this type of coverage is caught in headlines such as these: "Iran Bursting at Seams with Development"; "Shah Lifting Nation by Bootstraps with Help of Oil Revenue" (*Los Angeles Times*);[73] "Iran's Race for Riches" (*Newsweek*);[74] and "Instant Capitalists: With Shah's Backing, Millions of Iranians Soon Will Buy Stock" (*Wall Street Journal*).[75] As a correspondent for the *New York Times* wrote in 1970, the White Revolution represented "a sweeping program of reforms aimed at turning a primitive peasant society into an industrialized nation,"[76] and the writer found in "new office buildings, supermarkets, freeways and modern factories" ample evidence of an unprecedented pride and confidence that characterized the new Iran.

It is not that the media ignored problems caused by the shah's attempts at overnight modernization. On the contrary, the press—particularly after 1974—in many accounts emphasized the more exotic and bizarre evidences of disruption caused by pumping billions of dollars into a once poor economy. But the press in doing so assumed the tone of a bemused and only mildly disapproving uncle watching a favored nephew squander an unexpected inheritance in an impetuous and immature fashion. This benevolent and somewhat patronizing attitude of the press tended to obscure the possibility that the shah's version of economic development not only suffered from excesses but at its core was totally inappropriate to the actual needs of most of the Iranian people. This tendency of the press to leave basic assumptions unexamined was carried over into its failure to investigate the shah's assertions that major parts of his program had been a success.

An example of this is the regime's almost slavish belief in Western agricultural methods. Mechanized farming, for instance, which was urged by American advisers, proved disastrous in an arid country characterized by thin topsoil and sparse forestation;[77] in general the regime adopted an agricultural policy far better suited to a country with a large amount of arable land and a shortage of labor.[78]

Some other crucial aspects of the shah's version of modernization that went largely unchallenged in the press include gains claimed for the industrial sector, the economy, and social and health services, all of which fared little better than agriculture during the White Revolution. In essence, Iran's was a force-fed economy that suffered all the worst consequences of gorging: Inflation, increasingly inequitable distribution of wealth, the acquisition of and emphasis on inappropriate high technology and heavy durable goods, increasing unemployment and underemployment, and increasing dependence on foreign suppliers for goods and services.

Evidences of a severely distorted economy were everywhere in Iran, particularly after oil prices quadrupled in December 1973, but the American news media—despite passing attention to the more bizarre aspects—tended to overlook the warning signs. This was particularly the case during the White Revolution. One observer believes that this is the result of what he calls the Green Revolution Factor, which has it that American foreign-policy makers and the press invariably favor revolutions that involve technology, but frown on revolutions involving people.[79]

To be sure, Iran's rate of *industrial* growth was among the highest in the world. The problems lay in the reality that the industry being encouraged was Western in style and substance and better suited to the needs of developed Western countries. The industry that resulted from the White Revolution and later in the mid-1970s was heavily capital-intensive and pushed aside the smaller crafts and shop-type businesses where labor in Iran tended to concentrate. As a result, income gaps widened rather than narrowed, and by 1977 only an estimated 15 to 20 percent of the population could be said to benefit from the oil revenues.[80] Equally disruptive was the increasing dependence on oil revenue instead of on income earned by traditional exports.

The social sector under the White Revolution hardly fared much better. Under provisions of the reform plan, three national service corps came to be formed: Literacy, Health, and Extension and Development (the last one dealt with teaching agricultural methods). Young people with some secondary education went into the countryside for fifteen-month tours to help villagers improve their lives. A major problem resulted from the attitudes of the young corps members, who tended to be urban, middle class, better educated, and, therefore, often paternalistic or authoritarian in dealing with the "backward" peasantry.

The results of the various corps have been judged by scholars as mixed at best. According to one observer, for instance, the literacy corps had only comparatively limited effect:

> Sending 10,000 . . . teachers out to the villages annually was really not an adequate response to the educational needs of the country's 67,000 villages. Consequently, by 1978, some fifteen years after the inauguration of the Literacy Corps, only 62 per cent of Iran's rural youth of school age were enrolled in classes. The internationally acclaimed adult literacy classes . . . were equally unimpressive: in 1978 nearly 90 per cent of all rural women over fifteen years of age were illiterate, as were at least 60 percent of the men.[81]

Another explanation for the poor educational showing was the low government investment in education and the school system, particularly when compared with arms expenditures and money spent for a high-technology industrial base. According to a 1976 official government report, Iran had spent about 3.3 percent of the GNP since 1969 and 6 percent of the national budget on education. Yet the world's developed countries spend about 7 percent of GNP and 25 percent of national budgets in the same category.[82] Aside from the doubts raised by the *Christian Science Monitor,* however, these aspects of the White Revolution were left unexamined.

A news frame that portrayed the shah as a lonely leader at the top began to emerge by 1965, as suggested in the beginning to this dispatch in the *New York Times:*

> The pinnacle of power on which stands [the shah] of Iran is lonelier today than ever before. By attempting far-reaching reforms, Shah Pahlevi has alienated the traditional supporters of the throne—the landlords, 2,000 families who for many generations dominated the

economic life of the kingdom—without winning the support of those who might be expected to approve of his reforms.[83]

The article, which is not entirely uncritical of the shah, at least avoids the journalistic cliché about Iranians' near mystical reverence for the monarchy, although its discussion of SAVAK was decidedly understated: the shah "depends on the secret police and the army to keep him in power. Under the guidance of Gen. Hassan Pakravan, a respected and restrained official, Iran's secret police have been relatively controlled." What such control might be relative to is left a mystery. The reporter, Dana Adams Schmidt, concluded with the observation that the shah "finds it difficult to tolerate opposition, seeing in each expression of dissent a potential attack upon himself."[84]

Certainly, there were some fundamentalist ulama who were deeply disturbed by the shah's White Revolution when it was introduced in 1963. However, the apprehension of the fundamentalist clergy was not related to land reform or any other threat to their narrow material interest. The concern of the clergy in general and the fundamentalist elements in particular was due to the growing impact of the officially encouraged Westernization on the traditional values in the realm of culture. (One would assume that this phenomenon should be easily understood in the United States where the fundamentalist clergy have long been active against what they regard as legally protected permissiveness.)

This particular tension between the clergy and the state began in the mid-1930s when Reza Shah initiated his Westernization of Iranian life-style through the coercive unveiling of women. With the abdication of Reza Shah in 1941, the coercive measures of the state in the Westernization drive came to an end. The inauguration of the White Revolution in 1963 caused the clergy to fear a return to the forced Westernization of the 1930s. It is simply too facile to reduce the motives of the ulama to plain self-interest; on the contrary, most of the Iranian clergy opposing the shah did not object to the *concept* of modernization but rather took exception to the particular manner in which this regime's program was to be implemented.[85]

Furthermore, in the uprisings of 1963 that accompanied implementation of the White Revolution, there was a wide range of clerical response, ranging from ulama who supported the government to those who actively clashed with the military and the police in opposition to the regime. The great clerical majority probably was grouped somewhere in the middle, and adopted either a public position of neutrality, while privately voicing criticism, or a public position of qualified opposition.[86] There was also diverse clerical opinion on specific issues themselves. For instance, some religious leaders opposed the land reform, whereas others favored it.

The overriding issue in the minds of American journalists, of course, was land reform. The first observer to do a book-length study of land reform was the British scholar Ann K. S. Lambton, who wrote that "discontent [in 1963] prevailed among the religious classes and others. Land reform was not the only cause. The fundamental issue was a feeling, justified or not, that the use of arbitrary power by the government had exceeded all reasonable bounds."[87] The few ulama who condemned the land reform were motivated either by their own material self-interest or on the basis of the belief that it violated sanctity of private property under Islamic law.[88] But even in the instance of active religious opposition, several caveats could be noted, of which three are most important.

First, it is still a matter of scholarly dispute over just who among the clergy opposed land reform and for what reasons.[89] Second, it is a misrepresentation for the press to say that the clergy were "stripped of mosque lands." What is referred to in the press as clerical land was actually land donated by families or individuals to various religious foundations named after Shi'ite *imam*s, or saints. The revenues from these lands, called *vaqf*, were used to support various religious schools and programs. Under the first and most active phase of land reform, *vaqf* were among the exempt categories.[90]

Under the second phase of land reform—which most scholars consider to have been vastly scaled back for a variety of reasons, not the least of which were second thoughts about the program by the shah—religious or endowed lands were included to the extent that ninety-nine-year tenancies were granted to peasants who farmed them.[91] Indeed, according to Lambton, "the conclusion of tenancy agreements for *vaqf* property, one of the most difficult problems facing the land reform, was settled without open dispute."[92] A change of ownership did not occur, and proceeds still went for religious purposes.

The dispute concerned the *administration* of the proceeds by the state-run endowments organization, which decided how the money would be spent.[93] The state had always administered the funds, but with the advent of the White Revolution, the Office of Endowments began selectively rewarding those clerics and religious students who supported the shah with stipends and the like, and withholding support from those who had critical political views. It was generally believed that the SAVAK played the principal role in the selection process.[94]

The third point to be made about the implications of American press coverage of the clergy's opposition to land reform is by far the most important one. At no time, either during the White Revolution of the 1960s nor during the real thing in 1978, did the question of land reform *serve as a mobilizing issue for the masses.* In fact, until land reform was exposed as largely inauthentic, the peasantry seemed excited about its possibilities, and the urban masses remained indifferent in that the program did not affect them at all. Land reform for the masses was simply irrelevant as an antiregime issue.

In sum, then, the shah's White Revolution turned out not to be so revolutionary at all. It combined increased coercion and suppression of political life, discourse, and dissent with illusory reforms that in many instances worsened by far rather than improved the quality of the typical Iranian's life. As Prof. Amin Saikal has observed:

> The political system, which had been built largely to bolster the Shah's absolute rule, could not effectively cope with the capitalist-oriented social and economic changes to which the Shah aspired. It had denied Iranians the political "safety valves" that were necessary in order for them to cope with these changes, and to be able to express their consequent grievances, demands, and frustrations openly and legally.[95]

The shah failed to understand and his American advisers failed to tell him that this situation posed a crucial contradiction that could not be resolved through elaborate public relations, internal or external. The American press also failed to grasp the contradiction, persistently confusing aggregate growth with development, and presented a picture largely at odds with the facts of the shah's various reforms.

It was not that the information was unavailable. The CIA, according to one account, concluded that the White Revolution's planning was weak and that the shah assigned only a low priority to long-term economic planning. Moreover, an excessive amount was still being spent on arms. Most important, the land reform program could succeed only if the rural cooperatives were properly organized. The small allotments received by the peasants could never provide the necessary cash to farm the parcels successfully unless significant outside help was forthcoming. The CIA predicted that without such help, agriculture would regress—which it did.[96]

It was in this fashion that the shah structured social reform in Iran from 1963 to 1972 and unintentionally laid the foundation for what would become a classic example of social alienation, which culminated in the 1978 revolution. Yet the press failed to provide the independent sort of situational analysis so vital to a viable foreign policy. Instead, the myths persisted, as coverage of the shah's 1967 self-styled and performed coronation demonstrated.

In what was the longest analysis of Iran to appear in the *Times* since Salisbury's special report in 1961, Eric Pace told his readers that 75 percent of Iran's oil revenues was going to modernization and wrote of a "drastic land-reform program," of how the shah had brought industry to the towns and literacy to the countryside, of how he had sharply improved women's rights, and of how he had decided to celebrate these "successes" by putting on his father's diamond-encrusted crown.

In his lengthy paean to Westernization-cum-modernization, Pace wrote that the shah had "changed peasant life without the vast disruption of agricultural production that pessimists foresaw" and had broken the power of the "thousand families" in the countryside. Throughout, Pace touched only briefly on opposition charges that what the shah had accomplished had not been much and had been bought at the price of totalitarianism.[97]

Even when the press did mention the shah's harsh style of rule, he was still pictured as an enormously popular and successful ruler. A 1970 Associated Press dispatch, for instance, which ran in the *Times* under the headline "Reforms in Iran Bring New Hope," included a paragraph saying that "despite the trappings of a constitutional monarchy, there is no real democracy in Iran. The press is controlled, criticism of the Shah is forbidden and his power is absolute. Yet his personal popularity has soared with the White Revolution." The article had begun with this summary:

There is a new feeling of hope and pride in Iran, and it is evident in this sprawling capital with its new office buildings, supermarkets, freeways and modern factories. Much of the new feeling has been a result of the "White Revolution," a sweeping program of reforms aimed at turning a primitive peasant society into an industrialized nation.[98]

Even careful readers, given this sort of journalistic context, might be forgiven if they tended to overlook the darker side of the shah's regime. In brief, the largely sanguine picture portrayed by the American news media of what the shah had achieved did little to prepare American public opinion, elite or otherwise, for the fate that would eventually overcome the shah and Iran.

5

Further Illusions: 1963–1973

While the great bulk of space devoted to Iran from 1963 to 1973 centered on the assumed successes of the White Revolution, much to the shah's advantage, there were other aspects of the Pahlavi rule that also attracted the attention of the American press during this decade. Chief among these secondary areas were the panoply of the shah's coronation and his lavish celebration of 2,500 years of the Persian monarchy four years later; the general health of the Iranian economy; the nature of secular political opposition, which had come to include urban guerrillas by the early 1970s; and relations between the United States and Iran. Arguably, as much attention was paid the lavish royal melodramas as the other three categories combined.

News coverage of these events and trends reinforced the dominant theme sounded in journalism's treatment of the White Revolution, which we discussed in the preceding chapter. The picture of the shah that emerged in the American press during this period, in short, was of a necessarily autocratic reformer, whose efforts were not always appreciated by his subjects. The journalistic studio portrait of the shah as a man deeply committed to social progress seemed always to be in sharp focus. By comparison, the exceedingly rare snapshots of the shah as authoritarian ruler were blurred by journalists' use of extraordinarily considerate language, a routine willingness to extend him the benefit of the doubt, and a failure to seriously investigate charges about human rights violations. Most important, the press too often, although not always, let stand striking economic, political, and social contradictions, unremarked on, as if they were not contradictions at all.

The first of the shah's pomp-heavy affairs was his coronation in 1967, a fete he had to conduct for himself, given his lack of royal lineage. In an announcement of the affair months before, headlined "Proud as a Peacock," *Time* told readers that "few . . . would dispute his right to the crown."[1] Other major print media from the *Washington Post* to the *Reader's Digest* echoed the judgment of the shah as a Third World modernizer of unprecedented success.[2]

The *New York Times* gave front-page coverage to the event, which included the crowning of Empress Farah, and published several large photographs. According to the *Times* correspondent, the ceremony was a "blaze of pomp and splendor," which the shah had put off for twenty-six years until he had "consolidated his control over Iran and had brought to the country a measure of economic and social progress."[3] This vision, heavily promoted by the regime's public relations advisers, of a selfless man, patiently willing to forego his rightful place until he had achieved well-being for his people, was predominant in the American press. The only hint in the *Times* of his lack of popular support in the midst of rich detail telling of a Vienna-made gilded coronation carriage, his and her crowns encrusted with thousands of diamonds, golden scepters, and so on was a statement that informed readers, "He rules firmly with the support of the army and the government, whose premier he appoints. But his courtiers fear instability if he should die or be killed."[4]

Newsweek viewed the shah's crowning himself and his self-produced hoopla from a slightly more derisive perspective, but tempered the sarcasm with approving references to the White Revolution.[5] *Life* magazine commended him for waiting to take the crown until he could "thrust his country into the modern world through a series of important reforms."[6] *National Geographic* viewed the proceedings similarly.[7]

Four years after his coronation, in the fall of 1971, the shah staged a spectacular celebration marking a mythical 2,500-year anniversary of the founding of the Persian Empire and the establishment of the monarchy by the first shah, Cyrus the Great. Not incidentally, the international affair—publicized as a cultural festival—also honored Mohammad Reza Shah Pahlavi.

In Persepolis, center of the festivities and once the imperial capital before it was sacked by Alexander the Great, a city of fifty tents designed by the prestigious Jansen of Paris was erected for visiting dignitaries. Each canvas and plywood "tent" had twin bedrooms, two baths, kitchenettes, and servants' rooms. The shah and the empress occupied a special tent, larger than the others, equipped with marble baths and gilded fixtures. There was also a scarlet reception hall and adjacent dining hall, where all food served was flown in from Paris and prepared by chefs from Maxim's. The encampment was located amid lush gardens surrounded by thousands of specially planted evergreens. The outside perimeter was protected by barbed wire and well-armed soldiers. A sixty-mile road was built to connect Persepolis and Shiraz, another city involved in the celebration. Estimates of the cost for the fete ranged from a low of $16.6 million,[8] given by the Iranian government stung by criticism of lavish spending, to a high of $100 million, given in the *New York Times*.[9]

Whatever the cost, such splendor did not go unnoticed in the American press. Indeed, except for the White Revolution, during the 1960s and early 1970s no other single aspect of his rule received as much coverage as did—to use the shah's phrase—"the greatest show the world has ever seen."[10] Had an equivalent commitment of journalistic resources been made to investigating land reform claims or human rights abuses, the picture of the shah in the United States might have been far different.

There was a certain ambivalence to press coverage of the affair, however. On the one hand, the event received almost as much attention as, say, a coronation in England might receive. The press has always found a large audience for news of royal goings-on, whatever Americans may say about their antipathy to monarchy. On the other hand, some editorialists were irritated if not repelled by the shah's extravagance and lectured him accordingly. Too, some accounts, particularly those in newsmagazines, adopted a slightly condescending, sometimes smirking, tone toward the extravaganza.

Charlotte Curtis was dispatched from New York to cover the festival for the *New York Times,* and Sally Quinn reported for the *Washington Post.*[11] The series of articles written by Curtis, who was society editor at the time, focused on the lavish side of the event, as the beginning to one of her articles indicates: "The Shah of Iran established himself tonight as one of the world's great party givers. For sheer grandeur, his gala in a silk tent will be hard for any nation to surpass."[12] Another typical article closed by telling readers, "Some of the emeralds in her [Empress Farah's] crown were the size of golf balls. Her diamonds were only slightly smaller."[13]

The last piece filed by Curtis, a retrospective analysis headlined "After the Ball: Has Shah Achieved Lasting Gains?" included the observation: "So far, nobody but the Iranians view Persepolis as either another Congress of Vienna or anything resembling a summit conference. But the Iranians, nearly 85 per cent of whom are illiterate peasants, are delighted. They see themselves as having arrived, and no wonder."[14]

Aside from Curtis's inflated estimate of the illiteracy rate and the number of peasants in Iran, there is some doubt about how many Iranians were delighted by the festivities, which might explain why the shah had felt compelled to order widespread "preventive arrests" of potential troublemakers and to ring the Persepolis site with hundreds of soldiers. Curtis did have occasion to note in one of her articles that publicity surrounding the spectacular event may have backfired. According to Curtis, the shah felt compelled to conduct a series of interviews with journalists to answer repeated questions about "what his critics are calling a wasteful spending in a developing country." The shah was quoted as responding angrily, "Why are we reproached for serving dinner to 50 heads of state? What am I supposed to do, give them bread and radishes?"[15]

As for magazine journalism, *Holiday* published its account under the headline "Iran: Model Middle East State—Celebrating 2,500th Anniversary."[16] *Newsweek* ("Iran's Birthday Party")[17] and *Time* ("Iran: the Show of Shows")[18] also covered the affair, as did *Life* magazine, which treated the festival in two issues.[19]

That the shah should receive sterner treatment from the American press for his extravagant spending and ostentation rather than for his increasingly repressive rule is worth noting. Nonetheless, the lavish style of the so-called 2,500th anniversary of the Persian monarchy— which had not existed between A.D. 640 and A.D. 1501,[20] a fact lost on the press—did come in for criticism. An editorial in the *New York Times* called the celebration "extravagantly overdone" and twitted the shah for a "Scheherazade dream world of air-conditioned tents for attending heads of state . . . [who will] sit on velvet-covered 'thrones' and be served food from Maxim's of Paris by waiters in

$800 uniforms airlifted from Switzerland." Lectured the *Times*, "This may be in the best tradition of Persian potentates, but it hardly befits a modernizing nation still heavily in debt and afflicted with widespread poverty."[21]

The editorial, which included in passing the first mention to appear in the *Times* of CIA involvement in the 1953 coup, made reference to an Iranian people growing "increasingly restive under the shah's autocratic rule" and criticized the shah for identifying himself with Cyrus, who "after all, was an oriental despot." The editorial concluded with this thought: "The moderate liberalism that marked his [the shah's] 1963 reforms is more becoming to this twentieth century heir of Cyrus."[22]

The case of the Persepolis festival points to a major flaw in American press treatment of Iran from 1963 to 1973 and underscored a contradiction that went unremarked and unresolved. As was demonstrated by the *Times* editorial on the anniversary celebration, there was *occasional* criticism of the shah's spending habits in the press, and there were references to the deep poverty of the country. Yet the press during the same period routinely gave the shah high praise for remarkable social and economic gains and generally looked the other way or excused his lack of political progress. Moreover, the Iranian economy from 1963 on was pictured as a model for the Third World.

On balance, therefore, infrequent and carefully couched criticism of the shah's *personal* spending excesses simply could not carry the force of far more sustained praise of his purported overall economic progress. Certainly, such criticism as there was did not systematically raise questions about how much *structural* economic change had occurred. How this situation resulted in a one-sided public relations advantage for the shah can be seen in a sample of editorials and stories about Iran's economy during the decade of pseudodevelopment.

According to a 1967 editorial in the *Times*, for example, what had once been one of the "more inefficient and corrupted of American overseas aid efforts" was now a success story. In the judgment of the *Times*, "Iran's development success is encouraging, a credit to the shah, who has been diligent in promoting social and economic—but unfortunately, not political—reforms."[23] Over the years, a continuing string of upbeat stories was published in newspapers and magazines with such headlines as "Executives Help with Iran's Growth"

(1968);[24] "Shah of Iran, in Power 25 Years, Is Proving to Be a Successful Revolutionary" (1968);[25] "Iran's Prosperity Thrives Like Bubbling Oasis" (1968);[26] "A Prosperous Future Is Seen for Iranian Province" (1970);[27] "A Welcome for Capitalists: Iran's Booming Economy" (1970);[28] "Steel Joining Oil to Spur Economy" (1970);[29] and "Prosperity, Vitality Mark Iran's 2,500th Year" (1971).[30] Some news analyses did balance praise for the shah's economic program with consideration of less flattering aspects,[31] but the vast majority did not.

Economic contradictions were not the only ones lost in the generally sanguine picture of Iran portrayed by the American mainstream press. The continuity and scope of the internal political struggle against the regime were left largely unexamined as well. Even as opposition to the regime came to include urban guerrillas by the early 1970s, the press continued to ignore long-standing warning signals and to persist in the view that the shah enjoyed widespread support among his people.

Moreover, what press criticism there was of the shah's methods of dealing with his opposition was generally muted and overshadowed by exceedingly positive coverage of the White Revolution. As a result, critics of the shah's increasingly totalitarian regime in the United States and Europe were effectively disarmed just as international concern was beginning to mount. As with its portrayal of the White Revolution, the *Christian Science Monitor* was an exception to this pattern. Throughout the rest of the prestige press, however, there was an absence of serious analyses of opposition to the shah.

A 1965 news feature in the *New York Times* went so far as to trivialize the suppression and fear that after the late 1950s had become a permanent feature of life under the shah. According to correspondent Thomas F. Brady, "Iranians are said to be like American G.I.'s: Their morale is sound only when they grumble. Members of the upper middle class of Teheran . . . sustain this reputation with a pretty constant barrage of conversational complaint against the Government, the 'regime' and even the Shah." The writer did not assay what the opinions of other classes might be.

After establishing that the grumbling was hardly revolutionary, Brady went on to write: "Teheranis particularly *enjoy* denouncing Savak, the special security police, as an instrument of repression and thought control. But the complaints seem self-contradictory. If Savak were as brutally efficient a gestapo as the Teheranis suggest, they would all be in jail for subversive talk" (emphasis ours).[32] Brady concluded his piece with a humorous anecdote that had a punchline involving the overzealousness of SAVAK. The absence of a sustained and close look by American journalism at the nature of political repression in Iran left the attentive reader little context in which to place the free-floating fragments of political news about Iran that were published.

The disjointed, shallow, and, finally, apologetic reporting was matched by the tepid opinions of columnists and editorialists. A 1972 analysis by the *Times* foreign affairs columnist C. L. Sulzberger was typical of the perspective dominant in the higher reaches of prestige journalism and is worth quoting at length. Headlined "Still a King of Kings," the column began by tracing the dissimilarities between Cyrus the Great and the shah, but then changed direction by asserting:

> Yet the profession of kingship is still dynamic here today. . . . The present Shah, in his own way, has sought to impose revolution upon his backward country, hampered by superstitious inheritance, corruption and failure to develop its rich potential. He has dictated agrarian reform and social changes that have been opposed by conservative church leaders and landed proprietors. He has ruled as well as reigned, seeking to demonstrate that active kingship can be a modern profession.[33]

Having framed the argument in terms eminently favorable to the shah, Sulzberger went on to quote the shah:

> One mistake the United States made was trying to sell your kind of democracy to countries like Iran. . . . There are no democratic regimes in the area around Iran. Democracy of the Western type, when applied in underdeveloped countries, becomes only a weapon for subversion. My philosophy of government is that when the people are sufficiently educated and gathered into real political parties they can form the basis of Western democracy.[34]

Sulzberger left these assertions to stand unexamined and unchallenged, failing even to point out that the absence of political parties had more to do with the shah's repression than with regional deficiency. Instead, the columnist closed with a peroration that was ambiguous at best:

That is the dream of today's King of Kings and in many respects he has advanced significantly along his chosen road. But it takes time to budge Asia. There is a long, long way to go before the facade of democratic vitality and countrywide progress is replaced by reality and rule by the Shahinshah becomes his reign.[35]

In the same year of Sulzberger's column, the *Times* reported that a United Nations panel had found a consistent pattern of human rights violations in Greece, Portugal, and Iran, including the arbitrary arrests of hundreds of political dissidents, secret trials, and in many instances, executions.[36] There was no follow-up by the *Times* on the panel's findings.

The strongest stand taken by the *Times* on the absence of freedom in Iran was a single editorial published in 1967, which described the shah as a "benevolent dictator." This was the only occasion in twenty-five years when the *Times* used the term "dictator" to describe the shah. After praising the shah for his maturity and the White Revolution, the editorial observed:

It is mainly in the area of political philosophy that his record as reformer is meager. The Shah's victory over Premier Mossadegh and his National Front in 1953 was followed by suppression of all political opposition. Today in Iran there is only a facade of democratic freedoms. A sullen urban opposition asks what use there is in giving women the vote if the elections are not truly free.[37]

The editorial went on to say that "economic reform without much political reform has made for an uneasy combination in Iran, detracting unnecessarily from the shah's great accomplishments." How much effect three paragraphs of criticism in a six-paragraph editorial can have on the shape of opinion is doubtful. What is remarkable is that the editorial is the best evidence that the *Times* was fully aware of the shah's methods. Yet from 1953 to the revolution in 1978 the *Times* did not publish a major story on human rights violations in Iran. Instead, the views expressed in Sulzberger's column, written five years after the editorial appeared, would prevail. The end result of such journalism could only be, at best, the conclusion that the style of the shah's regime was cause for concern—but hardly alarm—a misperception left uncorrected until at least 1975.

By contrast, the American news media had demonstrated no such hesitancy to criticize the alleged lack of freedom during Mosaddeq's last year in power, during which time the press routinely described Premier Mosaddeq as a dictator. Even in death, Mosaddeq could stir strong emotions in the American press. An Associated Press obituary in 1967, for instance, asserted that Mosaddeq had ruled with an "iron dictatorship compounded of terrorism of his enemies and demagogic appeals to mobs in the bazaars."[38] No such description of the shah ever appeared in the mainstream American press.

Aside from the gadfly *Nation*,[39] the *Christian Science Monitor* was the only news organization to consistently raise questions about repression in Iran. The *Monitor's* treatment of the absence of freedom in Iran, while hardly a crusade, by comparison with the rest of the prestige press was exceptional. Over the years, articles that ranged from the declining quality and freedom of the Iranian press[40] to the nature of Iranian student protest in the United States[41] were published by the *Monitor*. During the 1960s, the work of Geoffrey Godsell was particularly noteworthy. For instance, an article written by Godsell in the same year as the piece by Thomas F. Brady of the *Times* on "grumbling" in Tehran put a decidedly different interpretation on things. According to Godsell, the "increasingly authoritarian" shah had a major liability: "The absence of any broad basis of political support at home."[42] Unlike Brady, Godsell included no humorous anecdotes about SAVAK. Instead, Godsell told his readers: "To dare to criticize him [the shah] within Iran today can be a most dangerous thing. Iran is in effect a police state for any politically articulate Iranian. And all political organizations are banned except the officially approved New Iran Party."[43]

In a dispatch published days later under the headline "Increasing Iranian Opposition Smolders," Godsell described SAVAK as a "secret security organization" that kept "close watch on any potential troublemakers. Criticism of the government—let alone protest—is strictly controlled." In stark contrast to the *Times* and other news organizations, which usually described the shah's opponents as either Communists or religious fanatics, Godsell offered the considered judgment that "between the two extremes linked with the murder of Premier Mansour and the attempted assassination of the Shah, there is a sullen and alienated body of opinion—mainly in the cities—bitterly opposed to the government."[44]

To some degree, Godsell's reporting was offset by the *Monitor's* editorial page. For example, in a 1967 editorial, with the headline

"Realpolitik in Iran," the *Monitor* anticipated the logic of Henry Kissinger by arguing:

> Certainly Iran is still not the crowned democracy on the Scandinavian model which some of the more idealistic young Iranians want it to be. But the Shah's position after a quarter of a century on the throne has proven a point: that his government is less rotten than its fiercest critics have often contended. What outside critics have perhaps overlooked is the strain of ruthless realpolitik that always has been present in the government of Iran—at home and abroad.[45]

Some of its editorials to the contrary, the *Monitor* was the only major news organization to give publicity in 1971 to the protest of Iranian abuses by prominent French intellectuals, including Simone de Beauvoir and Jean-Paul Sartre, and examine the nascent guerrilla movements.[46] Indeed, an editorial in 1972, under the headline "Contradictions in Iran," was the only mention in the mainstream U.S. press of European newspaper criticism of the shah's handling of guerrilla suspects. According to the *Monitor,* "The underground opposition is an embarrassment to the Shah, but the repression used to combat it daubs an ugly black spot on the image of the new Iran."[47] Commendable in our view as the work of the *Monitor* may have been during this period, its voice hardly carried strength equal to the combined volume of received opinion in other prestige newspapers, the wire services, and the newsmagazines. Indeed, the *Monitor's* exception very clearly demonstrated the rule.

Of all the aspects left underreported by the mainstream press during the period with which this chapter is concerned, 1963–1973, none would have greater long-range significance than the emerging relationship between the United States and Iran, a relationship that would find its ultimate expression in the Nixon Doctrine. Most Americans were not even vaguely aware of the emerging centrality of Iran in the constellation of perceived American strategic interests. Moreover, the press did little to further the general understanding that the United States had replaced Great Britain as the chief quasi-colonial power in Iran and was rapidly replacing England as the symbol of foreign domination and imperialism in the popular mind.

Arguably, the most important of these journalistic failures was to make plain the emergence of Iran as a critical player in the post-Vietnam Nixon-Kissinger strategy which began to evolve in the late

1960s. Instead, the two themes that dominated coverage during this period, besides the theme of the shah as modernizer, were (1) Iran as unconditional ally and first line of defense against a Soviet move in the Persian Gulf region, and (2) Iran as an island of stability in an inherently unstable part of the world.

The major turning point in Iran-U.S. relations, the advent of the Nixon Doctrine, went virtually unnoticed in the American media. To be certain, Vietnam preoccupied journalism, and what attention was paid the Middle East tended to focus on the Arab-Israeli confrontation. There is also something to be said for the case that a doctrine such as the Nixon-Kissinger strategy, in its broadest sense, is "uncoverable," given the inherent limitations of the *American media as system*. Questions of doctrine per se do not usually have the points of focus, or in the jargon of the industry, "news pegs," that result in "breaking" stories or sustained news coverage. Matters of doctrine, therefore, are usually left for the columnist-pundit to deal with.

Conventional practice to the contrary, the concrete implications of a given doctrine can readily lend themselves to news reportage. To the extent that the answers to the questions of who gets what, when, and why are determined by doctrine, the media are perfectly capable of apprehending cause-and-effect relationships. While reporters may maintain that this is not so, or that it is not their charge to place specific actions within a broader doctrinal context, or that it is not within the bounds of professionalism and objectivity to do so, mainstream journalists demonstrate no such inability or reluctance when, say, the doctrine and actions of an adversary such as the Soviet Union are concerned. In instances such as the Hungarian revolution, the invasions of Czechoslovakia and Afghanistan, or Russian assistance for Angolan rebels, the press did not hesitate to draw a clear line between action and doctrine, real or imagined.

The Nixon-Kissinger strategy, or Nixon Doctrine, was developed during the late 1960s and early 1970s as a response to the failure of the American military presence in Vietnam and represented a major shift in U.S. foreign policy. The change in policy also marked a key turning point in U.S. interest and attentions toward Iran; the country's importance as an oil producer and its strategic possibilities in the Persian Gulf region caused Washington policy makers to revise their view of the shah's importance.

The larger strategy of picking surrogates in various regions led, almost inevitably, to the selection of the shah as the key deputy of the United States in the Muslim Middle East. For his part, the shah was a proven friend to America, and his strategically important land was perceived as the most stable Islamic society in the region.

Undergirding the Nixon administration's new enthusiasm for Iran was the reality that by 1968 Britain, beset by economic difficulties, had tired of the burden imposed by its role in the region and had decided to speed up the already planned withdrawal of its forces from the Persian Gulf. This action, Washington believed, would create a "vacuum of power," which had to be filled either by America or by a powerful ally. Iran fully qualified as an ally but was not sufficiently powerful. It was against this backdrop that arms sales and transfers to the shah began, an arrangement which would eventually come to constitute the largest such arms deal in world history. Nixon agreed to sell Iran virtually any conventional arms it wanted.[48]

In one of the few major pieces in the *New York Times* to specifically point to the changed character of Iran's strategic role, Tad Szulc told readers in his front-page account, "Acting with British-American blessings, the [shah] has accepted responsibility for the security of the Persian Gulf after Britain removes her protection and armed forces from Bahrain, Qatar and the seven Trucial States."[49] According to Szulc, writing from Washington:

> By 1975, when the present program of military deliveries and training is completed, Iran is expected to be a major Middle Eastern power and an element of stability in the volatile gulf region, American officials say.
>
> Unpublicized United States credits, including the rare participation of the Export-Import Bank, are financing the current secret deliveries of the F-4-E model of the supersonic Phantom fighter-bombers. The bank usually refuses to finance sales of military equipment. Officials of the bank declined this week to discuss the Iranian credits.[50]

Szulc's detailed reporting was not matched again in the *Times* or in other mainstream news organizations.

From the August 1953 coup until the final days of the Pahlavi dynasty the United States treated Iran as a client state, sometimes more generously than others. To be sure, from the beginning of its involvement in Iranian affairs the United States had perceived the Iranian military as the principal instrument of its strategy in the country. Until the inception of the Nixon Doctrine, however, U.S. military assistance to Iran consisted of loans and grants, which amounted to about $1.8 billion between 1950 and 1970. In addition, thousands of Iranian military personnel were trained in the United States.[51] But on balance, until the Nixon Doctrine made itself felt, the shah remained dissatisfied with Iran's place in the American list of priorities. For instance, the shah was decidedly unhappy with the terms of the 1964 U.S.-Iran Military Sales Agreement, a four-year plan that provided up to $50 million a year for the first two years and $100 million yearly for the last two. Sales under the provisions of the agreement were to be reviewed each year and approved only after Washington was convinced the purchases were not interfering with economic and social reform in Iran.[52]

Because the Pahlavi rule lacked legitimacy or any significant base of popular support from its beginnings, the shah had always been especially eager to expand the coercive dimension of his power, particularly in times of popular challenge from below. This impulse was not entirely lost on American policy makers and politicians, and did not reassure them. Sen. Hubert H. Humphrey, for instance, was quoted as remarking in dismay in 1961, "Do you know what the head of the Iranian army told one of our people? He said the army is now in good shape, thanks to U.S. aid—and it was now capable of coping with the civilian population. That army isn't planning to fight Russians. It's planning to fight the Iranian people."[53]

The Kennedy administration several times refused the shah's request for more and better weapons and instead urged social reforms on the shah. Such reforms, an extension of Kennedy's "alliance for progress," would supposedly enlarge the middle-class support for the shah and preempt the opposition. The White Revolution was the eventual response, but the yearning for a bigger arsenal remained unfulfilled. The new attitude of unqualified American enthusiasm toward his regime generated by Nixon and Kissinger, therefore, was a welcome development for the shah.

Circumstances never provided the opportunity for a major test of the shah's mettle as regional policeman, but several conflicts in which Iran became involved offer some indication of the shah's eagerness and potential for keeping "subversion" in check. His sending of troops to fight leftist-led rebels in Oman's Dhofar province in

1973,[54] for instance, and his public support for North Yemen in its dispute with Marxist South Yemen are but two examples. Another was his close and cordial relationship with Israel.

In return for the shah's helpful willingness to serve U.S. interests in the region, the Nixon Doctrine established a policy of giving the shah anything he wanted (with the sole exception of nuclear weapons) to assist him in fulfilling his new responsibilities. The sales of conventional arms to a non-Western country without any restraint on their quality, quantity, and variety was an extraordinary departure from the past. A surprising aspect of this dramatic change in arms policy was that it went largely unchallenged in Congress, where it found bipartisan support, and in the press and the academic community. This must be attributed in large part to the reputation for brilliance, given currency largely by the press, that Henry Kissinger enjoyed at the time. His policies for the Middle East were nearly beyond criticism. As late as July 1977, when some questions concerning the logic of unrestrained arms sales to Iran were being raised in Congress, Senator Abraham Ribicoff expressed the sentiment of many of his colleagues: "Iran is one of the most important allies the United States has. When you realize that 50 percent of the world's oil comes through the Straits of Hormuz and the only armed forces to protect it are Iran's, to refuse him arms would be sheer stupidity on the part of the United States."[55]

As a result of the carte blanche given him by the Nixon administration, the shah began an arms buildup unprecedented for a Third World country. By 1970–71 the shah's defense budget had risen to a $1 billion share of a $10 billion GNP.[56] In 1973 the Pentagon announced that it had consummated a $2 billion arms deal with Iran, the largest ever until that time.[57] By 1974 nearly half of the Pentagon's total arms sales ($3.9 billion) were being made to the shah, who was on his way to commanding "the most extensive armoury of weapons outside America, Russia and Europe."[58]

By 1977 Iran was the largest arms customer of the United States, and at the time of the revolution the shah had either contracted for or had already spent in cash (or in an exchange of oil) $15 to $20 billion for weapons since the buildup began. Simply put, he had used Iran's only exportable resource, oil—which by his own estimate was expected to be exhausted by the turn of the century if 1970 production levels were maintained—to become the biggest customer for arms in world history. Toward this end, he received enthusiastic encouragement from the Nixon, Ford, and Carter administrations.

Whether because of a preoccupation with Vietnam or general indifference, the increasingly complex and deepening military and economic relationship between Iran and the United States was left largely unexplored in the press during the critical period from 1963 to 1973, at which point coverage began to increase slowly. In 1974–75, the attention paid Iran by the media increased dramatically. Once it became more a focus of media attention, the type of treatment Iran received in the press did change noticeably, and a critical attitude of sorts began to develop. But during the crucial early and mid stages of American involvement in Iran, the mainstream press constructed news frames that contributed importantly to misperceptions of enormous significance.

6

The New Persian Empire: 1973–1977

Between the restoration of the Pahlavi dynasty in 1953 and
its revolutionary demise in 1978, Iran was most visible in the American press during the initial stages of the White Revolution (chapter
4) and after the Arab-oil boycott in 1973–74, at which point the
coverage increased sharply, particularly in regard to the gold-rush
aspects of Iran's economy and arms purchases by the shah. Indeed,
from 1973 to 1977 the American press devoted as much space to Iran
as it had done for the previous nineteen years.

More significant, during this period the mainstream press for the
first time began to raise troubling questions about the shah's regime,
especially concerning his quest for military power, method of rule,
and repression of human rights. To be sure, this new journalistic
sensibility retained many of the previous assumptions and misperceptions. For example, the press did nothing to challenge the presumption that Iran was anything but a stable and reliable ally. Nonetheless, there was a major sea change in the journalistic portrayal of
Iran, and the reasons for this shift in news frames offer some important clues to understanding the complex relationship between the
press and foreign policy.

Why the press began to pay closer attention to Iran and became
more critical in the mid-1970s had to do with several factors, probably none of which can be said to include a realization of the shah's
despotism or the bankruptcy of his modernization plans. Rather, the

criticism had more to do with the transformation following late 1973 of a client comprador into an increasingly arrogant ruler who insisted on equal footing for Iran as a world power, who lectured Americans on the need to tighten *their* belts, and who engaged in a spending spree of spectacular proportion at the expense of the industrial world's consumers. That the press was not more critical, given these developments, is a testament to the hold he retained over U.S. policy makers, corporate America, and American journalism.

Whatever the reality in 1973, the popular perception in the United States was that a serious energy crisis was at hand and price-gouging Arabs were to blame. Editorial cartoons of fat-cat sheiks laughing at the West all the way to the bank to the contrary, it was the non-Arab shah who seized the opportunity posed by the shortfall and led OPEC to increase its prices by *70 percent*. In discussing the decision to raise prices to unprecedented levels, the shah declared that the industrial world "will have to realize that the end of the era of their terrific progress and even more terrific income and wealth based on cheap oil is finished."[1]

Iran, the world's second largest oil exporter at the time, began a period of conspicuous consumption that could not help but erode its erstwhile favorable image in the United States and earn the suspicion and enmity of the news media and Americans, who suddenly found themselves paying what they thought were outrageous prices for gasoline and vastly inflated prices for other goods produced by industries dependent on petroleum for energy.

As Iran's annual oil revenues jumped from $4 billion in 1973 to $21.4 billion in 1974,[2] the shah and his regime came under closer scrutiny in the press. It would be a mistake to assume, however, that the new critical attitude readily translated into improved coverage. Journalists rarely pointed out that *quadrupled* oil profits, in part extracted from the American consumer-on-the-street, made it possible for the shah to pay his way in the American scheme of things as set forth by the Nixon Doctrine.[3] In other words, Americans (and, of course, others throughout the world) through higher prices were actually paying for the shah's arms buildup without knowing it.

Certainly, under the assumptions and goals of the Nixon Doctrine, Washington had everything to gain under the changed situation dating from 1973, as did many important economic sectors in the United States, ranging from arms manufacturers to high-technology industries. Such a possibility, however, was never widely assessed by the mainstream news media. Instead, Nixon, Kissinger, and later Ford were portrayed as strongly opposing the increases. As a result, Americans, for the most part, have a historical memory of the period which is based almost wholly on a belief that the only force at work was OPEC avarice.

Notwithstanding the failure to examine the possibility that Iran's enormous windfall profits might be serving the Nixon administration's strategic objectives, the press in 1973 did pay far closer attention to Iran's arms acquisitions than it ever had paid in the past. Too, coverage began to take on a new critical edge, although emphasis tended to be on how well the shah might serve long-range U.S. interests rather than on the impact of unprecedented arms purchases on Iranian society.

Early in 1973 and well before the Arab oil embargo, the shah contracted with U.S. firms to purchase more than $2 billion in military equipment ranging from F-4 Phantom fighter-bombers to helicopter gunships. At the time, it was described as the largest single arms deal ever arranged by the Pentagon.[4] According to a *New York Times* account, "The deal was entered into on the ground that it would be highly profitable in helping American arms manufacturers caught in a post-Vietnam slump in orders and in helping to redress this country's deficit in balance of payments."[5] The news frame picturing the shah as helping out the American arms industry was a common one throughout much of 1973.

Such economic good news to the contrary, occasional clouds were evident by the summer of 1973. The shah's visit to Washington in July on a shopping trip for sophisticated weaponry, for instance, led Drew Middleton of the *Times* to write, "Iran's development into the primary military power between Israel and India has reached the point at which there are misgivings in the United States and in Western European governments." Middleton advised readers that the concern was caused by Iran's protective attitude toward Pakistan, which could bring about an arms race between Iran and India, Pakistan's nemesis. Still, Middleton cited unnamed Western intelligence analysts to back up the shah's claim that Iran's military expansion had goals far more suitable to U.S. interests: (1) protection of oil shipments from the Persian Gulf through the Strait of Hormuz to Japan, Western Europe, and the United States; (2) insurance against the dissolution of Pakistan; and (3) the deployment of military forces strong enough to deter "Soviet-inspired adventures in the Persian Gulf by Iraq."[6]

An editorial in the *Times* two days later expressed concerns similar to those raised in the Middleton piece, although, like its reporter, the *Times* was careful to give the shah every benefit of the doubt. Indeed, the first five of the editorial's seven paragraphs sang the shah's praises. Headlined, "The Persian Market," the editorial described the shah as an admirable ruler, given "the tradition from which he springs and the climate in which he operates," and said his ten-year-old White Revolution had "gone a long way toward transforming the feudal Iranian society and building a viable economy that will not remain dependent on oil revenues."[7] However, the editorial cautioned, the shah's "emerging ambitions for Iranian hegemony in the Persian Gulf and Indian Ocean areas" might pose a danger by diverting spending from domestic development and by heightening tension with "apprehensive neighbors."[8]

By far the majority of stories about Iran and arms in 1973 and 1974 were topical and dealt simply with what was purchased from whom and at what price. But by 1975, as concern increased among power elites outside the White House about the extent of the buildup, the tone of press coverage and editorial opinion changed. An example of new resistance to the policy of giving the shah everything he wanted was the bill introduced in early 1975 by Rep. Les Aspin to block the sale of six destroyers to Iran for an amount estimated at $700 million. According to a *Times* account of the move, the action came at "a time of mounting criticism of the build-up in military sales to the Middle East."[9]

The reference to "mounting criticism" suggests an important characteristic of the relationship between the press and foreign policy. Not until such misgivings become manifest among various power elites outside the presidency does the press usually begin to open up news frames about a client state. So long as a consensus exists around an administration's policy, the press throughout the cold war has raised few questions. But if *significant* elements of Congress, say, begin to question an administration's policy, mainstream journalism will usually pay attention because such questioning in itself constitutes "news." The press may even follow suit because such elite criticism *legitimizes* dissent. The point here is that once again the press is following rather than leading the way.

By the mid-1970s the *Washington Post* had come to take a particularly strong stand against the arming of the shah, perhaps in part because of its intense dislike for the Nixon administration. Certainly, the *Post* had not been a strong critic of the shah over the years. Motives aside, a January 1975 *Washington Post* editorial warned of "mindless sales of arms" in the Persian Gulf.[10] One year later, another editorial gave warning of a "network of commitments that are becoming steadily more dangerous and onerous" and of a "mindless American policy of supplying our most advanced military technology to Iran [which] is increasingly likely to get both countries into trouble."[11] Another 1976 editorial blasted Nixon for his decision to arm Iran as "secretive," "high-handed and irresponsible statecraft."[12]

A 1976 editorial in the *Los Angeles Times* sounded the major concern evident in most mainstream editorials of the period: The U.S. could be dragged into a war not of its own choosing because Iran, lacking the technical, industrial, and educational base to support such sophisticated equipment, could not operate its new weaponry without day-to-day American assistance. Yet if the shah should become embroiled in an unapproved fight, it would be difficult if not impossible to pull out the ever-swelling number of American personnel or order them not to do their jobs. The editorial concluded with this admonishment: "In the future, the wisdom of massive arms sales should be studied *before* rather than *after* the fact. And Congress should be much more zealous in seeing to it that long-range implications are taken into account."[13]

While the shah and his arms purchases came in for journalistic criticism, by far the most attention was paid the economic and developmental aspects of what by 1973 was being called the new Persian empire. As we have argued, this increase in press interest in Iran after 1973 was largely because of the effects of the oil price increase.

The causes for the increased attention paid Iran after 1973 aside, criticism directed at Iran's arms-buying spree and, later, the shah's human rights abuses should be balanced against the dominant news frame during the period, which was suggested in this headline from the *Wall Street Journal:* "The Renaissance of Modern Iran." George Melloan, a member of the *Journal*'s editorial page staff, admiringly wrote from Tehran in terms of a modern fairy tale in which the shah's political skills had combined with historical circumstance to elevate "Iran to a new and unique position."[14]

By 1974 the Iranian boom was common fare for the mainstream

press, as these headlines indicate: "Iran: A New Persian Empire? How the Shah Has Harnessed Oil Revenues and a Purposeful Development Policy" (*Christian Science Monitor*);[15] "An Exuberant Prosperity, Fed by High Oil Prices is Transforming Tehran" (*New York Times*);[16] and "Shah of Shahs, Shah of Dreams" (*New York Times*).[17]

While stories about the country's prosperity tended to dominate news of the economy, the problems encountered along the way were not neglected. The *Christian Science Monitor* wrote in 1974 of many obstacles to spreading the benefits of the boom, most particularly a serious lag in transforming the agricultural sector.[18] The *Washington Post* issued an editorial warning about Iran's "price-swollen oil revenues, which far exceed the absorptive capacity of its economy,"[19] and even the usually optimistic *New York Times* wrote, "Iran, where civilization flourished while Europe was barbarian, is today a country that cannot feed itself. The [shah] promises greatness, but 70 percent of the people are illiterate and 60 percent live at subsistence levels."[20]

By 1975 some journalistic attention began to be paid Iran's looming deficit as the shah persisted in his grand schemes and outspent his revenues despite a drop in world requirements for oil, although the space devoted to the subject never equaled its importance.[21] Despite the attention given Iran's new problems by the press, the full measure of the country's disastrous spending was never made plain. The terribly overheated economy usually was portrayed more as a sideshow than a potentially explosive situation in the making, and even those articles that did warn of possible catastrophe were overshadowed by the generally optimistic tenor of the mainstream press. Yet by 1975 the economy's terminal symptoms had become obvious.

As early as 1973 some mainstream scholars had warned of serious problems, including Prof. Marvin Zonis of the University of Chicago, who argued at a congressional hearing that obvious material progress was terribly misleading. According to Zonis, "One can visit the Hilton, La Residence, the Key Club, the Darband, the Imperial Country Club or one of the staggeringly large number of boutiques in Tehran and not realize he is in one of the poorest nations in the world."[22] Also testifying was Prof. Richard Cottam, who described how social progress was effectively blocked by bureaucratic red tape, corruption, and the shah's unwillingness to share power. Cottam told committee members, "I know of no more successful public relations operation than the Iranian Government's," yet he argued that a close look behind the scenes would reveal "scandals that would make Watergate look like nothing."[23]

Interestingly, until the 1978 revolution and the hostage crisis, the mainstream press made little use of academic opinion about Iran. Whether in 1953 or 1976, professorial comment in news stories about Iran was almost totally absent. The academic perspective was limited to a rare guest commentary or a letter-to-the-editor. For reasons not entirely clear, in 1978 and particularly during the Iran hostage situation, journalism turned far more readily to the university for assistance in understanding the fast-moving events.[24]

By 1974 Iran's oil revenues were approaching $1.5 billion a month, and the "hyperboom" was well under way, yet the emphasis was on current expenditure rather than new investment,[25] and the volume of imports had increased by 39 percent.[26] According to British journalist and author Robert Graham, "By early 1975 the Iranian economy was almost out of control. During the first quarter of the new Iranian year . . . government spending was up 208 per cent on the same period the previous year,"[27] and imports had increased almost 100 percent over the same period in 1974.[28] Inflation was rampant, rents spiraling sometimes to 60 percent of pay, and the land cost of housing was at 47 percent.[29] According to Graham, from March to August 1975 the government would admit to an increase in the consumer price index of 28 percent, whereas the real rate was probably closer to 35 to 38 percent.[30] While many of these facts surfaced in the American press in fragmentary form, they did not receive the kind of treatment that might have challenged Washington's view of Iran.

The weight of evidence suggests that concerns about whither Iran were usually submerged in far more favorable accounts of the country's economic progress. How this process worked can be seen in the analysis of a lengthy journalistic appraisal of the new Persian empire that was published in the *New York Times* Sunday Magazine in 1974 with the headline "Shah of Shahs, Shah of Dreams." Author David Holden, a correspondent for the Sunday *Times* of London, included a number of considered judgments that were hardly complimentary to the shah and cast doubts on the economic course upon which he had set forth. Yet throughout his piece the pros far outweighed the cons, and Holden tempered his criticisms in a way that was typical of much of the American press. For instance, Holden wrote, "While the Shah's ambitions are indeed spectacular, it is hard not to feel they outreach the dreams, and perhaps even the *capacities*, of his people" (emphasis ours). Holden then wrote:

> In his impatient, Napoleonic vision of history, Iran is destined to become the Japan of West Asia—one of the five great powers of the world by 1983. But in the minds of his amiable, devious and immensely respectful people such a goal still seems remote. Although they may bow down with relish before his power, they seem less likely to rise to his great expectations.[31]

Such paternalism might be written off as Tory imperial nostalgia were it not an example of a thematic thread, albeit less crudely stitched, that can be found throughout so much of the American press's coverage of Iran, particularly in 1953, 1963, and 1978.

One type of story that frequently appeared during the mid-1970s was the kind that focused on mismanagement of the wealth brought by oil. The tone of these stories was far more condescending than alarmed. While critical at the first level of analysis, this type of story usually dealt only with economic issues and left the clear impression that if the chaos caused by the influx of petro-dollars could be brought under control, development would proceed apace. Rarely did a consideration of the political dimension enter stories of this type, and the contradiction posed by an essentially feudal regime and modernization went largely unexplored. To quote a State Department officer in a single sentence, as *Newsweek* did, that "Iran is a dictatorship in everything but name,"[32] simply did not provide the potentially concerned reader with the background or sustained analysis necessary to judge the shah's regime adequately.

Beyond the question of arms purchases and the suitability of the shah's development policies, the OPEC price increases had put in motion economic forces that would pull the media in opposite directions. On the one hand, the press voiced a sort of populist lament about the unfairness of the sources of Iran's new wealth, while at the same time being dazzled—if not blinded—by the opportunity the riches held for American industry, business, and trade. How these conflicting currents could transform quadrupled prices at the gas pump into a bonanza for corporate America can be seen in the signing of a 1975 trade deal between Iran and the United States. In retrospect the agreement may have clouded the vision of the media at precisely the time the press was beginning to pay more critical attention to Iran; good business, in short, may have undercut good journalism. As a result, forces that would ultimately lead to the revolution continued to be ignored or go underreported.

Under the terms of the unprecedented compact of March 1975, Iran agreed to purchase some $15 billion in American goods and services over a five-year period. Another $7 billion was earmarked for the construction by American companies of up to eight nuclear plants. The bilateral trade agreement, according to the *New York Times,* represented the largest such business accord in history.[33] An editorial in the *Los Angeles Times* welcomed the deal by arguing, "The $15 billion trade agreement between the United States and Iran is staggering, yes, but not as some would suggest, frightening. There must be uneasiness, however, on two aspects: One-third of the money will be spent on arms, and a fair share of the balance will buy eight nuclear power plants." Having sounded this muted warning, the *Times* concluded with this observation: "On balance, the United States can look with favor on what [the shah] is doing. He is applying the precious resource of his country, petroleum, to the task of modernizing a largely agrarian and primitive state."[34]

While the *Los Angeles Times* did not make clear who might have been uneasy with the deal, the overwhelming weight of evidence indicates it was not the mainstream American press. Journalists generally greeted the pact with enthusiasm. C. L. Sulzberger of the *New York Times* wrote a typical treatment, pointing out that the $15 billion deal was the "largest business accord ever arranged; even the Marshall Plan involved far smaller commitments." He also told his readers that the bilateral trade agreement "runs overwhelmingly in U.S. favor," adding that oil was only a minimal part of the deal.[35] What had been a lucrative market now became a gold rush for American business, and coverage tended to center on the shah as superconsumer. As a review of the *Wall Street Journal Index* quickly verifies, nothing quite like the subsequent wave of spending had ever hit corporate America before. To expect the press to engage in a close and critical investigation of the phenomenon in the face of such a boon for American business is simply unrealistic, given the corporate values of modern media.

Moreover, it should be pointed out that the failure of the press to go beyond convenient assumptions about the shah's Iran during this heady time was not singular. Washington, of course, was positively sanguine about its ally's fortunes and future, but more important, significant parts of the cultural apparatus as well found it expedient to look with favor on the Pahlavi dynasty. It is not unreasonable to conclude that the press, in some important measure, took its bearings from those areas of the private sector that usually might be expected to serve as a corrective in the foreign policy arena, but where Iran was concerned, it chose to confer legitimacy on the shah instead. The transfer of respectability to the shah's regime by think tanks, universities, and prominent individuals was as much a thriving business as the transfer of arms and high technology.

Universities ranging from Stanford and Harvard to MIT and Columbia set up special research and development or educational programs at the behest and with the funding of Iran. In the largest such deal, according to the *Christian Science Monitor,* Georgetown University contracted for $11.5 million to aid Iran's Ferdowsi University in developing schools of agriculture, economics, and engineering.[36] The University of Southern California and Pepperdine University awarded honorary doctorates to the shah and his wife in return for $1 million endowments.[37] David E. Lilienthal, former chairman of the Tennessee Valley Authority and the Atomic Energy Commission, undertook to study and strengthen Iran's civil service,[38] and former Secretary of State William P. Rogers became legal counsel in the United States for the Pahlavi Foundation, nominally a charitable foundation but effectively a front for royal investments.[39]

A particularly striking example of the willingness of some intellectual entities to rent out their reputations was the liberal Aspen Institute of Humanistic Studies, which in 1975 undertook to organize the Aspen/Iran program. According to Joseph E. Slater, Aspen's then president, the effort was intended to provide "Iranians with new modes of outreach and new opportunities for international contact, enriching non-Iranians through their associations with Iran and uniting Iranians and non-Iranians alike in consideration of the major global problems that plague our increasingly interdependent world."[40] Originally, Aspen was to have received $3 million from the Pahlavi Foundation to run the Iran program, but actually got only $750,000 before the revolution severed the relationship.[41] Functioning almost as an intellectual escort service, Aspen named Empress

Farah Pahlavi an honorary trustee, and Iran's ambassador to the
United Nations, Fereydoun Hoveyda, as a special adviser.[42]

In the fall of 1975, the institute organized the Aspen Institute/
Persepolis Symposium in Iran, which brought together more than a
hundred leaders from fourteen nations to "look at values in transition." At the end of the conference Slater and Robert O. Anderson,
chairman of Aspen's board and principal shareholder and chairman
of Atlantic Richfield Company, presented Empress Farah Pahlavi
with Aspen's Special Award for Humanism.[43]

There can be little doubt, given the historical evidence, that the
transfer of respectability by corporate and elite America to Iran,
coupled with Washington's enthusiasm and journalistic myopia, sub-
ordinated consideration of the continuity of opposition to the shah
and the accompanying protest that characterized the domestic Iranian
scene throughout the 1970s. The depth of illegitimacy of the regime
in the minds of Iranians and the absence of authentic stability in the
society remained to be discovered by Americans in 1978.

Nonetheless, after 1973 the press did begin to carry more news
about the absence of political freedom in Iran. Why this should be
so had to do with a series of developments inside and outside Iran
which were impossible for the journalistic establishment to ignore.
Following the bloody uprisings of 1963, opposition to the shah's
regime became a constant, although some periods of political and
armed resistance were more intense than others. Increasingly, torture, imprisonment, and executions became tools of the state in an
attempt to deal with political, social, and later, economic unrest.
Sources of protest included students, professionals, the religious
community, and guerrilla groups. The protests also took many forms
and resulted from varied points of conflict with the regime.

Religious protests were rekindled on a massive scale in 1975,
when the shah announced the end of the multiparty system—subser-
vient and ineffectual as it may have been, it had some symbolic
meaning to desperately hard-pressed Iranians—and the beginning of
a single-party state dominated by the shah's Rastakhiz (National Resurgence) party. Initially, the press treated the shah's maneuver in a
perfunctory way and gave it little attention, perhaps because announcement of the $15 billion trade agreement came only two days
later.[44]

As implications of his move began to sink in, however, American mainstream journalism began to have misgivings. In a column that came as close to open criticism of the shah as any he ever wrote, C. L. Sulzberger pointed out that the shah in his memoirs, *Mission for My Country,* had written:

> If I were a dictator rather than a constitutional monarch, then I might be tempted to sponsor a single dominant party such as Hitler organized or such as you find today in Communist countries. But as a constitutional monarch I can afford to encourage large-scale party activity free from the straitjacket of one-party rule.[45]

Sulzberger failed to point out that the shah's multiparty system had been an elaborate political charade in the first place, but he did write that he "found it odd that, speeding toward economic parity with the four democracies [West Germany, Japan, France, and Britain] . . . , Iran's regime has found it desirable to move abruptly to a single-party state." Although he found nothing "Hitlerish or Communistic" about the new institution, he found nothing democratic either.[46]

Although news accounts increasingly raised questions about the shah's one-party state, these concerns were usually offset by emphasis on the shah's commitment to social progress and unflattering references to his opponents, who typically were identified as terrorists, Communists, or fanatics. For example, an article by Eric Pace published in May 1975 on the revamping of the political system framed the shah's efforts in the context of his efforts to court public opinion and uncritically repeated the regime's notion that the one-party system would lead to greater citizen participation.[47]

An account of protests in the religious city of Qum by *Washington Post* reporter Andrew Borowiec dealt with the shah's ruthless treatment of his opposition but cautioned that it "is not inconceivable that Moslem traditionalists are supplied with funds and weapons by Marxists" and added that "the religious fanatics are against the land reform (*already completed*), emancipation of women, alcoholic beverages and the general and rapid Westernization of Iran's major cities" (emphasis ours).[48]

Even after the one-party system was initiated, the mainstream American press continued to use every possible alternative to the word "dictatorship" or "police state" in describing various aspects of the shah's absolute power, although by 1976 harsher terms came to be more frequently used. Pace, for example, wrote of a "press loyal to the Shah,"[49] and of a "Teheran press which faithfully reflects the views of the Shah,"[50] whereas the reality was that newspapers critical of his majesty were shut down and their editors and reporters jailed and in some cases executed.

Until 1976 the closest a Pace dispatch came to putting a name on things was in a December 1975 story, which referred to the shah as a "dictatorial monarch."[51] The majority of other American journalists showed similar restraint in descriptions of political life under the shah, despite the reality of Iran: a one-party state in which rigid press censorship was enforced by a feared secret police, opposition was outlawed, and all decision-making power rested in the hands of one man.

A long analysis of the changed Iranian political scene in the *Washington Post*, while avoiding charged language and taking an even-handed line, nevertheless presented a noticeably different picture than the one provided by the *Times*. From the mid-1970s on, the *Post* generally took a far more tough-minded view of Iranian politics than did the *Times*.

Under the headline "Shah Cracks Political Whip," *Post* writer Andrew Borowiec informed readers that the shah had issued a "stern warning" to the growing middle class in Iran to "toe the line or else." In discussing the new party, Borowiec was the only journalist to point out that it had replaced the "previous two rather fictitious parties." Contradicting the *Times* and its assertion that Iranians were flocking to join the new party, Borowiec wrote, "It was no surprise that the politically numbed and disinterested Iranians generally stayed away from the polls [June elections]. According to the best estimates available, only 35 to 50 percent of the electorate bothered to vote." He was also one of the few journalists to note that guerrilla actions against the government had increased significantly following the creation of a one-party political system.[52] Unlike his earlier piece on religious opposition in Qum, Borowiec stayed away from broad generalizations about "Islamic-Marxists" and "religious fanatics."

By 1976 news accounts of armed resistance to the shah were common in the U.S. press. In most instances, the violence was attributed to "Marxist and Islamic-Marxist terrorists" by the government, an explanation usually passed on by the press without comment or clarification. However, the press by this time had begun to add the adjective "alleged" to the government's use of the terms "terrorist" and "Marxist."[53]

By the mid-1970s the Iranian regime's repression of dissidents had attracted the attention of international human rights groups, several of which investigated the claims of the opposition elements and issued reports highly critical of the shah's government. These reports persuaded a number of prominent Western writers, academics, and artists to lend their support to the activities of dissident Iranians abroad. The reports also compelled the press to pay more attention to the abuses of human rights in Iran.

As early as 1973, probably as a result of Iran's increasingly visible high profile, more frequent references to—if not lengthy analyses of—the shah's harsh style of rule began to appear in the American press. Moreover, references to the shah's commitment to democracy, which once appeared routinely in news accounts, disappeared completely. The dominant frame became one of concern if not alarm for the shah's handling of dissent. Typical of background phrases that began to find their way into mainstream journalism was one used by a *New York Times* writer to describe SAVAK in a not altogether flattering 1973 profile of Iran: "The country's secret police organization . . . has been ruthless in suppressing political subversion."[54]

While the protest of a group of American writers and scholars, including Kurt Vonnegut, Jr., and Noam Chomsky, over the jailing of twelve Iranian journalists, writers, and film makers was buried by the *Times* on page 18,[55] the influential newspaper finally did publish an article dealing specifically with human rights violations in September 1974.[56] The first major international human rights organization to receive much publicity for its work on Iran was Amnesty International, which released a report in 1974 describing the shah's regime as among the most repressive in the world,[57] and by 1976 references to human rights abuses had become routine in press coverage.

Eric Pace of the *Times,* for instance, had finally come to conclude that Iran was a "hereditary dictatorship."[58] Additional publicity about Iran's practice of terror and torture was generated by an International Commission of Jurists report presented by the U.N. body in Geneva in May 1976,[59] and the publication of a book by an Iranian poet and former political prisoner, Reza Baraheni, whose charges, however, were usually relegated to the book review pages and who did not receive nearly the same degree of media attention as have, say, Eastern European dissidents.[60] Indeed, the point must be emphasized that news items about the shah's abuses did not usually receive front page or drumbeat coverage. Even so, stung by criticism, officials of SAVAK began responding publicly to the charges by human rights organizations and the press.[61] A September 1976 congressional hearing on human rights violations in Iran added to SAVAK's image problems,[62] although the hearings did not receive widespread publicity, as did reports that its agents were spying on dissident Iranian students in the United States.[63]

As the Carter administration's declared policy on human rights received more attention, so did abuses in Iran,[64] although few journalists noticed that the policy had made little difference on actual American behavior toward the shah. Indeed, the press seemed to believe that the policy might be having some effect on the shah's practices, as this headline from the *Christian Science Monitor* indicated: "Iran Feels Impact of Carter Human-Rights Message."[65]

Any credit due the mainstream press for its increased concern with human rights in Iran must be tempered with several major qualifications. First, most coverage of the question came in the form of fleeting references submerged in larger news stories. Indeed, by comparison with the attention paid other aspects of Iran under the shah, human rights received very little space. In the main, the American *mainstream* press slighted the human rights story, choosing instead to concentrate on economic and foreign policy subjects.

In 1975, for instance—the high point for U.S.-Iran economic and foreign relations—the *New York Times* published only three items whose major focus was human rights violations in Iran. One was an excerpt from an article critical of Iran's human rights policy, which had been published abroad,[66] and the second was a letter-to-the-editor protesting artistic repression under the shah, which was signed by, among others, Muriel Rukeyser, Arthur Miller, and Kurt Vonnegut, Jr.[67] The third instance was a cautionary (if not condemnatory) column about the lack of civil rights in Iran by John B. Oakes of the *Times*.[68] By way of comparison, during 1975 the *Times* published some 150 articles on dissidents and human rights violations in the Soviet Union.

A second consideration, to be kept in mind when judging press performance on the human rights aspect of the Iran story, is that while the press was content to report the story as *other* individuals or organizations developed it, mainstream journalism did not actively pursue it. In this sense the press was finally forced to pay some attention because of reports from such diverse groups as Amnesty International, International Association of Democratic Lawyers, International Federation of Human Rights, International League For the Rights of Man, International Commission of Jurists, and Writers and Scholars International. Even so there was no American equivalent to the exposé in the *Sunday Times* (London) which revealed SAVAK's use of physical and psychological torture to deal with the regime's opponents, despite the wealth of journalistic resources and investigative talent in the United States. (Indeed, the *Times*'s study did not even receive widespread attention in the American press.)[69] A series of hardhitting columns by Jack Anderson,[70] two articles in the *Washington Post*,[71] and a treatment by CBS's "60 Minutes" *after* the revolution were notable exceptions.[72]

The argument can be made by journalists, of course, that the press *could not* pursue the human rights story in Iran, precisely because it was a police state. A variation of this explanation was advanced by the *Post*'s Andrew Borowiec, who wrote:

> In a tightly controlled country such as Iran, unofficial information is scarce, contact with opposition groups is illegal and virtually impossible, verification of the official version of incidents is extremely difficult. Rumors abound, diplomats are reluctant to share whatever information they manage to collect for fear of jeopardizing their sources.[73]

The problem with this argument is that it presents journalism's problem only as one of circumstance not choice. When adversary police states, such as the Soviet Union or Poland, are involved, American journalism is confronted with precisely the same problems in news gathering as it experienced in Iran. Yet the difference in quantity and quality between coverage of human rights abuses in the Soviet bloc and such coverage in Iran is striking. Moreover, the *Sunday Times* (London) was working under the same constraints as other foreign journalists, yet managed to produce a major story on human rights violations. Finally, in this regard, how was it that organizations ranging from Amnesty International to the International Commission of Jurists were able to collect human rights information about Iran, and American journalists were not? For one thing, such organizations listened to the testimony of Iranian exiles, whereas American journalists did not. Ironically, since the fall of the shah, the U.S.

news media now gives generous space to the charges of exiles against the Islamic Republic.

A third reservation about press performance centers on the failure of prestige journalism to regularly raise the issue of human rights in editorials, which can serve as important signals to policy makers concerned about where the limits of public support may lay. As with news accounts, editorials did not focus on human rights abuses per se, but rather touched on the matter within a larger context. Even on the exceedingly rare occasion when the major thrust of an editorial dealt with the shah's methods of dealing with dissenters, most mainstream editorials hardly had the sound of ringing condemnation. In an editorial on student protests against the shah's 1977 visit to the United States, for instance, the *New York Times* at once criticized the shah for his human rights policies, commented on the contradiction posed by the regime for the Carter administration, admitted that there had been some recent improvement in the lot of some political prisoners, and then argued that the United States had little direct influence over Iran in any event. The editorial concluded by advising the administration not to suspend arms sales but to restrain them and base them on assessments of the military situation in the region.[74] Eminently reasonable and sensible as the editorial may have sounded, the writer still could not bring himself or herself to call the shah a dictator.

Our final reservation about coverage of human rights in Iran was the context into which charges of abuse were almost always put. Invariably, news accounts balanced discussion of the absence of even modest political freedom with a virtual litany of assertions about the shah's social accomplishments or his general popularity. The result was a journalistic admixture of criticism and praise, with the emphasis usually falling on the latter. Rarely if ever has the American press accorded such consideration to rulers with a record like that of the shah.

True, as this chapter has demonstrated, mainstream press coverage of Iran in the mid-1970s did reveal what can reasonably be considered negative comment in many news accounts of the shah's chosen course in Iran. The shah himself often complained about the bad press he received in the United States. Given this fact, many observers of the press (and even some of its usually eager critics) may be puzzled by the claim we make here that coverage of Iran was distorted at all, particularly to the degree we argue. After all, didn't some news stories in the 1970s describe the shah as "autocratic," "often oppressive," or even "dictatorial"?

The seeming contradiction disappears if one makes the distinction between the criticism of means and the questioning of ends. It is true that the shah's *methods* did frequently receive critical coverage, but his *motives* and *goals* went almost unquestioned, while those of his critics were either denigrated or ignored. The cumulative result was that the American public got a picture of an impulsive, impatient, sometimes imprudent man who played rough but who had the best interests of his country at heart and was, in any event, headed in the right direction. Typical of this journalistic approach was a 1974 *Washington Post* dispatch that early on in the piece informed readers:

> The Shah runs a very tight state, a police state. He makes it clear to all his 33 million subjects that Iran is what it is today and will be what it will be tomorrow because he, the Shah, is personally shaping its destiny. The Shah is driven by a compulsion . . . to force Iran into industrial and economic competition with the developed nations of the West, and to do it in record time.[75]

Lest the reader get the wrong impression, though, the writer added some five paragraphs later: "Some of the Shah's critics (there are critics, although they speak very softly) say he suffers from an over-inflated ego. Others call it megalomania. Nevertheless, the great majority of Iranians *all but worship him*" (emphasis ours). This sort of conclusion served to underwrite the notion that whatever else the shah was he was firmly in control and would remain so.

In this regard, even though the press began to cover human rights abuses, journalists continued to overlook the main story, which was the shah's growing estrangement not only from the general population but from the dominant political and entrepreneurial elites as well, a phenomenon that was the local outcome of a feudal political order pursuing a program of socioeconomic modernization. At a time when the prestige press might have played a useful role as a reality check for Washington, it continued to perpetuate the official myth that Iran was an island of stability in the Middle East's sea of troubled waters.

Ignoring the reality that most social scientists agree that the legitimacy of a government cannot be secured by force, the press came to confuse the passivity born of coercion with consent of the governed. Perhaps more important, American journalists seemed oblivious to the reality that political instability is the companion of modernization. For the general relationship between modernization and instability is a fact of history. Moreover, in a society where economic modernization takes place within a feudalistic political order, the resultant instability can become explosive. One does not have to subscribe to a leftist or a liberal perspective to acknowledge the logic of this relationship. For instance, Samuel P. Huntington, an influential member of the American foreign policy elite, has nonetheless argued that a key aspect of modernization is the demand for increased participation in politics. He writes:

> Revolution is thus an aspect of modernization. It is not something which can occur in any type of society at any period in its history. It is not a universal category but rather an historically limited phenomenon. It will not occur in highly traditional societies with very low levels of social and economic complexity. Nor will it occur in highly modern societies which have experienced some social and economic development and where the processes of political modernization and political development have lagged behind the processes of social and economic change.[76]

The press, in short, did not perceive clearly that the process of forced modernization accompanied by the absence of participatory politics could only result in a model of *instability*. To the extent that such a failure results from assumptions about whether Third World peoples have the capacity to demand participation in politics, journalism is likely to repeat such errors in judgment in the future. Moreover, journalists missed the point that a country does not have to be rich or modernizing to have a stable political system. Similarly, to be rich and modern does not guarantee stability.

Even in serious attempts by the press to come to grips with the realities of Iran there was always missing the recognition of the inherent contradiction between feudal political structure and the modernizing process. For example, a 1977 six-part series in the *Washington Post* by a reporter for *Life* magazine, Richard T. Sale, represented on the one hand a significant effort on the part of a major newspaper to bring readers a coherent understanding of Iran and contained on the other many of the failings that we have discussed.

For Sale, whose wife was the daughter of a member of the shah's cabinet, it was not the shah's overcentralization of power, finally, that was blocking modernization, but rather the "agricultural, peasant based, religion-ridden nature of Iranian society." Much of what Sale had to say of the shah's progress, or lack of it, was highly critical. For example, he was the only mainstream American journalist to write unequivocally that "land reform in Iran has been a failure." Too, he clearly recognized that for modernization to succeed in Iran, agriculture had to keep pace with industrialization. But Sale's ultimate judgment was not that feudal politics was at root the problem. Rather, he concluded his first article by arguing, "What the Shah is attempting may lie not beyond the capacity of his vision, but beyond the character of his people."[77]

One of the very few American journalists to recognize the profound contradictions at the center of the new Persian empire was Frances FitzGerald, whose highly regarded book on Vietnam, *Fire in the Lake,* won the National Book Award. A 1974 piece of hers in *Harper's,* "Giving the Shah Everything He Wants," was—and is— arguably the best-informed piece of journalism about Iran ever to appear in a mainstream American periodical.[78] FitzGerald's lengthy study of a society gone terribly wrong demonstrated an astonishing grasp of the shah's Iran that seems positively prescient in light of subsequent events. Unlike the great majority of her colleagues in the press, she clearly understood the incompatibility of feudal politics and authentic development.

What is apparent in FitzGerald's work, beyond her refusal to accept uncritically the view of official Washington, is the scholarly and wide-ranging research that supported such assertions as her flat statement that the shah had never made a serious attempt at development. Absent were undocumented claims about the shah's modernization program or facile assertions about the religious fanaticism and irrational motives of his opponents. Using impeccable evidence, FitzGerald instead systematically demolished the dominant myths of the Pahlavi regime from modernization to the shah's reliability as an ally.

In place of the usual clichés and prefabricated prose, FitzGerald presented a closely reasoned, carefully documented case for a society in the grips of terror, massive repression, economic chaos, cultural anomie, and in a word, disintegration. The article stands as a model for what journalists of intelligence, sensitivity, and talent can accomplish—if it *occurs* to them to do so. What was possible for Fitz-Gerald to know was possible for others as well. If even a few other reporters had mounted a similar effort over the years, there might have been far less surprise in the United States at the events of 1978.

Yet American journalism, in spite of contrary evidence, too often confused the coercive rule of a monarch with stability. Even the shah's 700,000 armed men, finally, could not provide him with real stability. In fact the regime turned out to be so weak and incoherent that in the face of the first sign of serious challenge from the populace in 1978, it began to disintegrate from within.

7

The Press and the 1978 Revolution: West Meets East

Most analysts now rank Iran as a foreign policy disaster for the United States second only to Vietnam and are unanimous in the judgment that an enormous failure of intelligence kept Washington from taking the necessary steps to head off the debacle.[1] Usually this failure of the formal intelligence apparatus is discussed with a view toward how the revolution might have been averted or contained and the shah kept in power. A significantly different concern, which we happen to share, holds that adequate information might have opened debate over the wisdom of U.S. policy and a generation of U.S. foreign-policy makers' shortsighted moves that undermined the emergence of a secular, progressive, nationalist alternative to the shah.

Questions aside of whether Washington could or should have done something to preserve the shah's regime, there is little doubt that policy makers and Congress were surprised by the shah's lack of staying power. At least in theory, it is precisely when the formal means of gathering foreign policy information break down for whatever reasons that the press can play its most important role in an open society. Journalism, by providing an alternative situational analysis, can, if nothing else, stimulate a policy debate that makes it politically more difficult for policy makers to pursue a perilous course. The press can play this role, however, *only if* the journalistic system is operating independently of the government's formal policy-making apparatus. If, on the other hand, journalism is taking its cues from policy makers whose own judgments are deeply flawed, the result can be a dangerous exercise in circular delusion.

Our argument in this chapter is that just such a closed information loop was the rule during much of the 1978 year of revolution, as it had been during the previous twenty-five years, although toward the end of the revolt some segments of the mainstream press did begin to manifest doubt about the shah. Unfortunately, the modest improvement in reporting was hardly an effective counterweight to a quarter of a century of stereotypes planted in the public mind about Pahlavi governance. In short, as a result of years of wrong assumptions about the country, its people, and the shah, American journalism performed predictably, thereby truncating public debate on one of the most important foreign policy developments since the end of U.S. involvement in Indochina.

The explanations for the performance of American journalism during the revolution were essentially the same as those of the previous quarter of a century. Indeed, the subtle interplay of ethnocentrism, ideology, and wishful thinking that had informed reporting about Iran since 1953 became even more of a factor in the fast-paced tumult of the 1978 revolution.

As we argued in the preceding chapter, the American mainstream press for a range of reasons gradually grew more critical of the shah's regime after the 1973 oil embargo. However, this tendency toward criticism was cut short by the emerging revolutionary challenge to the shah's regime. From January 1978 and the first demonstrations in Qum until early fall, much of the U.S. press reverted to form and fell into line with Washington's view of affairs.

At first the press tended to ignore the shah's opposition, then to denigrate it, much as had been the case during the 1963 uprising. In this regard, during the first phase of coverage, the press accepted the regime's and Washington's contention that the shah's problems were wholly the work of Islamic reactionaries and Marxists. An editorial in the *Washington Post* in September 1978 summed up this point of view when it argued that "frenzied opposition from traditional religious elements" combined with "communist subversion" produced a "poisonous brew."[2]

Until the end of the summer of 1978, during the year of revolutionary demonstrations, neither policy makers nor journalists realized the general hostility toward the monarchy and that the grievances of the Iranian people and the political weakness of the state had reached the point where the shah could no longer rule effectively. A growing relative deprivation and a sharp sense of moral and cultural emptiness, combined with the shah's unwillingness to share political power, had produced an explosive society.

The fuse was lit by what most observers now agree was a spectacular case of bad judgment. In January 1978 the shah attempted to discredit the Ayatollah Ruhollah Khomaini as an opposition leader by launching a highly personal attack on him in a leading daily newspaper and the semiofficial voice of the regime. Far from discrediting Khomaini, the newspaper article provided the critical mass of the revolution; a comparatively insignificant act, as so often is the case where rage and alienation have long gone untended, set in motion forces far beyond the shah's expectation or imagination. What to this point had been essentially a series of secular protests involving university students, lawyers, writers, former National Front types, and so on was now on the verge of being overtaken by a mass movement that was largely motivated by religiocultural concerns and symbolism. Thus the situation resulted in as complex a revolt as has occurred in modern times.

Perhaps it is a metaphor for the twenty-five-year relationship of the American press to Iran that the *New York Times* in early 1977— just as political opposition was gaining serious momentum—*closed* its bureau in Tehran, leaving not one American reporter stationed in the country,[3] despite the unprecedented economic and strategic relationship of the United States to Iran. Until the revolution there had never been more than one or two news bureaus in Tehran at any given time. The *Times* rotated its reporters regularly, usually on a six-month basis. The Iran story for the most part was covered from Washington, D.C.; by Iranian stringers; from such Middle East jumping-off spots as Beirut and Cairo; or by American news reporters or correspondents who flew into the country for several weeks of fact finding and then returned home to reflect and to write their stories.

This kind of *absentee journalism* was hardly the only cause of the failure of the mainstream media in Iran, however. Merely having a large number of correspondents in a friendly client's capital does not guarantee a closer examination of the forces at work in the society. Nevertheless, how and where correspondents are deployed obviously has some effect on how much attention will be paid a subject and often determines how it will be portrayed as well. Not having correspondents of long residence on the scene may certainly have contributed to the delay which kept most of the news media from fully discovering the Iranian revolution until the fall of 1978, or about ten months after the protests in Qum, which were the bloodiest in Iran since the 1963 uprisings.

Most important, the press confused the religious idiom of the revolution with wholly sectarian motives and gave currency to the theme that religious reaction and not a quest for participation and equity explained events in troubled Iran, ignoring the reality suggested by anthropologist Michael M. J. Fischer: "The causes of the revolution, and its timing, were economic and political; the form of the revolution, and its pacing, owed much to the tradition of religious protest."[4] Beyond a tendency to stress these simplistic and distorted general themes, which we will discuss at greater length later in this chapter, coverage of several specific aspects of the revolution is open to criticism as well.

The question of the revolution's level of violence, for instance, was raised repeatedly by the media, but in such a way that made little distinction between state violence and the tactics of those in revolt. It is not unreasonable to assume that an American audience might conclude that Iranians were in armed revolt, given the probably cumulative effect of routine references to "bloody clashes," "a year of bloody disturbances," "violent upheaval," "rampaging mobs," "anti-shah violence," and so on. A typical treatment was this beginning of an Associated Press dispatch, which appeared in a metropolitan California newspaper under the headline "Moslems Riot; 13 Die in Iran": "More than a dozen persons were killed Sunday during violent clashes between government forces and Moslems enraged at desecration of Iran's holiest shrine by military gunfire."[5]

Aside from isolated instances, Iranians did not take up arms against the shah's forces until the last two or three days before the collapse of the regime, and even then street fighting was confined to bands of youths in the major cities. The blood spilling was almost entirely one-sided. Demonstrators often *did* engage in attacks on property, particularly public buildings and banks, which may explain the media's choice of words. But for more than a year literally millions of Iranians faced tanks and machine guns with little more than moral outrage. To be sure, the shah was indecisive, and military personnel often had no desire to shoot. Yet it remains true that the revolution was fought with empty hands, unlike the revolt against Somoza in Nicaragua or the resistance to a Soviet-controlled regime in Afghanistan, and the people, not the military, did the dying.

While the press did repeatedly refer to actions taken by the shah's troops and police, the failure to make a sharp distinction between armed and unarmed resistance to the regime made it appear as though both sides were equally engaged in violent acts. One measure of who was doing what to whom, of course, is the number of persons injured or killed by government forces. Again, there is no certain way of knowing how many died or were injured during the revolution; reasonable estimates, based on hospital and grave registrations and other similar forms of evidence, put the figure at approximately 10,000 killed and at least three times as many wounded.[6]

Press coverage of an equally significant and specific dimension of the revolution offers evidence of a shortcoming of a different sort. Journalists failed either to comprehend fully or to portray completely the enormous popularity of the revolution. The great majority of Iranians wanted an end to the institution of monarchy and the Pahlavi regime. The Iranian revolution was probably the most popular in modern history. Yet the American press, to the extent that it dealt with the question of popular support, tended to view and depict the overwhelming sentiment for an end to the shah's rule as mere "fanaticism." As Eric Rouleau, French journalist and expert on the Middle East, has explained, exceptionally rare was the Western observer who "pointed out the pitfalls of labeling an entire people fanatics simply because they were virtually unanimous in expressing their will."[7]

In this vein, journalists were inclined to center on street demonstrators engaged in seemingly exotic behavior; on urban lumpen; and on Muslim fundamentalists and leftist activists, an approach that ignored or overshadowed the important roles played by students, women, industrial and other salaried workers, and the middle- and upper-middle-class elements. In brief, the *cross-class* nature of the revolution, which was unprecedented in modern revolts, went largely unreported. To be sure, the urban masses (rural involvement was small) provided great numbers for street demonstrations, but the leadership for the revolt (including mollahs) came from the middle classes.

The media did cover in some detail the series of strikes, both localized and general, which began in the summer of 1978, took hold in the fall, and continued until the end of the revolution, and the press perfunctorily pointed out the various elements of society participating in them. An Associated Press dispatch of October 1978, for instance, told of striking hospital workers,[8] and a November dispatch gave details of striking bank employees, shopkeepers, power workers, and oil-field workers.[9]

What was largely missing from these accounts and most others was a pointed analysis of the *significance* of this widespread opposition to the shah and of the complex motives involved. Too, we could not find a single editorial or column in the mainstream press that commented favorably on the strikes, found them the slightest bit remarkable, or praised workers willing to strike for moral and political reasons rather than out of sheer economic self-interest. There was a similar absence of news stories or news features that gave strikers a human face. The rich and compelling detail of individual and collective human struggle, in the main, was remarkably absent in press accounts.

Students of the American press who argue that it is not the role of journalism to go beyond the surface of events but simply to state the objective facts would do well to compare American news coverage of, and editorial comment on, strikes in Poland and resistance to martial law there with the attention given the strikes in Iran in 1978. Where Poland is concerned, the Solidarity movement, its leaders, its tactics, and its achievements are well known to the attentive American public, and sympathy and admiration for their cause and conduct among Americans cannot be in doubt. In the case of Iran in revolt, the opposite was true.

In the absence of a different sort of coverage, students of Iran's revolution are left to speculate about what the American public might have thought, had they known, of wealthy Iranians contributing generously to pay the salaries of striking oil workers; of the same oil workers, already the best-paid workers in the society, refusing bribes in the form of even higher wages, and producing only enough oil for domestic consumption; of blood donors besieging hospitals to help those wounded in demonstrations; of shopkeepers stocking and selling only enough goods and foodstuffs to sustain their customers; of public services and offices at a standstill for months at a time; of a sense of unity and a spirit of cooperation in all sectors of society that was as palpable as it was unprecedented. These aspects of the revolution were readily apparent and susceptible to journalistic treatment, as is demonstrated by the work of *Le Monde*'s Eric Rouleau, among a few others, and nonmainstream "opinion" magazines in the United States, such as *Inquiry* and the *Nation*.

Yet it would appear that because of preconceptions about the nature of the revolt, and because they saw resistance to the shah as little more than fanaticism, mainstream journalists did not develop the human interest stories or supplementary analysis that would place the strikes in context. As a result, the American public got only a superficial view of the strikes, despite the fact they were among the most successful in history (far more so, say, than in Poland), represented a major turning point in the revolution, and finally, paralyzed the society and weakened the regime so that capitulation became inevitable.

As we have argued in earlier chapters, in the realm of foreign affairs, at least on a day-to-day, crisis-to-crisis basis, it is most likely to be the mainstream press that provides the public with its definitions. Even though the definitions often originate with foreign policy elites, it is the press that gives currency to the political and cultural vocabulary which is used to discuss events in popular discourse.

These definitions or labels and the vocabulary that comprises them, to the extent that they produce patterns, can be said to form contexts within which a foreign client is perceived by the public. In the process of this definition and perception building, images and themes are established which in turn come to provide for media audiences the basis for judging whether a particular event is good or bad, reassuring or dangerous, deserving of support or worthy of contempt. In no other political instance can this process be seen at work so clearly as in a revolutionary situation or rebellion against established authority. The press through its explanations of situations of this sort, intentionally or otherwise, bestows on or withholds legitimacy from those in revolt.

Any useful analysis, therefore, of how the press operated during

Iran's revolution must include an examination of the concrete themes, definitions, patterns of assertion, and frames of reference that were provided by journalists in covering the revolutionary developments of 1978. The media's interpretations of Iranian reality during this period clustered around two poles: The first locus had to do with what Iranians in revolt were against, and the second had to do with what they were for.

Revolutions are rooted in discontent, and how the nature of this discontent is presented by the press largely shapes the general public's judgment of the revolt it causes. In the case of the Iranian revolution, the primary explanation in the mainstream press of the discontent was the presumed opposition of the Iranian people to Shah Mohammad Reza Pahlavi's program of modernization. Various subthemes emerged, too, but the notion of the Iranian people's resistance to social change remained the dominant one, despite the reality, in the words of Iran scholar Nikki R. Keddie, that the "combination of inflation, shortages, and large and evident income-distribution inequities probably contributed more to growing discontent than did the standard factor cited in the West of 'too rapid modernization.'"[10]

A preoccupation in the press with modernization in Iran was not something new, as we have discussed in preceding chapters. In its coverage of the 1978 events, the press again accepted the tenets of the White Revolution as accomplished givens and therefore tended to view the revolutionary movement through a lens essentially ground and polished by the shah. These themes which dominated the first nine months of news media coverage of the revolution can be clearly seen in a United Press International dispatch filed in August 1978: "Iran clamped martial law on three more towns yesterday to *halt rioting by religious extremists opposed to the shah's liberalization* of the Moslem nation" (emphasis ours).[11] Yet another UPI writer described a clash between riot police and "conservative Moslems" opposed to the shah's plans to modernize Iran.[12]

A veritable journalistic litany grounded in this assumption came to dominate not only wire service reports, but newsmagazine accounts, and news stories, analyses, commentary, and editorials in major newspapers as well. Rarely were sources given or evidence presented for such a view of the shah's goals or his accomplishments. Rather, the claims were simply asserted in authoritative tone and manner, as if they were beyond reasonable debate.

An important subtheme that characterized the first six months of coverage of the revolution, until events rendered the contention unsupportable, was the notion that Marxism might be significantly involved as a revolutionary catalyst. The press with few exceptions demonstrated a willingness to ratify the shah's claim that "Islamic-Marxists" were at the bottom of his problems, and usually failed to consider other sources of opposition, which were clearly neither Marxist nor religious.

For all its interest in the possibility that Marxists were lurking behind the revolutionary scenes, most of the news media's attention remained focused on the religious nature of the ideology of the rebellion. Yet aside from occasional and usually brief references to the man, the U.S. press did not fully discover the Ayatollah Ruhollah Khomaini and his importance to the movement until November 1978, or eleven months after the revolution began. By contrast, a French television team headed by Maurice Sevend had conducted a filmed interview with Khomaini in Najaf, Iraq, 21 September 1978, and an interview with Khomaini by Lucien George appeared in *Le Monde* in May.[13]

It may be some measure of the lack of understanding of Iranian history by American journalists that it took them so long to discover Khomaini, given the penchant of the American media to explain politics, revolutionary or not, in terms of personalities. Three of the few early attempts at considering the forces behind insurgent Islam were articles published during the summer of 1978 in *U.S. News & World Report*,[14] the *Wall Street Journal*,[15] and a single-page treatment by *Time*.[16] All three identify the Ayatollah Mohammad Kazim Shariatmadari as a leader of consequence, but Khomaini merits short mention only in the *U.S. News* analysis.

The first interview with Khomaini in the U.S. press was published in *Newsweek* on 6 November.[17] It consisted of six questions together with brief responses from the religious figure. Once discovered, however, Khomaini quickly became an object of journalistic fascination and conjecture. Coverage in the weeks before and after the Ayatollah's return to Iran following his fourteen-year exile gave the clear impression that Khomaini had made the revolution, instead of the other way around. According to a *New York Times* report of Khomaini's departure from France, "[Khomaini], the man who brought down the Shah and has called for a new Iranian Islamic republic, left here today to return to his country."[18] A *Los Angeles Times* reporter, in a dispatch filed several weeks later, identified Khomaini as the man "who masterminded from his exile in Paris the downfall of Shah Mohammed Reza Pahlavi,"[19] while a UPI story filed from Tehran in mid-February 1979 began with the assertion that "crack units of the Shah's Immortal Brigade surrendered today to the forces of Ayatollah Ruhollah Khomaini, apparently completing his takeover of Iran."[20]

This tendency to see the politics of a country as revolving around and synonymous with a strongman was neither new to press coverage of Iran in particular nor to the Third World in general. For years, as Frances FitzGerald perceptively argued in an article written during the revolution;

> the assumption [of the press and official Washington] was that the Shah was the only person who counted in Iran; that the country, being underdeveloped, had no politics in the sense that advanced countries do; and that Iranians, being apolitical, would simply accept a dictatorship as necessary and good for them. The foreign-policy establishment has traditionally made similar assumptions about almost all Third World countries.[21]

For Iran, such treatment by the press reduced a mass movement that had complex and long-standing forces behind it to the product of the iron will of one man. It was precisely because Khomaini did not possess supreme political power that he was prevented from imposing his vision of a theocratic state from the beginning; to make such a move by fiat, he realized, would not succeed. He and his closest supporters turned to political means to achieve their goal; the irony is that they proved far more effective in this pursuit than their opponents, who thought the clergy politically unsophisticated.

The consensus view among journalists during the 1978 revolution was not limited to the personalities involved. There were other areas of broad agreement as well, which can be said to have contributed in significant ways to the American public's perceptions of events in Iran, at least until events overcame them. Among these other subjects were the journalistic treatment of, first, the shah's prospects for survival; second, his royal pedigree; third, the departure of the shah from Iran, and fourth, the return of the Ayatollah Khomaini after fourteen years of exile.

Typical of journalistic assessments of the shah's chances for successfully resisting the tides of revolutionary change—at least in the
early stages of the revolt—was *Time* magazine's June assessment:
"Few believe that the Shah is in any danger of being overthrown.
Iran's monarch still has the machinery of power firmly in his hands.
The Shah also has a broad base of popular support, particularly in
the army and among farmers and a newly created industrial working
class."[22]

American readers might have been in a better position to evaluate
the place of the shah in the hearts of his countrymen if they had
known something of the shah's history. Typically, though, they were
usually told only that he was restored to his throne in 1953 after a
showdown with Prime Minister Mohammad Mossaddeq. Repeated
use by the press of the vocabulary of royalty (allusions to the Peacock Throne, the Pahlavi dynasty, the empress, the crown prince,
and so on) gave Americans—who, despite national mythology to the
contrary, are fascinated with royalty—the clear impression that the
shah's kingly credentials were impeccable, no matter what else might
be said about the man. Actually, of course, the dynasty of His
Imperial Majesty Mohammad Reza Pahlavi, Shahanshah (King of
Kings), Aryamehr (Light of the Aryans), was exactly two genera-
tions old.[23]

Events leading up to the actual departure of the shah from Iran in
mid-January focused on the short (thirty-eight days) and unhappy
tenure of Shapour Bakhtiar, whom the shah, in a last-minute attempt
to salvage his rule and the "monarchy," had named prime minister
earlier that month. The major failure in the press's treatment of Bakhtiar's abbreviated time in office was the tendency to go along with the
State Department's public position that there was a government.
Bakhtiar had opposed the shah for years, true, but he was not a
staunch opponent of the monarchy per se and believed the best solution for Iran was a regency council. Bakhtiar's position, in short, was
that the shah still could reign but not rule.

The U.S. press tended to miss the point (and so did Bakhtiar) that
popular opposition to the shah by January 1979 had long since been
transformed into a revolutionary movement that unequivocally demanded an end to the monarchy, titular or not. Mere return to adherence to the 1906 constitution, with its provisions for a monarchy
along British lines, was no longer the issue.

Bakhtiar opted, however, to defend a discredited constitution and to seek a vote of confidence from a parliament that had essentially been hand-picked by the shah and which Bakhtiar himself had derided only weeks before as little more than "a house of puppets." The result was that Bakhtiar was not regarded by the Iranian people even so much as an illegitimate ruler; he suffered the ultimate indignity of being considered of utterly no consequence at all.

Despite this reality, the press usually covered Bakhtiar as if he mattered, falling into line with the next-best-choice scenario of the U.S. foreign policy establishment. In fact, although the press seemed not to take note of it, there was no *political* authority between the fall of the shah's first compromise prime minister, Sharif-Emami, on 6 November 1978 and the disintegration of the military on 11 February 1979. There were only the forces of coercion on the one hand and the moral force of Khomaini's decisive leadership on the other, with literally nothing between: a classic revolutionary vacuum existed.

Yet as late as a year after the turmoil began, as a systematic review of the media revealed, the press still had not used the term "revolution" to describe occurrences in Iran. The *Christian Science Monitor* had raised the question of terminology earlier in an editorial (11 December 1978), all the while hedging its bets, when it told readers: "But if the eyewitness report of events by Dr. James Bill on today's Opinion and Commentary page is accurate, Iran is in a state of revolution." The *New York Times* began using the term on 25 January 1979, or a week before Bakhtiar was forced to flee and the struggle was ended. The *Washington Post* followed suit in early February on the return of the Ayatollah Khomaini to Iran. Much of the rest of the press, including the wire services, did not make regular use of "revolution" until after the Bakhtiar government fell on 11 February.

How the mainstream press covered one other event, the departure of the Shah from Iran, is worth considering before moving on to an analysis of how journalists treated the revolt's religious dimension. There is almost a wistful quality to many of the news accounts and editorial assessments of the shah's leave-taking on 17 January 1979 for a "vacation" in Egypt. Such a tone tended to create the image of a saddened, tearful, and ill-treated sovereign whose ungrateful people, in mindless fashion, had driven him from his country. He was forced to leave, the press would have its audiences believe, simply for having tried to drag his subjects into the twentieth century. That the shah should emerge as a sympathetic figure and Iranian revolutionaries as ingrates stands, perhaps, as another metaphor for the historic relationship of the American news media to Iran.

To be sure, other media at the time of the shah's departure—and, indeed, during much of the latter part of the revolution—included brief mentions of the grievances of Iranians. It can be argued, however, that such a considered judgment was (1) overshadowed by the mass of coverage, as we have outlined it in this chapter, and (2) hardly adequate to the chore of describing a regime characterized in 1974 by Martin Ennals, secretary-general of Amnesty International, as having the worst human rights record in the world.

Most important in this regard, while our study revealed that the press frequently used terms such as "stern-willed," "determined," "autocratic," and in rare instances, "iron-fisted," to describe the shah, we could find no use of the terms "tyrannical," "brutal regime," or "despotic rule," all of which journalists have used to describe other regimes in the region and throughout the world which are considered "unfriendly" to U.S. interests. Moreover, in our study of the entire year of revolution, we could find only *a single instance* in which the mainstream media used the term "dictator" to describe the shah, and that came in a positive context. According to a November 1978 *Washington Post* editorial, it was a curious matter that "the shah—a dictator, after all—has not been using the full power available to him to take the situation in hand."[24]

Of all the factors at work in the Iranian rebellion, perhaps the most baffling to the U.S. press was the emergence of religion as a revolutionary force. Yet it is precisely such a dynamic that American journalists are likely to have to interpret in the future, given the likelihood that Islamic nationalism will continue to provide the idiom for political rebellion in the region. Islam in general and Shi'ism in particular greatly mystified and, equally important, deeply disturbed the American press, which can be described as nominally Christian but effectively secular.

In short, the American news media's portrayal of the motive forces of the Iranian revolution went far beyond a view of Iranians as being merely anti progress. According to the consensus press view, the deepest source of Iranian discontent transcended the realms of economics and politics. Instead, as the press saw it, the revolution was the result of something more fundamental: religious reaction. The Iranian people, in this view, were given to blind faith in a profoundly irrational, antimodernist religion that appealed to man's darkest and basest instincts. This view of Islam in general and Shi'i in particular dominated press coverage throughout the revolution and was quickly established as the received wisdom in journalistic discussions of what the Iranian people were opposing and what they hoped to achieve.

At least one journalist, Meg Greenfield, writing in *Newsweek*, recognized the problem inherent in the cultural confrontation between East and West when she argued in a column on the Middle East, headlined "Islam and Us," that "no part of the world is more important to our well-being at the moment—and no part of the world is more hopelessly and systematically and stubbornly misunderstood by us." The ignorance and shallowness which characterize American perceptions of the Islamic Middle East, Greenfield contended in her essay, might be compared to the ignorance born of European arrogance that governed Columbus as he first encountered "Indians" in the New World. We have come to look on the Islamic peoples of the Middle East, Ms. Greenfield argued, as Indo-Europe's slow learners.[25]

The major source of perceptual error for the American media in reporting the Iranian revolution is contained in the truth that revolutions (and journalism as well) always involve two dimensions of human existence—the objective and the subjective. The press badly faltered in dealing with the former and proved totally inadequate to the challenge of the latter.

American journalists are trained to concentrate on an assumed objective reality by reporting only that which is verifiable, readily observable, and subject to the laws of evidence. Questions aside of whether objectivity can be achieved, in theory by journalism's professed standard the press ought to have recognized the serious economic and social problems rampant in Iran under the shah. Journalists ought to have been capable of more accurately judging, for instance, the White Revolution. In practice, subjective factors always dictate how objective conditions are to be interpreted, and journalists saw Iran through an ideological and cultural haze that distorted the motives of the Iranian people and legitimized the motives and behavior of the shah.

Revolutionaries perceive their activities as a struggle for freedom from what they regard as an oppressive and illegitimate social structure. This objective dimension, therefore, relates to the coercive, deceptive, and exploitative conditions of everyday life, all of which are neither mysterious nor difficult to measure. Under the Pahlavi dynasty, Iran was viciously class-ridden. The maldistribution of income was intensified rather than diminished by the flow of petrodollars into the Iranian economy, and little of the oil wealth penetrated the rural areas.

Moreover, the extent of repression was unprecedented in Iranian history. Thousands were executed or imprisoned, torture was routine, criticism of the shah was automatically considered treason, and opposition to massive inequality was branded as a crime against the state. The secret police (SAVAK) was the most powerful bureaucracy in the country. That these objective conditions could be ignored or misinterpreted in the American press up to the final collapse of the regime is largely the result, as we have suggested, of subjective factors at work in the character of the revolution and in the realm of American journalism.

Objective conditions, of course, in and of themselves do not constitute a necessary and sufficient cause for revolution. A harsh life does not logically lead to the politics of revolt. Those who come to fight for revolutionary change must also have a commitment to myths or ideas that promise a more satisfying society.

In the case of Iran, as opposed, say, to Poland in revolt against Soviet dominance, the *subjective* thrust of the revolution in its religious form and its opposition to a pro-Western regime were almost intuitively rejected by American reporters. In other words, the subjective motivational forces of the revolution clashed with the subjective internalized values of reporters, which led journalists to overlook or misjudge objective conditions. The journalists' pronounced cultural discomfort with the religious character of the revolution, furthermore, was reinforced with an ideological bias that filtered Iran's past and present through the lens of narrow American self-interest.

Whether it was the *New York Times* or the *Washington Post, Newsweek* or *Time*, the wire services or the television networks, the American mainstream news media tended routinely to characterize the Iranian uprising as more the work of turbaned religious zealots than the reaction of people outraged by a repressive regime. According to a standard interpretation offered by United Press International, "The protests against the government were begun by conservative Moslems who opposed the shah's liberalization program and demanded a return to rule by Islamic law."[26] And in the view of an Associated Press writer, "modernization has collided with ancient social and religious traditions, whose proponents refused to budge."[27]

American journalists' preoccupation with one "ancient social and religious tradition," the ceremonies surrounding the holy month of Muharram and its special day of worship, Ashura, is worth particular mention at this point because the way the media covered these events provides some insight into overall coverage of the revolution. According to an article in *Newsweek:*

> All week, the chants echoed cross Iran. In the holy city of Qom, religious zealots taunted the army from roof tops with slogans warning the Shah and his Empress to "get out of Iran." In the alleyways of Teheran's ramshackle bazaar, street toughs ripped open their shirts, pounded their chests and chanted: "The flower garden of religion I shall water with my blood." Iran was *revving up* for the annual holy day of Ashura, when perfervid Shiite Muslims—the Shah's fiercest foes—literally whip themselves into a frenzy. Late last week, the violence began (emphasis ours).[28]

Newsweek's account was illustrated with a photo of a crowd of protesters, most with fists raised, captioned with the "garden of religion" quote; another photo of a small group of young men engaged in self-flagellation, captioned, "Frenzy: flagellation ceremony last year"; a photo of mourners bearing a stretcher with a body wrapped in traditional white mourning robe; and a picture taken at a crowded Mehrabad airport in Tehran, captioned, "Western evacuees jam Teheran's airport: 'My children are terrified'." The *Newsweek* account continued:

> Demonstrators defied the military government in scattered clashes that left scores—if not hundreds—dead. Every day, the sprawling Behesht-Zahra cemetery south of Teheran echoed with the *wails* of women mourners in their long black chadors as another dozen or so bullet-riddled bodies were washed, wrapped in white shrouds and buried. Spurred by religious fervor, the fresh wave of dissent left Iran all but paralyzed again (emphasis ours).[29]

A similar mood was evoked by the beginning of *Time* magazine's account of the same period: "After two weeks of mounting tension, the *frightening* holy days ended last week—and the Shah still sat upon the Peacock Throne" (emphasis ours).[30] During the same period, *Time* told its readers, "These days marked the climax of the holy month of Muharram, on which Iran's devout Shiite Muslims traditionally take to the streets in a *frenzy of reproach and self-flagellation*" (emphasis ours). A picture of chador-clad women accompanied the article and had as its caption: "Women in Tehran *wail* for youths slain in anti-Shah clashes" (emphasis ours).[31]

It is not unreasonable to argue, in our view, that the context which results from the Kiplingesque emphasis, tone, and word choice in coverage of this sort has predictable results, particularly in the larger context of the media's coverage of the revolution throughout its course. By largely ignoring the profound political and moral significance of Muharram and Ashura and instead concentrating on its more "exotic" aspects, the press cannot help but create for American readers living in a Christian culture a sense that Iranian revolutionaries were more shackled by religious superstition than interested in political freedom.

The background of the ceremonies was alluded to in most accounts, but in such a superficial way as to render them even more seemingly senseless. Sketchy references to the slaying of Hosain and self-flagellation, for instance, hardly gives the uninitiated a sense of the rich complexity of what was involved. Such a brief mention cannot reasonably be expected to inform readers that for all Shi'ite Muslims throughout the world the month of Muharram symbolizes Islam's injunction against, and the believers' obligation to resist, tyranny and illegitimate government, an injunction with particular significance to Iranians in 1978.[32]

If a dangerous kind of ethnocentrism is not at work in the instance at hand, how is the use of terms such as "wail," "turbaned," "frenzy," and "frightening" to be explained? Would it occur to American reporters covering the Vatican, moreover, to make mention of the biretta worn by Catholic clergy, or refer to priests as "black-robed," as reporters consistently described mollahs throughout the revolution? Or to describe Western women at a funeral for their sons as "wailing"? Or to use the verb phrase "revving up" to characterize Christian preparations for Easter? Or to describe priests opposing Polish martial law as "religious fanatics"?

Moreover, self-flagellation is practiced in Iran by an insignificant number of people; the practice is discouraged by many religious leaders, and some have even rejected it as sacrilegious. It was as if French reporters, say, were to observe a Pentecostal snake-handling ceremony in the American South and then to conclude that such behavior characterized typical American Christianity.

There were some American journalists who in their work did avoid making overreaching claims about the motives of the religious opposition, including Youssof M. Ibrahim, who at various times reported for the *New York Times* and the *Wall Street Journal*, William Branigin and Jonathan C. Randal of the *Washington Post*, and Middle East veteran Joe Alex Morris of the *Los Angeles Times*, who was killed while observing a confrontation between demonstrators and the regime, the only journalist to lose his life during the revolution.

Branigin, who had reported on and off from Iran for several years, was one of the very few American journalists to seek out leaders of the religious opposition early in the revolt. For example, a January 1978 dispatch included a sympathetic hearing for Ayatollah Kazem Shariatmadari.[33] Branigin in most of his dispatches was careful to delineate between opposition factions and include mention of secular grievances.[34]

Similarly, Branigin's colleague at the *Post*, Jonathan C. Randal, who has spent considerable time in the Middle East, also looked for sources of opposition beyond the religious,[35] although occasionally resorting to mainstream clichés about revolutionary motives. One of his April 1978 dispatches, for example, was an analysis that strongly criticized the shah for having quadrupled oil prices in 1973 and injecting "the lion's share of the new oil money directly into the already badly strained Iranian economy." However, Randal prefaced his criticism with this observation: "Rarely would contemporary history appear to provide such an example of a people's ingratitude towards a leader who brought about an economic miracle of similar proportions [to Iran's]."[36]

A month later Randal characterized the struggle as "a battle between church and state" and asserted that the religious opposition's quarrel with the shah "focuses on the Shi'i sect's demand for a return to the liberal 1906 constitution and their opposition to land reforms imposed by the shah."[37] He did point out that as the "shah's government became increasingly autocratic, the mosque came to provide the principal arena for dissent." And by November, *Post* writer Jay Ross had come to conclude that while the government claimed that opposition consisted primarily of Moslems opposed to the emancipation of women and seizure of church land, "the real reasons appear to go much deeper—unfulfilled economic expectations and lack of political freedom."[38]

One of the few newspaper articles to focus on the human interest side of the struggle was written in late 1978 by the *Times*'s Ibrahim, who was the only American reporter to even mention Dr. Ali Shariati, whose thinking was a major intellectual force in the revolt. Ibrahim began his piece by focusing on the miserable existence of a typical slum-dweller in Tehran. The piece also profiled resistance to the shah in the bazaar and among university students. According to Ibrahim in perhaps the strongest passage to appear in a major American daily newspaper during the revolution: "The fear of torture, prison, arbitrary arrest, and the ubiquitous presence of Savak seems overwhelming. Phone conversations are guarded, and dissidents prefer to see journalists away from their hotels, where they are sure Savak monitors all entries and exits."[39] He went on to describe the brutal experiences of an intellectual who had suffered imprisonment and torture at the hands of the secret police.

Exceptions aside, for the most part, American journalists, as they had since 1953, persisted in repeating the regime's claims about the opposition as if they were beyond reasonable doubt. The absence of even routine journalistic attribution to authority was perhaps the most obvious indicator of how certain reporters were about their facts.

Perhaps the least understood aspect of the events of 1978 to American reporters was the role of Shi'i Islam as a mobilizing and legitimizing force in the revolutionary movement. At least for four centuries, Shi'ism has been a principal source of national feeling for the vast majority of Iranians. For the Shi'i beliefs, rituals, and symbolism serve as a vital social cement and as such, are as much a cultural-anthropological phenomenon as a religious one. Iran today is the only country whose population is predominantly Shi'i.

Imam Hosain is the most significant religio-political hero for Iranians, regardless of their socioeconomic status. The drama and symbol of Hosain's life and death convey a common message to villages, tribes, and urban dwellers. It was no coincidence, therefore, that popular resistance during the 1978 revolution reached a climax of sorts during the holy days of Muharram in December, a time that commemorates the death of Hosain.

In all this, it should have been clear to journalists that the Shi'i tradition of resistance in Iran has not been categorically or predominantly opposed to political and economic change. Many Shi'ite leaders actively supported the liberal 1906 constitution, for instance. Yet we could find only *one* considered judgment that suggested such a possibility in our survey of mainstream coverage of the revolution, and this was a single passing reference in the thousands of words published by *Time* during 1978–79: "The mullahs, for all their abhorrence of the decadent excesses of modernism, have traditionally been political progressives and nationalists in their outlook."[40]

The contemporary radical Shi'ite movement in Iran grew as a result of widespread disillusionment with Western reformism and Soviet Marxism—two of the main sources of opposition ideology in Iran for fifty years. For roughly ten years before the revolution began, an unprecedented resurgent interest in a radical interpretation of Shi'i developed among politicized Iranians, particularly the new generation of theology students. Politically, the surprising aspect of the new radical Shi'ite movement was its widespread appeal, an appeal that cut across classes to touch Iran's merchants of the bazaar, religious leaders, students, urban masses, and professionals.

As early as 1962, a group of moderate Shi'i intellectuals formed the moderate to liberal-left Movement for the Liberation of Iran to oppose the dictatorial practices and the sociocultural excesses of the regime. The leaders of this organization included the popular theologian Ayatollah Taleqani, Prof. Ezatollah Sahabi, and Prof. Mehdi Bazargan, who later would become prime minister of the provisional revolutionary government. Taleqani and Sahabi until the revolution were serving seven-year sentences at Evin Prison. Bazargan had been in and out of prison many times for the two decades before the revolution.

The most productive and influential theoretician of this revived Shi'i movement was Dr. Ali Shariati, a graduate of the Sorbonne. Regardless of their historical accuracy or their place in the Islamic theological literature, Shariati's writings had a profound impact on the Iranian revolutionary movement.[41] Yet he was completely ignored by the American press; as was noted earlier in this chapter, the only mention of his name—and a passing one at that—was by Youssof M. Ibrahim, then with the *Times*.

Many prominent politicoreligious thinkers, including Ayatollah Taleqani, Mehdi Bazargan, Ali Shariati, and Abolhasan Bani-Sadr, favored modernization and rejected many aspects of the traditional past. They were interested in native authenticity, not glorification of the past. They knew very well that despotism, special oppression of women, the claim of divinely given power, extreme inequality, super-exploitation of peasants, self-flagellation, tribalism, internecine warfare, superstition, intolerance, and political distrust and insecurity were some of the enduring—if not dominant—elements of the national Iranian tradition.

These thinkers also knew that popular sovereignty, political equality, majority rule, land reform, public education, emancipation of women, equitable distribution of national wealth, equality before the law, judicial independence, and constitutionalism (to which they passionately aspired) were all imported modern ideas. The efforts since the later nineteenth century to introduce democratic and egalitarian concepts within Islam do not change the reality that as political objectives, contemporary progressive ideas originated in the secular West and are associated with modernity.

Because of the constraints of popular culture, the regime's ability to suppress religious writings and mosque gatherings was severely limited, and so protest, denied a secular incubator, moved inevitably into the religious realm. Even so the religious opponents of the regime had to use generalized religiohistorical symbolism and metaphors to communicate their immediate concerns. Under these circumstances, progressive politicoreligious thinkers could only express abstract discontent and appeal to the dissatisfaction or alienation of their audiences, but they were unable to engage in the kind of critical discourse that would result in presenting a coherent alternative to the existing political order, nor were they able to formulate concrete solutions to the problems facing the country. In the end, conservative religious forces with vague references to an Islamic republic would reap the benefits of these circumstances.

The functional alliance between the antiregime clerics and the progressive forces (both religious and secular) began in the upheavals of 1963 and continued, however inactive and ambiguous, through

the remainder of the 1960s and 1970s. During these years there was
no open distinction between the fundamentalist and the progressive
clerics. The *significant* distinction was made between the clerics who
opposed the shah and those who either were silent or cooperated with
the regime. As the regime succeeded in suppressing the progressive
elements, secular and religious, the fundamentalist mollahs became
increasingly influential in the opposition movement.

The mollahs, who in their preachings or writings indirectly criticized the shah's regime for turning the country away from Islam,
were not organized before the revolutionary demonstrations. Beginning in the summer of 1978 various political factions and personalities, both clerical and nonclerical, coalesced around the name and
figure of Khomaini and gradually created a network of nationwide,
mosque-centered, neighborhood organizations. These organizations,
called *komiteh*s, played a decisive role in mobilizing mass support
for the revolutionary demonstrations and were remarkably decentral-
ized. Khomaini came to symbolize the unity of the antishah forces,
and his sudden elevation to the unchallenged position of leadership
enabled him to exert tremendous influence on the course of the revolutionary movement.

Yet there was no national organization to manage the affairs of the
revolution. There were only hundreds of local committees performing public tasks that ranged from forming food co-ops and providing
aid to striking workers to caring for persons wounded in demonstrations. By the fall of 1978 every neighborhood mosque had become a
revolutionary headquarters as well as a place of worship and public
speaking. And as the movement grew and the fall of the regime
neared, the most fundamentalist mollahs came to dominate the network of mosque-centered organizations throughout the country.

To sum up, the disparities and disorienting effects of the pseudodevelopment schemes produced the objective conditions of revolt.
At the same time, the repressive measures against secular progressive dissidents were successful, and hence opposition politics was
forced into the only other possible idiom—popular religion. Progressive politicoreligious writers and activists used this unintended
and unexpected opportunity to appeal to the alienated and promote
rebellious consciousness. However, as the revolutionary movement
grew in size and intensity, fundamentalists proved better equipped,
both organizationally and ideologically, to take advantage of the so-

ciopolitical mood of the general populace, particularly the urban poor, to serve their own exclusive objectives.

It is against this richly complex historical background that the religious thrust of the revolution must be regarded. Iranians, although not particularly pious as a people nor given to religious observance (mosque attendance before the revolution, for instance, was nominal at best), nevertheless turned to the traditional value system represented by Shi'ism as a means of expressing their profound rejection of the shah's repression and mindless pursuit of things Western. Religion provided the vehicle for protest, simply because (1) pseudodevelopment had produced a state of anomie in the society; (2) secular alternatives were effectively repressed; and (3) the radical version of political/oppositional Shi'ism appeared to be an authentic ideological alternative against the shah's dictatorship and his blind drive for Westernization. This turning inward to indigenous values was reflected in the revolution's motto: "Neither East nor West!"

While acknowledging the structural and historical limitations on politics that exist in all places at all times, we maintain that real choices of political action concerning issues of power and authority were made by competing actors in the crucial years of 1978 and 1979. It was not fate or some law of history that shaped the course of the Iranian revolution. Rather, it was, on the one hand, the decisive and skillful leadership of Ayatollah Khomaini and, on the other, the fragmentation and confusion of the secular forces that enabled the fundamentalists to establish their hegemonic control over the Iranian state and society. Somewhere between the clergy's assertion of leadership and its acquisition of total power, there was an opportunity for secular forces, which they failed to seize.

In all this the American press paid much attention to the fanaticism of the fundamentalists but virtually ignored the internal politics of the revolutionary movement in general and the surprising political astuteness of the mollahs in particular. American reporters neither understood nor correctly interpreted the forces at work, and instead, using shallow and highly ethnocentric stereotypes and frames, portrayed the revolt as simple religious reaction. Specifically, journalists missed the significance of Shi'ism as a cultural force; failed to comprehend the symbolism at work; concentrated their attention on fundamentalist elements of the religious community to the virtual exclusion of the progressive component; and in general let a deeply rooted suspicion of the mixing of politics with religion form much of their analysis.

For the most part, during much of the revolutionary period and practically all the period that followed, the media, in the words of Prof. Edward Said, reduced "all aspects of the diverse Muslim world . . . to a special malevolent and unthinking essence. Instead of analysis and understanding as a result, there can be for the most part only the crudest form of us-versus-them."[42]

During the year of revolution, we could find only three or four articles written at any length which dealt with the religious dimension of the revolution, and the thrust of most of these is caught in this 5 January 1978 *Washington Post* headline: "The Darker Forces of Islam."[43] To the degree that Islam was dealt with other than in passing references, the consensus view agreed with the assessment of *Post* writer Stephen S. Rosenfeld in a column headlined "Breaking the Link with Modernity" cited earlier in this chapter. Rosenfeld, it will be remembered, found a "chilling message" in a "dark new force" at work in the world, that force being, of course, Islam's "particular relationship to modernization." According to his view, it was becoming increasingly apparent that modernization and Islam were incompatible: "Modernization in the sense of conventional economic development and political liberalization shrivels."[44]

Such a judgment as Rosenfeld's, of course, leaves the reader to assume that under the shah and therefore Western liberal capitalism, economic development and political liberalization flourished in Iran, which, of course, could not be farther from the truth. But beyond this misapprehension is a set of assumptions about the religious opposition to the shah's regime, and about the Iranian people, which is bound up in Rosenfeld's contention that

> the suspicion is unavoidable that Khomeini is popular precisely because Iranians know he harbors such [reactionary] views and because, in their current disposition anyway, they share them. This is a dismal thought for us of the democratic West, who usually regard "the people" as basically a progressive entity whose will, if followed, will produce a good society, but it is not easily dismissed.[45]

In his analysis, Rosenfeld, like most American journalists, completely ignored (or simply was ignorant of) contemporary Iranian political history, particularly the Mosaddeq era. Clearly Mossadeq was the single most popular Iranian leader until the rise of Khomaini. Yet Mosaddeq's vast popularity was hardly based on religious reaction or antimodernism. How then do Rosenfeld's views of the Iranian people square with the other single most important mass movement in modern Iranian history?

To understand better why the view presented by Rosenfeld and much of the press was grossly oversimplified and ethnocentric at its core, it is necessary to take a closer look at the common explanations in the American news media of religious behavior and opposition to the shah, most of which (1) centered on the clergy's narrow material- or self-interest having been violated by the shah's modernizing plans, (2) portrayed the religious community and its leadership as *monolithic,* and (3) depicted the great masses of Iranians, beset by bewildering modernization, as eager to return to a sort of Dark Ages.

The line of logic followed by most American journalists was this: The clergy, stripped of mosque lands during the White Revolution, embittered by the shah's emancipation of women, and aghast at the idea of a modern world, whipped a petulant and easily manipulated population into a frenzy, which in turn led to the shah's downfall. Yet it is simply too facile to reduce the motives of the ulama to plain self-interest; on the contrary, most of the Iranian clergy opposing the shah did not object to the *concept* of modernization but instead took exception to the particular manner in which this regime's program was to be implemented.[46] The dominant journalistic view, as we have suggested, ignored the complex nature of the revolution and presented a distorted view of secular as well as religious motives. More important, such a view simply did not square with the historical record.

Once again it becomes crucial to make a distinction between the past and the present, to distinguish between why and how the revolution occurred, on the one hand, and what has occurred since, on the other, keeping in mind the larger point here that politics and not natural laws were at work. Although elements of the ultraconservative clergy eventually gained the upper hand after 1979 and have behaved in ways that Rosenfeld and the press said they would, this does not mean that the tendencies they represent or the steps they have taken in the present were in the minds of most Iranians at the time of the revolution. The prejudice of reporters toward Islam should not be confused with knowledge.

Similarly, an injunction not to confuse what has happened since

1979 with the motive forces of the revolution is particularly critical for a retrospective consideration of another issue that preoccupied American journalists: the question of women's rights. Doubtless, the defense of equal rights for women in the Islamic world touches the most sensitive traditional nerves. And there is no question that the ulama as a whole have reactionary and rigid views on the rights and humanity of women. Yet the American press in 1978 greatly distorted the significance and complexity of the issue in the Iranian revolution.

There were two separate claims in the usual press portrayal of the question of women's rights in the Iranian revolution: (1) the shah acted as the emancipator of Iranian women; and (2) antipathy toward the emancipation of women was a primary motivation of the ulama in their opposition to the shah's regime. These contentions constitute falsehoods that contain an element of truth, and for that reason the task of dissecting them requires elaboration.

To be sure, the fundamentalist mollahs were contemptuous of unveiled women and the liberal fashion of dress. They were also bothered by the rapid increase in the number of women in the clerical work force and in institutions of higher learning. Too, Khomaini himself had written violently against women's liberation from traditional bondage and the Family Protection Law.[47] Yet there is absolutely no evidence that opposition to women's rights or support for veiling was an *organizing* or *mobilizing* issue for the masses. Not even the most conservative religious tracts or pamphlets cited lifting of the veil, giving women the vote, or encouraging women to attend universities as reasons for opposition to the regime.

The massive participation of middle-class women, particularly students, in the revolutionary demonstrations of 1978 and the often enormous risks these women were willing to take in confrontations with the police or army were clear proof that antipathy toward the emancipation of women could not have been a motivating force. Iranian women attending European and American universities in 1978 were equally enthusiastic about the revolution. Furthermore, such distinguished Iranian writers and intellectuals as Symin Daneshvar, Homa Nategh, and Symin Behbahani actively supported the revolution. Thus it is simply false to claim that resentment toward unveiling or expansion of opportunities for women was a primary cause of the rebellion against the Pahlavi dynasty.[48]

Similarly, the press's view of the shah as the emancipator of women had more to do with his effective public relations apparatus than with reality. It is true that under the Pahlavis *upper- and middle-class* women gained a degree of liberation from their traditional bondage. Despite his own low opinion of women, for instance, the shah probably came to believe by the mid-1960s that the integration of women into the work force made economic sense. The Family Protection Act of 1967, later repealed and passed in stronger form in 1975, introduced some significant reforms in divorce and family law which had been based on strict adherence to religious law.[49]

At the same time, though, women in the privileged classes were pressured by the social milieu constructed by pseudomodernization to use their newly found freedom in conformity with Western standards. Given the shah's own views that "women count only if they're beautiful and graceful and know how to stay feminine" and that women "have produced nothing great, nothing!"[50] there is some reason to believe that giving women the vote was more for the sake of appearances than the commitment of a liberated male. Since there were no free elections, the newly franchised half of the population simply created a highly visible constituency that could exalt the shah for his enlightenment.

In actuality only educated women could use the Family Protection Act or benefit from the employment opportunities opened to the clerical work force. Yet, there was no serious effort by the sociopolitical establishment to create an atmosphere in which the increasingly aware Iranian woman could be more creative and authentic in the process of change from tradition to modernity.

When the revolutionary upheavals of 1978 began, many middle-to upper-class women participated in the mass demonstrations, often wearing veils as a symbolic way of protesting pseudomodernization and of showing support for lower-class Iranian women who wear the veil as a matter of habit. The truth of the matter is that the overwhelming majority of Iranian women wore the veil before the revolution and continued their habitual practice after. Whatever the nature of convention, of course, it remains repugnant to force women to wear (as under Khomaini) or not to wear (as under Reza Shah) the veil. But the fact remains that although the present regime enforces the wearing of a chador, or scarf, for women appearing in public, it does not mean that this was an issue in the general discontent that produced the revolution.

As for Khomaini's early writings opposing the equality of men and women, few Iranians were even aware of them. Iranians thought of Khomaini above all else as a spiritual leader who had decisively opposed the shah's dictatorship. Perhaps the most compelling evidence that antipathy toward women's rights was *not* a mobilizing issue is that Khomaini felt it politically prudent during the revolution to play down his real feelings in this regard.

The American news media, in short, did not first examine the facts and then conclude that the opponents of the shah were motivated by opposition to modernization or liberalized women's rights. On the contrary, reporters, like U.S. officials, accepted the characterization of the opposition provided by the shah's propagandists and overlooked the reality that more than half a million public employees participated in the general strike. They included teachers, oil workers, engineers, technicians, judges, bureaucrats, professionals, and industrial workers. These elements, which played a crucial role in the revolution and are now oppressed by the new order, were as a group overwhelmingly secular in their political orientation.

The major problem with American coverage of the Iranian revolution, in retrospect, was not the mere fact that little was known about Islam; quite to the contrary, it lay in the media's pretending that a great deal was known and in presenting a view of Iran's revolution that was dictated more by official Washington than by reality. To the extent that this was so, as Walter Lippmann once remarked in a much different context, "misleading news is worse than none at all."[51]

Beyond the question of what the media knew or did not know of the religious dimension of Iran's revolution, there is the question of ethnocentrism and ideology. At the first level of analysis, there can be little doubt that American reporters were deeply suspicious of and perhaps repelled by the traditionalist Shi'i symbolism, a symbolism that served as a unifying bond between the middle class and the poor, urban and rural, intellectual and lumpen, in the one-year struggle against the shah's regime.

Certainly, media coverage triggered in the American public a strong ethnocentric reaction against the revolutionaries. The one-year media diet ranged from headlines that screamed "Iranian Mobs Riot," "Anti-Shah Rampage," and "Chanting Mob Packs Streets of Tehran" to routine references to "anti-modernization fanatics" and assertions that for Muslims masochism is the preferred way to demonstrate devotion. For the U.S. press, the Iranian revolution was a difficult international event to cover because it was both anti-West and anti-Communist. There is a general tendency among the media to discredit contemporary revolution, and usually it is the label of "Communist" or "Marxist" which is used to accomplish the task. The familiar labels made no sense in the case of Iran, however, particularly since the revolutionaries did not use weapons. The press, therefore, found new labels, such as "religious fanatics," "Muslim fundamentalists," and "Islamic Marxists," to reflect discredit on a popular revolt.

The effect of discrediting a popular anti-Western rebellion is also to confirm one's own sense of ethnocentric superiority. An ethnocentric view, in turn, in its most virulent form can lead to racism. Where ethnocentrism leaves off and racism begins is a matter for debate, but in our discussion here, we believe that the dividing line is drawn on the distinction between accomplishment and the capacity to accomplish. Ethnocentrism fosters the belief that one culture has achieved more than another and is therefore superior. This attitude does not necessarily deny the possibility of the second culture's "catching up." Racism, on the other hand, depends on a view that another people do not have the *capacity* for "civilized" or modern political accomplishment. Therefore, the culture in question is considered *inherently* inferior. In the United States, of course, most people have come to associate racism only with the color hierarchy, which in itself is an ethnocentric belief; using this standard, they would be hard pressed to understand how their attitude toward the Iranian revolution could be considered racist; insofar as the Iranian people come close to meeting the Anglo standard of whiteness. The point here is that, of course, racism can be based on any perceived "otherness," if the perception of difference is pronounced enough, as the world learned to its horror from the Holocaust.

It was the idea of the capacity of the Iranian people that was most often denied by the press. The American people were encouraged to doubt whether the Iranian people are capable of authentic interest in freedom or whether they are capable of achieving political stability without a dictator or foreign influence. By portraying the Iranian people as backward and shackled by religious superstition, the news media at the very least erected an ethnocentric barrier between the revolutionary aspirations of Iranians and the sympathies of the American public and reinforced the views of foreign policy elites that the best the country could hope for was an Americanized shah.

To argue that media distortion of the motives of Iran's revolution was wholly a function of the ethnocentrism, orientalism, and suspicion of religion of American reporters is to oversimplify and mislead, however. There is evidence that the media will treat ethnicity, religion, and politics differently under different circumstances. For instance, there are stark differences between how the press portrayed Iranians in revolt (religious fanatics or zealots) against the shah, and Afghans (freedom fighters or Muslim militiamen) rebelling against a Marxist regime. Similarly, the press has not seemed profoundly bothered by the Catholic church's opposition to the regime in Poland. Moreover, in its coverage of the Middle East, the press has celebrated such "good" Muslims as Anwar Sadat (*after* Camp David).

In sum, although ethnocentrism plays a major role in press coverage of the Third World, inconsistencies in journalistic behavior make it necessary to look elsewhere for both a necessary and a sufficient explanation of why the press performs as it does. In this regard, in chapter 9 we shall argue that in the realm of geopolitics, ideology is the constant for the media, and ethnocentrism is but a variable.

For Americans who had only a casual, often inaccurate sense of Iran before the revolution of 1978, press coverage of the sort sampled in this chapter had, in our view, predictable results. We will elaborate on this possibility and what consequences such a development holds for the foreign-policy-making process in a later chapter, but one possible measure of the effects can be offered at this point. In January 1979, after a year of revolutionary upheaval, the departure of the shah and the return of Khomaini, an ABC News–Harris Survey was conducted on what had transpired. Although, by 55 to 25 percent, Americans agreed with the charge that the United States had made "'a bad mistake in backing the Shah as long as we did' because of his abysmal human rights record, by 52–24 percent, a majority of Americans would prefer a military take-over in Iran to a 'government dominated by extreme Moslem religious leaders who would be popular with the Iranian people.'"[52]

A finding of this sort takes on both particular and general significance when viewed against subsequent revelations that at the time of the poll the United States government was actively pursuing the possibility of sponsoring just such a military coup. Press coverage, in short, might well have paved the way for the U.S. government, had it so decided, to intervene once again in the internal affairs of Iran without fearing American public opinion.

8

Journalism as Capitalism

In the contemporary world the first draft of popular history is composed by mainstream journalists. Moreover, the press accounts concerning matters of international significance are likely to be the only draft the general public will ever see. A proposition of equal importance is that the popular classes' view of foreign affairs is less a reflection of actual events than of the journalists' perception and interpretation. These realities demonstrate the ultimate importance of journalism in the foreign policy setting, for they constitute the principal sources of what power the press wields in the foreign policy arena.

The role and function of the journalist as historian-in-a-hurry, in turn, logically poses an inevitable question for a society that prides itself on its openness: What if the draft of history produced by mainstream foreign correspondence is seriously flawed, as we argue was the case in Iran? As we noted in chapter 1, this is not a particularly bothersome question for those who view the world from what we termed the elitist or cynical perspectives. Yet for reasons we have already advanced, we believe the question to be of vital importance. Indeed, we argue that any worthwhile appraisal of the future of U.S. relations with the Third World should take into account the opinions of the general as well as the attentive American publics concerning the predicaments of the Third World. And any such evaluation ought to consider the causes of faulty press performance and its effects.

Toward that end, it is our thesis that the failure of the press in reporting the realities of U.S.-Iran relations, not unlike similar failures that have occurred with disturbing regularity since the cold war began, has its basis in the press's inability or unwillingness to exercise judgment independent of that of official Washington; this possibility is as contrary to the conventional descriptive view of the press as staunch adversary as it is to normative expectations held for the press in democratic theory. This lack of critical judgment by the mainstream press results from a subtle interplay of ideology and the nature of the media as an industry; ideology, however, is the dominant aspect. While mainstream journalists and academics will readily admit the shortcomings of the mass media as an industry, few will accept the position that ideology is a significant factor in journalistic behavior. Indeed, it is precisely the denial of possessing such an ideological orientation that is at the core of the American journalistic credo. That the debate over ideology in the media is hardly a new one does not diminish its importance, and an analysis of why the press behaved as it did in Iran may offer a fresh perspective for those concerned about how and why the press performs as it does.

In this chapter we will offer an analysis of the role of economics and the importance of structural-organizational factors in media behavior. Such an analysis will revolve around a central question: To what degree do the commercial goals and bureaucratic nature of the media dictate how foreign news will be covered? The answer to this question can be neither exact nor generalized. Yet we reject the tendency to overemphasize the economic and bureaucratic factors at the expense of examining the ideological influence in the press coverage of major foreign policy issues. We will discuss the ideological dimension at length in the following chapter.

Perhaps the most commonplace explanation for why the American press covers the world as it does, an explanation advanced as often by those who criticize the news media as by those who defend it, has to do with the commercial nature of the American system of media. The press behaves as it does, proponents of this school of thought argue, simply to keep profits as high and costs as low as possible. Those who hold this view maintain that the content of the news is determined mainly by what will "sell newspapers." Economics and not politics is what dictates how the press covers the world; the largely impersonal forces of the market are what finally matter, rather than the subjective dimension of ideology.

The importance of the market-forces explanation of media-in-situation and its widespread acceptance in journalistic circles, the academy, the general public, and among reformist critics cannot be overemphasized. Among other outcomes, this devout belief in economic determinism establishes the givens from which much of the reasoning about the media's coverage of foreign affairs derives. Such a presupposition largely defines the questions that are asked, imposes the boundaries of discussion, and in essence predetermines and informs the shape and substance of most media criticism of press performance abroad.

Prof. Bernard C. Cohen set forth the majority view in his benchmark analysis, *The Press and Foreign Policy.* He argued that "despite the implicit, reflexive, routinized character of the editorial task, one can observe certain persistent influences and sources of judgment being brought to bear on the treatment of foreign affairs news." He divided these possible influences into three categories: The first deals with what he calls "commercial criteria," the second, with the policy preferences of editors and publishers, and the third, with the tendency of most of the media to defer to the prestige press and the wire services in judgments regarding foreign news.[1] It is clear from his discussion of the subject that he considers the first to be the most important and unambiguous. In this regard, he concludes that "the commercial criteria affect chiefly the amount of coverage and its general character, which are long-term decisions, rather than influencing judgments on a daily basis against one particular news item and in favor of another."[2]

About the possible effect of media owners' policy preferences on coverage of events abroad, which is the closest Cohen comes to discussing the implications of ideology, he makes two crucial observations. The first is a heavily qualified judgment that such preferences may have an impact only "on some newspapers."[3] The second is that "editorial preferences and theories [about foreign policy] may come into play *within the bounds established by the ruling commercial considerations*" (emphasis ours).[4]

Echoing Cohen is this representative view of a press severely constrained by economic realities contained in an excerpt from a leading journalism textbook of the 1970s: "When editors compare notes on readership, they often disagree on which kinds of news are the most popular—sports, comics, the front page, or what. But when it comes to the least popular kind of news, they are unanimous. Foreign affairs takes the palm, hands down."[5] The authors go on to cite several early studies that support this contention and then conclude, "Little wonder that most editors have cut their foreign news to the bone."[6] Besides reader apathy, the authors argue, "editors have another good reason for downplaying foreign news: It is difficult and expensive to cover."[7] Finally, the authors point to the inherent problems that result from a pitifully thin network of correspondents abroad. The possibility that ideological bias might also pose a significant problem to journalism performance is not raised.

While the commercial imperative in foreign affairs journalism is certainly deserving of attention, overemphasizing it effectively deflects substantive criticism of the press and undermines serious challenge to the existing way of things by neatly turning the tables on those who come to suggest that ideology and not the profit motive is the necessary and sufficient cause for media behavior. In other words, if the iron will of the market is all that is at work, it follows that the press must have no agenda other than making money. Therefore those who come to question the "obvious" neutrality of the media must themselves perforce be ideologues. Such an equation is based, of course, on the presupposition that in American society material self-interest is presumed to be essentially neutral as opposed to ideological self-interest, which is not. More significant, the former is not considered in an unfavorable light, whereas the latter is.

Whether those who argue for a view of journalism simply as capitalism in action are consciously aware of the attractive protection and convenient defense offered by the commercial imperative thesis is not at issue. What becomes apparent from a review of the literature, however, is the tendency of mainstream journalists and their defenders to engage in a kind of diversionist plea-bargaining when confronted with evidence of shallow or distorted coverage of foreign affairs which reasonably could be construed as the result of ideological bias. Rather than admit operating under the influence of ideology, a felony, the journalistic fraternity cops a plea and admits only the pursuit of profit, which in American society is a misdemeanor at worst. Moreover, the media establishment will argue, in a variation of scarcity analysis, that there simply are too many stories in the world to cover and not enough journalists to cover them.

As a result of a debate framed in these terms, the attention of reformist critics is usually successfully diverted, and their energies

are given over to moralizing about how the media ought to think less
about profit and more about performance.[8] The result of such logic
is the inevitable conclusion that spending more money on news gathering will necessarily improve the quality of and diminish distortion
in news coverage, a notion that dominates press criticism in the
United States.[9] The media in turn respond to such arguments by in-
sisting that foreign correspondence is costly and the news it produces
is of little interest to the general public, and that journalism is doing
everything it can to serve the public within the reasonable constraints
of enlightened capitalism. And so the argument has gone for the
better half of a century, in circles, with its participants, in each other's view either unworldly reformers or philistines, locked into an
interminable and sterile debate whose never-changing parameters,
profit or social responsibility, all but guarantee circular reasoning.[10]

In the opening essay of a collection of his speeches on the press
and foreign policy, James Reston, the distinguished *New York Times*
political columnist and editor, set forth the conventional boundaries
for an examination of press performance abroad. Reston argued that
the relationship between policy, the press, and public opinion should
be analyzed "down in the pit where both officials and reporters operate under the tyranny of fact, deadline and decision." After having
implicitly claimed the logical high ground by demonstrating an eminently reasonable concern for reality, Reston continued:

> Academic monographs on ideal reporters and officials in a perfect
> world are not very helpful. The President has no choice between deal-
> ing with the military situation and the political tradition. He has to
> deal with both. Similarly, the owners and managers of newspapers
> and radio and television stations *are not likely to spend more time
> thinking about their duty than about their economic security.* I happen
> to believe that they would probably be better off if they thought more
> about their duty and less about their security, but that is not the way it
> is, and therefore it is probably more useful to try to understand the
> practical everyday conflict between reporters and officials and how it
> developed (emphasis ours).[11]

Reston is clear about the nature of the variables at work, three of
which—fact, deadline, and decision—constitute in his words a tyranny. It is fair to assume he considers the fourth, economic security
of media owners, to be just as tyrannical. Such an analysis, it will be

noted, neatly preempts the possibility of ideology's being cause for concern.

An analysis that emphasizes the commercial imperative to the exclusion of consideration of the role of ideology leads the student of the media and foreign policy into an intellectual cul-de-sac in at least three ways. First, by overstating the effects of the system's *operational* economics on deciding what gets covered and how thoroughly, such reasoning focuses attention away from the possibility that ideology is dominant. Second, the conventional commercial-imperative argument ignores the reality that resources in any industry are always finite and therefore, by definition, scarce. *Allocation* of scarce resources and not the scarcity itself, then, in the news business as in others is what matters. In the coverage of foreign affairs, as the case of Iran suggests, such allocation and the results it produced may not have been so much dictated by the profit motive or concern for costs as they were by ideological concerns. Finally, explaining all media behavior as a search for profit obscures the reality that a cost-benefits analysis of the process of journalism simply cannot explain why Iranians in revolt were "religious fanatics" and Afghans are "freedom fighters."

Of course, economic forces and the journalistic and bureaucratic routines they foster have a tremendous impact on the quantity and quality of press coverage abroad. But economic forces are not the only ones at work, and, finally, not even the most critical ones in terms of *how* a client state is portrayed. For instance, it would have *cost* no more to examine the claims of Iranian land reform than to sneak reporters into Afghanistan after the Soviet invasion of 1979. Indeed, the former would have been far cheaper and considerably less dangerous than the latter. A useful analysis of why the media behave as they do, therefore, must distinguish between what is the result of operational or systemic economics and what is not. Too often this distinction is lost in a priori assumptions about the status quo on both sides of the question.

Conventional analysis of superficial or inadequate coverage abroad usually begins with two propositions. The first is that Americans are not interested in foreign news, which makes it unprofitable to cover. The second is that the number of correspondents has dramatically dropped since the end of World War II (except during the Korean and Vietnam wars) in direct relationship to the increase in the amount it costs to keep a reporter abroad. According to the conventional argument, this fact, coupled with an alleged lack of general audience interest in the larger world, makes it economically impossible under the laws of supply and demand to expect more from the media.

The debate over the inability or unwillingness of the news media to devote more resources to compensate for a drastically reduced overseas press corps frequently turns on the question of audience interest in foreign news. Industry and much academic reasoning is that Americans in the main do not make serious use of the news media. Accordingly, the consensus among editors, publishers, and broadcast executives is that the typical American is simply not interested in foreign affairs, and thus it follows that it is neither economically efficient nor profitable to invest heavily in the gathering of news abroad. The factual basis for this first proposition, widely held as it may be among intellectuals and media decision makers, is open to serious question.

Moreover, it is one of the larger contradictions in American society that at the core of the democratic mythos, so often extolled in editorials, is the well-informed citizen, yet much of the press, academy, and government, in practice, more often display contempt rather than high regard for the citizenry. Whether it be a broadcast executive's decision to air "I Love Lucy" reruns instead of Senate hearings on Vietnam or the newspaper dictum to write for a nation that moves its lips when it reads, the common industry argument is that people are simply being given what they want, and what they want is not very much.

Despite the certainty with which news industry executives discuss the wants and capacities of the American people, the evidence is not all that clear. For instance, for nearly twenty years it has been conventional wisdom that most Americans get their news from television. This has been held to be unusually significant (and damning) because communications researchers are nearly unanimous in their belief that (1) people who make "serious" use of the media are most likely to do so with print media, and (2) because of its nature, television provides a far more superficial view of the world than do the print media.

Yet according to a persuasive analysis by at least one researcher, the notion that most people get their news from television is a myth.

Prof. Lawrence W. Lichty has argued that while people may *think* that TV is their major source, reliable marketing studies show just the opposite. In his analysis, based on "exposure" data collected by the Simmons Market Research Bureau in 1981, Lichty wrote that more than "two-thirds of U.S. adults or sixty-eight percent read at least part of some newspaper every day" and 12 percent of all adults read two or more newspapers each day, while fewer than one-third of U.S. adults watch either local or national TV news on a given day. Some 31 percent of adults read *Time, Newsweek,* or *U.S. News & World Report,* according to Lichty, and one-fourth of all adults read *Reader's Digest.*[12]

By contrast, Lichty argued that other data suggest that while the *total* audience for the three evening TV news programs on a given night may be large (about 50 million as compared to the 47 million for a single entertainment program such as "Dallas"), the TV news audience fluctuates widely:

> It is far more fickle than the audience for newspapers or magazines. Slightly more than half of the nation's TV households watch one of the network evening news programs at least once in the course of a month. But only *one percent* of all 78.3 million American TV households watches CBS's Dan Rather as often as four or five nights a week, and Rather presides over the nation's most popular network evening news show. The average for households that watch his program at all is five broadcasts per month (author's emphasis).[13]

The issue aside of where Americans are most likely to get their news, equally compelling evidence has raised doubts about the prevailing belief of editors that Americans are not interested in serious news. In 1978 a nationwide Louis Harris survey on public attitudes toward news revealed a major discrepancy between media assumptions and audience preference. According to the survey report, "Those who work in the media (editors, news directors and reporters) feel that only 5 per cent of the public expressed deep interest in world affairs being covered in the news media. A much higher 41 per cent of the public express deep interest in world affairs being covered in the news media."[14]

Perhaps the most comprehensive study ever conducted of reader preferences, which began in 1977 under the auspices of a media coalition of prominent professional and industry organizations, lends support to the notion that there is a considerable audience in the United States for foreign news. The survey indicated that a majority of the general public and three-fourths of the college graduates are more interested in international news and national news than in coverage of their own community. Asked about twenty-five categories of content, 84 percent of the respondents replied that they usually read international or world news, just two percentage points below the response rate for stories about the economy. Thirty-six percent of the sample picked international or world news as the category they cared most about.[15] According to Leo Bogart, a leading researcher in audience preference, "This high level of interest in international news cuts across every segment, dipping only slightly among those 18 to 24, those with low income and education and among rural residents." Moreover, concluded Bogart, "Newspapers would abandon an important part of their franchise if editors assumed that television has taken care of covering the world."[16]

The argument about American interest in foreign affairs aside, there is no doubt that the foreign press corps has been drastically reduced during the past forty years. The greatest number of foreign correspondents is thought to have occurred just after World War II, when there were an estimated 2,500 Americans regularly reporting from abroad.[17] In the 1950s there were some 280 correspondents in Western Europe alone.[18] Besides correspondents from the three wire services, Associated Press, United Press, and International News Service (which later merged with UP to become United Press International), reporters were posted abroad from a wide range of newspapers, including, of course, these: *New York Times, New York Herald Tribune, Chicago Daily News, Chicago Tribune, New York Post, Baltimore Sun, Kansas City Star, Washington Star, New York Daily News, Christian Science Monitor, Cleveland Plain Dealer and News, Toledo Blade, Los Angeles Times,* and the Hearst and Scripps-Howard chains. Magazines with correspondents abroad included *Saturday Evening Post, New Yorker, Reporter, Time, Newsweek,* and *U.S. News & World Report.* There were also overseas broadcast reporters from ABC, CBS, NBC, the Mutual Broadcasting System, and the DuMont Network.[19]

By 1975 American news representatives abroad—both U.S. citizens and foreign nationals—numbered about six hundred for all news media.[20] Foreign correspondence had become, more than ever, trickle-down journalism. At the top were two wire services, a few syndicated services (chiefly the *New York Times* syndicate and the *Washington Post–Los Angeles Times* service), correspondents from a few prestige dailies and the three newsmagazines, and the news staffs of the three television networks.

The consensus leader in foreign affairs journalism, of course, both in resources and influence, is the *New York Times*. In 1978 its syndicate served some 250 of the nation's most important dailies, and it had the largest staff of foreign correspondents of any newspaper: thirty-four.[21] Still, this total was under half the number of *Times* correspondents deployed around the world in the 1950s.[22] Other newspapers and the number of correspondents they had abroad in the late 1970s were the *Los Angeles Times* (18), *Washington Post* (13), *Wall Street Journal* (12), *Christian Science Monitor* (8), and *Baltimore Sun* (6). Each of the three television networks and newsmagazines field fourteen to twenty foreign staff correspondents.[23]

Because of the steadily and dramatically declining overseas press corps, American daily newspapers have come to depend increasingly on the wire services for their picture of the world. Yet for the past decade, the Associated Press, which serves some 1,330 clients, or 80 percent of American newspapers controlling 90 percent of daily circulation,[24] has done so with only about 75 offices abroad staffed with eighty to ninety American correspondents at any given time.[25] United Press International has averaged about sixty-five to seventy staff correspondents. Each of the wire services may also have employed several hundred "locals," who are usually nationals of the country they cover and therefore subject to the pressures their governments can bring to bear. The wire services sometimes have used locals to cover major countries, including Indonesia, Turkey, and until 1978 and the revolution, Iran.[26] Additionally, the news agencies rely heavily on stringers, who are employed on a piece-work basis and are of varying degrees of competence and reliability.

How thinly the American foreign press corps has been spread can be seen in a comparison offered by Mort Rosenblum, formerly AP bureau chief in Paris, editor of the *International Herald Tribune,* and a correspondent with wide experience in Africa, the Far East, and Latin America:

Considering the system's other problems, the number of correspondents abroad is even more inadequate than the totals suggest. By comparison, the AP and UPI each have as many reporters in their Washington bureaus alone as they have based overseas. The New York *Times* covers its home town with a hundred reporters, three times as many as it has overseas. But, because of distances, official meddling and other obstacles, it can take three times as many reporters to cover the same sort of story overseas as it does in the United States.[27]

The domestic counterparts of the foreign press corps, it should also be noted, who cover the White House, Department of Defense, and the State Department are equally few. There are only about 150 reporters on what might be termed the defense and foreign policy beat, or about 10 percent of the national press corps working in Washington.[28]

Rosenblum has also made the point that "proportionately, news organizations in a number of countries cover the world more thoroughly than the American media." According to his calculations:

> In Japan, eight newspapers and two news agencies had 222 correspondents based on six continents in 1978; five broadcasting companies had another ninety correspondents. The largest newspapers keep fleets of private aircraft and well-equipped bureaus. More than a hundred reporters accredited by Japanese news organizations were based in six American cities during 1978. One Spanish daily newspaper with a circulation of around 150,000—the circulation of the Phoenix, Arizona, *Republic*—keeps staff correspondents in four world capitals and full-time stringers in another five.[29]

In part, the dramatic drop in the number of American foreign correspondents can be attributed to the disappearance of some major urban newspapers. But the main cause, according to most industry sources, is the increased cost brought about by inflation in the United States and abroad and the plunge of the dollar on world money markets. According to one authoritative source, by the late 1970s it cost $80,000 to $140,000 to keep a single American correspondent abroad.[30] *Time* magazine's managing editor has put the cost even higher. In 1980 he told members of the Overseas Press Club in New York City that *Time* had twenty bureaus abroad and thirty-four correspondents. "The average cost per correspondent in 1980 will exceed $200,000. This is 245 per cent higher than in 1970, when the cost per correspondent was $83,000."[31] A *Los Angeles Times* executive estimated that the cost for his newspaper to support a foreign bureau was about $150,000 a year, or about triple the cost of fifteen years ago.[32]

The major consequence of a decimated foreign press corps has been the development of a kind of overseas "pack journalism," to borrow the phrase used by Timothy Crouse in his landmark study of the press and presidential elections, *Boys on the Bus*.[33] Another phrase used to describe the phenomenon of shifting large numbers of reporters from country to country, news event to news event, trouble spot to trouble spot, is "parachute journalism," which alludes to the practice of putting reporters into a news situation after it has developed.

While many journalists involved in gathering and distributing foreign news are disturbed by the meager resources they have to work with abroad, they also are frequently quick to argue that the problem is in large part mitigated because the typical journalist is a generalist rather than a specialist. The belief that a generalist in journalism is usually superior to the regionalist or specialist is rooted far more in journalistic myth than established fact. Yet, according to longstanding tradition, an effective journalist needs to know only a little about a lot. Tough-mindedness is an adequate substitute for systematic knowledge of a country, its political and cultural history, even its language. The possession of a highly suspicious mind, the willingness and capacity to ask perceptive questions, and the ability to write under deadline are often thought to be sufficient qualities for the conduct of journalism abroad.

At least based on our studies of press performance in the Middle East in general and Iran in particular, the traditional assumptions about the generalist have not been borne out. The shallowness of coverage of both the revolution and events that preceded it, taken together with a journalistic view of Iran that corresponded closely to the image the shah and his American supporters wished to project, leads inevitably to quite different conclusions than those suggested by supporters of the generalist school of reporting.

First, it cannot be reassuring that coverage of a country of Iran's importance to the United States was left largely to Iranian nationals until the revolution. According to Juliet Pearce writing from Tehran for the *Washington Post* in 1975 at the height of U.S.-Iran relations,

"With the exception of a handful of foreign staff correspondents all representatives of the foreign press are stringers (part-time correspondents) or Iranian nationals. These men know exactly their place and the conditions of continuing employment in Iran."[34] As Pearce implies, it simply was not logical to expect Iranian correspondents to be candid about the regime in the type of police state that Iran was under the shah.

Second, it is equally illogical to expect the three hundred or so Western correspondents, only one of whom spoke Persian,[35] to make much sense of the revolution on suddenly finding themselves "parachuted" into its midst. It is precisely under such conditions of ignorance, insecurity, and indecision that reporters are most likely to seek the reassuring comfort of the quintessential "pack."

Thrust into a revolutionary situation in an alien culture, lacking a coherent understanding of the historical forces at work, confronted with the intense pressure of successfully outdistancing equally eager and beleaguered competitors working under similar deadlines and limitations, the typical reporter can only fall back on what appears to be the safe path. It is precisely under such conditions as these that the nonregional specialist is most likely to defer to the views and judgments of senior reporters from certifiably establishment news organizations, of which the *New York Times* probably is first among few equals. In this regard, reporters are likely to become part of a *hermetic* group, as media scholar Todd Gitlin has suggested:

> Reporters covering the same event find it convenient [and prudent] to borrow angles, issues, and questions from each other. Borrowed frames help them process a glut of facts—on deadline. Especially when reporters are in unfamiliar social territory, and when enough of them are clustered in that unfamiliar territory to constitute a social group, they are liable to become a *hermetic* group, looking around the circle of reporters, rather than outward to the event, for bearings (author's emphasis).[36]

According to a 1985 estimate by the director of Israel's Government Press Office, there are not usually more than thirty American staff correspondents resident in the Muslim Middle East—an area almost as large as Europe and remarkably heterogeneous—on a regular full-time basis. And, as he points out, this handful does not divide up the territory but rather tends to compete in the same places

for the same stories.[37] Moreover, if one of this small group of reporters should develop an expertise, it is far more likely to deal with
some aspect of the Arab-Israeli strife than with, say, Iran.

Even if a correspondent should decide to report from a perspective
different than the pack's, his or her editors at home, who endlessly
compare their organization's coverage with the coverage of others,
are likely to grow uneasy with the disparity and, in turn, encourage
the field reporter to rejoin the fold; sometimes the encouragement is
subtle, sometimes not.

Similarly, particularly under crisis conditions in a client state, the
unsure generalist is simply not going to risk going against the view
of official Washington or the consensus of academics who are in the
service of the status quo; at times such as these, ideology is more
than ever likely to inform reporting. Finally, the generalist-reporter
in a situation such as Iran is likely to find far more reassuring and
believable an interpretation of events offered by a suave, English-
speaking, obviously congenial representative of the regime than in
the version offered by strangely costumed, oddly customed, and frequently hostile "natives."

It seems self-evident, given the conditions and assumptions under
which American journalists worked in Iran, particularly during the
revolution, that reporters were "hermetically sealed off" in many
more ways than those suggested by Gitlin. Finally, the theory of
generalism simply does not meet the test of the evidence provided by
coverage of Iran, nor does it logically appear to serve the interests of
journalism or the goal of an informed public. Columbia University's
Prof. Edward Said, whose book *Covering Islam* examined the press
and the hostage crisis among other topics, has made a similar argument:

> No matter how gifted the individual, he or she cannot hope to report
> places as complex as Iran or Turkey or Egypt without some training
> and a lengthy residence in a place. Consider, for instance, that James
> Markham, the capable and gifted man who reported the Lebanese
> Civil War for the [New York] *Times* in 1975–76 had just come from
> Vietnam, and after only a year in the Near East was sent to Spain;
> during John Kifner's absence in Teheran, the entire Levant was re-
> ported intermittently for the *Times* by Henry Tanner, a man stationed
> in Rome, while Marvine Howe, the former Beirut correspondent (who
> was also supposed to cover Jordan, Syria, Iraq, and the Gulf) spent

one year in Beirut right after her stint in Portugal, and in the autumn of 1979 was moved to Ankara.[38]

By way of contrast to the American norm, Said offers as a model of journalistic conduct in the Middle East the example of Eric Rouleau of *Le Monde,* who speaks Arabic and has reported from the region for nearly twenty-five years, and David Hirst of the *Manchester Guardian,* also fluent in Arabic and a fifteen-year veteran.[39] Rouleau's work in particular probably represented the finest and most informed journalistic effort during and following the revolution. (In 1985 Rouleau was appointed French ambassador to Tunisia.)

Even when reporters do not find themselves operating under crisis conditions, the expectations for the generalist in foreign affairs reportage seem unrealistically high. An intriguing if disturbing insight into the everyday life of a foreign correspondent operating according to the dictates of generalism was provided by an *Esquire* profile of Flora Lewis, Paris bureau chief of the *New York Times.* Ms. Lewis's comments are particularly revealing in the context of our arguments in previous chapters about the American press and its portrayal of religion in Iran.

According to Ms. Lewis, in 1980 during the hostage crisis she was asked by her New York editors to take on a task of "staggering" proportions. Her special assignment: ferment in the Islamic world. "They had a meeting in New York, and someone said, 'Jesus, nobody knows what the hell's going on in Islam. Let's send Flora.' So they called me up, and I went. It was crazy; I wasn't even sure how to use the material I would gather," Ms. Lewis recounted. After "frantically" making arrangements, the *Times* bureau chief set off for London, Cairo, Algiers, and Tunis, finally to return with "twenty notebooks and ten pounds of paper," at which point she "sat down to write."[40] Of the problems with which she had to contend, Ms. Lewis said:

> On the Islam project . . . I needed a rather extensive file on the Philippines. It turned out that the Asian bureau couldn't spare anyone to do that either—they had their hands full with the Cambodian war and the mess in South Korea and the political crisis in Tokyo—so someone just had to put together a package for me out of New York.[41]

At the same time she was working on the "Islam project," Ms. Lewis was working on several other stories simultaneously. "One was a music piece about a young American composer over here. And I had been following the NATO missile decision for some time; and although New York wanted me to drop that . . . I was eager to take time out for the NATO meeting," she said. Spreading herself too thin, reported Ms. Lewis, has always been a problem. "I dabble. I'll write about a gastronomic binge, I'll write about NATO, I'll do an interview with Nureyev, I'll do a political piece. I don't know a hell of a lot about anything."[42]

The arguments for the generalist as an adequate substitute for at least a regional specialist seem patently weak, given the historical record. Moreover, the case made for generalism is a suspiciously convenient one for those concerned with profit making in journalism. To use specialists requires a far larger and more expensive work force, of course, than does the use of roving generalists. That many working journalists also happen to subscribe to a belief in the superior value of the generalist does not render the practice worthwhile; it would not be the first time that economic necessity and preference have been successfully transformed into ethical or professional standards, even when the transformation works against the best interests of those performing a task and those who consume what is produced.

As we suggested earlier in this chapter, conventional debate over press coverage of international affairs, to the extent that economic factors are at issue, has tended to focus on the profit-seeking role of the media, sharply increased costs for maintaining correspondents abroad, what the news industry has done to adjust to soaring costs, and finally, whether diminished foreign affairs coverage is simply a function of a lack of public interest. In short, the usual sort of discussion has generally proceeded from the fundamental assumption that the media operate in a free market where supply and demand are what count.

Yet at the same time that the number of correspondents abroad has fallen, so has the number of separately owned units of media in the United States decreased dramatically. To speak of the forces of the market operating, given the degree to which economic concentration has embraced the American mass media, is to insist on myth at the expense of contemporary reality. Journalistic competition today is among giants. Both the top and the bottom of the funnel through which foreign news flows to the American public have gotten smaller and smaller.

For press critic Ben H. Bagdikian, "Modern technology and American economics have quietly created a new kind of central authority over information—the national and multinational corporation." Bagdikian, the undisputed American authority on ownership concentration in the mass media, in his 1983 book, *The Media Monopoly,* has made what appears to be an unassailable case that by the 1980s most of the major American media, including newspapers, magazines, radio, television, books, and movies, were controlled by only fifty corporations.[43] Citing ample evidence throughout the book to back up his case, Bagdikian pointed out:

> Most of the fifty biggest firms have a direct stake in foreign investments and, therefore, in foreign policy of the United States. There is almost no country in the world in which a subsidiary of the fifty media companies does not have a significant investment. One major media company alone, CBS, has foreign subsidiaries headquartered in thirty-four countries, ranging from Argentina to South Africa.[44]

Arguing that the problem caused by intensive economic concentration in the media is as subtle as it is profound, Bagdikian wrote:

> In a democracy only one condition justifies a private publisher's imposing his personal politics on the decision of what to print: that a wide spectrum of other ideas has equitable access to the marketplace. If a small number of publishers, all with the same special outlook, dominate the marketplace of public ideas, something vital is lost to an open society. In countries like the Soviet Union a state publishing house imposes a political test on what will be printed. If the same kind of control over public ideas is exercised by a private entrepreneur, the effect of a corporate line is not so different from that of a party line.[45]

News media executives continue to insist that it is precisely the existence of a free marketplace of ideas, ruled only by unfettered economic forces and private ownership, which will keep the media free. Because of ownership trends over the past twenty years or so, however, such a market no longer exists, if it ever did, and the citizenry must now depend wholly on the goodwill and sense of social responsibility of media owners for open discourse, surely an historically unreliable supposition. Moreover, it is particularly within the realm of news of international events that smaller, nonchain or corporate, independently owned voices are least likely to be heard and therefore can hardly be considered a countervailing force.

Contemporary trends in media ownership present a far greater danger than the mere reduction of journalistic forces abroad and require a different type of analysis than the one usually put forth by reformist critics whose major goal appears to be convincing corporate journalism to act responsibly and provide more generous support for foreign-news gathering. However, it would be a mistake to assume, as is popularly done, that the *major* threat from economic concentration is direct and blatant owner control of content for narrow partisan advantage. Certainly there was no evidence to explain coverage of Iran in these terms. The problem is far more subtle and is bound up in the tangled relationship between the press, foreign policy, and ideology.

9

The Journalism of Deference

Every organized form of work has a central ideal around which individuals who perform the work construct their self-image, whether they be blue-collar workers, day-care providers, account-ants, or physicians. This core ideal, which is as much a product of the ego as of the workplace, sets forth the reason for being for a type of work, establishes acceptable standards for performing it, delimits ethical boundaries for conduct, and perhaps most important, gives to the worker and sustains a sense of self-worth. For many occupations and professions, the central ideal is concrete, uncomplicated, and rarely the subject of debate. For other areas of work, however, the central ideals are less clear-cut and far more abstract, complex, and controversial. Such is the case with the notion of *objectivity,* which is the core ideal of contemporary American mainstream journalism.

Mainstream journalists—those journalists who work for print and broadcast organizations considered the dominant sources of infor-mation for the general public—have come to believe that the pursuit and practice of objectivity have created a news media system that largely is nonideological, no matter how ideology is defined. The development of objectivity as an ethical goal and achievable practice for the journalist is generally believed to be a triumph over the highly politicized press of America's distant past, particularly the late 1700s but also periods of the nineteenth and early twentieth centuries.

Objectivity has come to be seen in the journalistic community as synonymous with a mature, socially responsible press. Certainly members of the press will admit temporary and embarrassing exceptions to the central ideal, instances where the media clearly have strayed from the path of objectivity. But on balance, there is a deeply held and abiding belief that the news media in America are the most objective and nonideological in the world and that democracy is all the better for it. This shibboleth has been aptly expressed by Prof. John Tebbel, a noted journalism historian:

> The twentieth-century concept of a free press in a democratic society rests on the ideal of fair and accurate reporting, that is, the attempt to be as objective as possible in covering the news. It is the attempt to do so that counts, not the inevitable human failures.
>
> The governments of authoritarian countries share the belief that the ideal of objectivity is reactionary. There is no slightest pretense of objectivity in the press of those countries. They argue that there is no association of news and truth in the newsroom; consequently they impose their own truth on the news.[1]

The prevailing academic point of view, at least in schools of journalism, is that journalistic objectivity, essentially an Anglo-American invention and practice, is what delineates the press systems of the West from those of the Second and Third Worlds. Such an assumption usually presupposes that in the Western English-language tradition all points of view are available and that "presenting all points of view makes news objective."[2] By contrast, "The Second and Third Worlds see news in an altogether different light. Their emphasis is on what news does rather than on what news is. . . . Since they are not trying to sell news but to use it for a particular end, objectivity—i.e., presenting all viewpoints—is not only unnecessary, it is counterproductive."[3]

According to one examination of the differences between Western and Third World news ideals, "The concepts of objectivity and speedy dissemination in a free marketplace of ideas where journalists act as 'watchdogs' over the government are essential to an open and democratic society in the West";[4] on the other hand, "Most often ideological, political, cultural and socioeconomic realities in a Third World nation determine the type of news that nation reads, hears or views."[5]

The coeditors of a series of essays on comparative mass media systems, among others, have argued that Western journalistic objectivity, having been recognized as an impossible and unattainable ideal, is "rapidly being replaced by concepts of fairness, accuracy, and lack of bias."[6] However, they do not make clear how these "new" values might differ from the goals of the old objectivity beyond the suggestion that reporters are now allowed a freer hand to use subjective description. While such a metamorphosis may be under way in the realm of domestic reporting, and we have our doubts, there was little evidence of such a development in the coverage of Iran for twenty-five years.

It can be argued—and frequently has been—that the owners of media give little more than lip service to the ideal of objectivity; in this view, their overriding concern is profit, not service to the public. Often enough, small numbers of journalists have also voiced doubts about whether the press is achieving what it says it is. For some intellectuals, the issue has been whether such a thing as objectivity can even exist. Conventional leftists, for their part, argue that objectivity in the American media exists only as a deceptive myth to conceal the fact that the press serves the interests of its owners. Finally, there is ample evidence that the general public at times, and for a variety of often vague reasons, can become remarkably suspicious of the media's seriousness about objectivity.

This sometimes loud and often acrimonious debate notwithstanding, the belief in an inherently nonideological press is a fundamental article of faith held by most working journalists. This belief is neither disingenuous nor held lightly by the majority of news persons, despite the arguable case that their conviction does not accurately reflect reality. Moreover, it is neither helpful nor productive in analyzing the media, particularly in its relationship to foreign policy, to assume that journalists are not serious when they make the case for objectivity. Journalists as a group are no more hypocritical than any other. Despite a sometimes cynical and worldly pose, they believe as much in their credo as do others involved in intellectual or physical labor. They are no more insincere than are welders or college professors. Most mainstream journalists say they are nonideological, and they believe it; such a belief informs their life work in theory and simply cannot be easily dismissed as a pose by those who would understand the behavior of the American press, particularly in the foreign policy arena.[7]

In this chapter, we will raise several questions about ideology and the press and attempt some answers: What is the self-image of journalists and how do they sustain it? How free are the media of ideological restraints? Is conformity of thought about foreign affairs in the news media encouraged or challenged? Under what conditions do the media part ways with Washington? Is domestic dissent against policy given a fair hearing in the press, or is it neutralized? What is reasonable to expect of the news media in reporting foreign affairs in which the United States has a perceived interest?

Our analysis in this chapter proceeds from our firm conviction that the journalists who cover defense policy and foreign affairs as individuals are for the most part decent, caring, often well prepared in a general sense, and usually serious. Their commitment to accomplishing their professed goals and living up to their professed values is a deeply held one. Our analysis, then, will focus not on the sincerity or intentions of journalists but on what they actually achieve. If what they achieve is far less than what is sought, as we will argue is usually the case for coverage of defense and foreign policy, this does not result from their conscious infidelity to the values and mores of their profession.

This chapter's thesis is a simple one and was suggested by the arguments developed in the preceding chapter: To the extent that mainstream journalism failed in Iran, it did so for ideological and ethnocentric reasons rather than because of the economics of the industry or because the press was victimized by a manipulative U.S. government, as is more commonly argued in such failures. It was not because of news-gathering costs or unconscionable pursuit of profit, for instance, that *Newsweek* could tell its readers in 1973: "How safe a bet is Iran? Unquestionably, the Shah has many advantages. Iran's economy is improving rapidly and may soon be up to Southern European standards. . . . As long as the 53-year-old monarch is alive and well, in fact, the U.S. seems likely to be backing a strong horse."[8]

The case of the press and Iran, furthermore, is not exceptional. The American news media for some varied and complicated reasons since the inception of the cold war have projected foreign politics and conflict through an ideological lens ground by official Washington, which has given a distorted view of the world to the American public. News bias in coverage of foreign affairs, with the recent exception of some coverage of Latin and Central America, has been particularly evident in the media's treatment of political and armed resistance to dictatorial client rulers in the Third World, and of U.S. efforts to save them, either through direct intervention or by more circumspect means.

Such a thesis, of course, is not taken seriously by most working journalists. Through a commitment to professionalism and careful attention to the rules of objectivity, journalists genuinely believe they have managed to transcend the human condition and escape the limitations of bias. Indeed, it is not too strong to say that the belief in a triumph over bias through a commitment to professionalism is the a priori assumption of contemporary journalism's ethical rhetoric. Most journalists deeply believe that their profession has perfected the techniques of pursuing objective reality to the extent that personal values do not seriously affect their work. Steeped in the ethical rhetoric of a democratic press, they see themselves as tough-minded practitioners of a well-defined craft, with clear-cut rules to eliminate personal bias. That *class* or *West-centered* biases may be a problem simply does not occur to them. Indeed, as sociologist Gaye Tuchman has pointed out in this regard:

> Newsworkers take comfort that, in the aggregate, their accounts of events are true by noting that those accounts were independently produced by newsworkers in a variety of organizations, and so do not represent personal bias. As for the problem of professional or class bias, they revert to identifying the methods they use to gather and assess news as guarantees of objectivity.[9]

The question of value-free reporting may remain open for social scientists, but it is beyond debate for journalists. Journalism for American journalists is and ought to be the essence of anti-ideology. News persons, who themselves often take great pride in not subscribing to a closely prescribed set of ideas, believe that good journalism is the enemy of cant, doctrine, and dogma, which they suppose are the only significant characteristics of ideology. From the perspective of most journalists, then, to suggest that their reporting may be influenced by their values or the values dominant in their society is to impugn their motives. To say they are ideological is to insult them. In this regard, we believe the greatest hurdle American journalists have to overcome before coverage of foreign affairs will improve is their belief that they are nonideological.

Certainly in this discussion we do not mean to suggest that the pursuit of truth—if that is what is meant by objectivity—is not desirable. What divides opinion is disagreement over whether truths exist independent of social agreement about their nature; how best to discover them; how they are interpreted; and which ones ought to be emphasized. Leaving aside the question of whether objective truths exist or are socially constructed, in our judgment the nature of the American news media undercuts the *pursuit* of truth by encouraging and enforcing—where necessary—a particular set of rules for achieving objectivity, which, contrary to the expectations held for them, result in a highly skewed view of the world. This view as it concerns foreign policy is a perspective determined not by independent journalistic judgment but by foreign policy elites.

Journalists operate in a social system and are subject to its influences, direct and indirect. Correspondents who closely follow the dictates of professionalism and objectivity—which are not the same thing, yet have come to be considered so—simply are not exempt from the dominant social forces. The reality is that journalists, if they are to work and prosper in the mainstream media, often unselfconsciously come to adopt a particular ideological perspective despite the firm commitment of the reporter to fairness, balance, professionalism, and the value-free practice of his or her craft.

The reluctance of journalists to acknowledge the effects of ideology on their work may be centered in their definition of the word. What we mean by ideology here is a well-ordered world view shaped since World War II by the requirements of the national security state; such a world view is a generalized form of political consciousness, a perspective. We do not mean by ideology a set of doctrinaire, highly systematic, rigidly imposed categories, concepts, and definitions that lead the journalist consciously to shape his or her work toward a particular, focused political end. In the sense we mean it, ideology is to conscious doctrinal belief as white noise is to a Stravinsky symphony. We are using the term ideology in its broadest sense, not its narrowest; in particular, we do not here equate *ideology* with partisanship.[10]

Using the context of domestic politics as an example, ideology would be the writing of stories which reflect a general belief that

America probably can accommodate only a two-party system; partisanship would be the act of writing stories to put either Democrats or Republicans in a good or bad light. Similarly, in the context of coverage of defense or foreign policy, belief in the superiority of Western liberal capitalism as a model for development is ideological, while preference for a particular political scheme for achieving it in the Third World may be considered partisan.

Because the American news media in the late twentieth century have come to approach domestic *electoral* issues involving the two established political parties with some degree of evenhandedness and have become less openly partisan in the news columns, many journalists have taken this to mean that professionalism has overcome ideology. This conclusion, however, is not supported by the historical evidence. Specifically, the development of relatively unbiased news coverage of two-party domestic electoral politics has not meant an absence of status quo bias in coverage of movements, events, or personalities that are perceived as posing a significant challenge to the existing social order. There is ample evidence of an ideological cast to the mainstream media contained in case studies of press coverage of race, labor, the women's movement, the student movement, serious domestic political dissent from nuclear weapons and energy, radical alternatives to liberal capitalism, and so on. Most particularly, such bias is evident in coverage of domestic political dissent from defense decisions and of conflict situations abroad in which the United States has a perceived direct interest. Usually, these challenges have been met with bipartisan political opposition, which is precisely the moment when the dominant ideology can have its greatest influence on the press.

What matters most in a discussion of dominant ideology are *shared* biases, not individual opinions. It is precisely because a world view is so widely shared inside and outside the journalistic system that it appears nonprejudicial; such collective bias becomes received opinion and is thereby rendered invisible. As Kennett Love, who covered Iran in the 1950s for the *New York Times,* asked, "Is a fish aware of water?" Even when a journalist's personal opinion may not correspond to society's dominant ideology, which is entirely possible, the orientation of the system in which journalists work certainly does. And as with work in any industrial bureaucracy, the individual reporter's preference is not likely to prevail.

Most recently, mainstream reporters, their defenders, and often their detractors will frequently respond to the argument that the media have a status quo ideological basis by citing press coverage of Watergate as evidence of the willingness of the press to take on the establishment. Yet the general press became most active in the affair only after important elites and institutions, not the least of which was the judiciary, became alarmed about the actions of the Nixon administration and determined that they constituted a far greater threat to the existing political order than did Nixon's Democratic opponents. In this regard, persuasive arguments have been advanced that the role of the press was vastly overrated.[11] The popular press throughout the Watergate affair failed, indeed, to distinguish between a permanent cure of a cancer on the body politic and the much more likely possibility that Watergate justice represented only a temporary remission.

Regardless of how the press performed during Watergate, there is little evidence to support the thesis that a more balanced and questioning approach toward domestic party politics has been translated into a *sustained* ideology-free perspective on U.S. relations abroad. Occasionally, it is true, the media will appear to challenge the status quo in some important ways involving defense and foreign policy. During the Vietnam War, for example, the press under the prodding of a relentless Seymour Hersh brought My Lai to light, and William Beecher, then with the *New York Times,* revealed the secret bombing of Cambodia.

For the most part, however, these and other instances of revelatory journalism, important and promising as they may be, were exceptions and not part of a pattern. They often depended more on the enterprise of individual reporters than on routine journalistic practice, and usually gained currency despite the press system—not because of it. It is rare also that revelations such as Hersh's or Beecher's ever find their way into the press *before* influential elites in the country have defected from a given administration's foreign policy. The My Lai story, for instance, gained exposure only after the 1968 Tet Offensive and the surge of elite defections in the administration, Congress, and the private sector.

Perhaps the most famous press revelations during the Vietnam War were, of course, the Pentagon Papers. But even here, the decision of the *Times* and other newspapers to publish the secret history of the war was taken well after significant splits in elite opinion over the war had occurred, and after the central question in national debate had changed from Should we leave? to How should we get out? Also, it was plain that the Pentagon Papers held no secrets of state, only state embarrassments.

Yet another reason reporters tend to believe they are beholden to no particular viewpoint is that they have routinely reported embarrassments to the foreign policy establishment, a fact which above all others serves to confuse the issue of press independence. Attentive Americans, for instance, know of many of the U.S. government's interventions abroad. If these things are known, it follows that the press must be free of a statist ideology. Theorists and journalists who make this argument exhibit a selective historical memory and overlook the fact that the American audience usually learns of unflattering U.S. government behavior long *after* the capacity for moral outrage is diminished and the moment for organizing domestic political opposition has passed. Under these circumstances, those who wish to applaud the flame of a free press are mistakenly celebrating the ember as if it were the same thing.

For example, CBS did not broadcast its admittedly hard-hitting "60 Minutes" segment on Iran's secret police, the SAVAK, until March 1980 on the 120th day of the hostage crisis, or some twenty years after the terror apparatus had been established with the assistance of the CIA.[12] And, as we saw in chapter 2, the popular press did not generally raise the question of CIA involvement in the overthrow of Mosaddeq until some twenty-five years after it had occurred. What was common knowledge among students of the Middle East for a quarter of a century remained to be discovered by most Americans. And when CIA involvement did become widely known, the press—following Carter's lead—in the early days of the hostage crisis tended to dismiss the affair as "ancient history" even though the Persian translation of *Countercoup* by Kermit Roosevelt had become a bestseller in Iran, and what seemed ancient to Americans was vivid history to Iranians for the first time since the coup's occurrence twenty-five years before.

Yet the belief in an ideology-free press persists, despite obvious contradictions of which journalists seem simply to be unaware. James Reston of the *New York Times,* as just one example, apparently quite ingenuously was able to assert boldly in his book's introduction that "our job in this age, as I see it, is not to serve as cheerleaders for our side in the present world struggle."[13] Leaving aside his interesting and revealing presumption that a "world struggle" was under way (the book was published in 1967), it is perhaps useful to juxtapose his philosophy with his actions some six years earlier during the Bay of Pigs incident.

According to one authoritative account, Reston played a key role in convincing the *Times* editors to play down advance knowledge of the invasion of Cuba to the point that the story went virtually ignored. He is reported to have advised the then *Times* publisher, Orvil Dryfoos, to tone down the story, display it less prominently under a smaller headline than had originally been assigned, and eliminate any reference to the imminence of the invasion. He argued that these steps should be taken in the national interest.[14] Several weeks after the invasion foundered, President Kennedy is said to have complained of even this much publicity in the nation's newspaper of record, to which *Times* editor Turner Catledge responded by pointing out that a report of preparations for the debacle had appeared in the *Nation*. Replied Kennedy, "But it was not news until it appeared in the *Times*."[15] Kennedy's general point about the power of the *Times* to define news is well taken, if not his plaintive lament; it was precisely because the *Times* failed to give adequate mention to the invasion that other media failed to pick up the story until after the assault had begun.

The point to be made here is that the behavior of Reston and the *Times* is not an isolated example of decision making, either for the *Times* or the media at large. There have been many other instances where decisions were based not on professional considerations or the economics of news gathering but rather on ideological concerns and a conception of the national interest. There is ample evidence to suggest the truth of the possibility that the press is far more deferential to the state than it acknowledges. This evidence is contained in analyses of news coverage of a number of major stories in which U.S. interests have been or are involved, including Guatemala in 1954, the Dominican Republic in 1965, Chile in 1973, East Timor in 1975, Nicaragua in 1978, and the continuing stories dealing with the Soviet Union and defense spending, to cite only a few such case studies.[16]

Journalism's consistent willingness to suspend independent judgment and to accept Washington's frames, labels, and assessments has had predictable consequences. Thus Cuban involvement in Angola received sustained media attention, while U.S. involvement was played down; the absence of popular support for Polish martial law was made plain, but the illegitimacy of the shah went unnoticed; a pronouncement by the Philippines' Ferdinand Marcos in 1983 that antigovernment agitators and publishers who engaged in "propaganda" could be executed received only passing mention in the national news. It is not difficult to imagine the tone and scope of press coverage if a similar statement had been made by the Sandinista government in Nicaragua.

For American journalists, whether they realize it or not, the problems of coverage of foreign affairs involving U.S. interests are perpetuated by the body of rules, practices, and ethical shibboleths which exist to insure that the news reporter maintains detachment from his or her subject. In many ways, these rules tend to exaggerate instead of diminish the ideological tendencies of press coverage of events abroad.

The prevailing historical view is that the concept of objectivity was first applied to journalism as a result of the realization of publishers that the press, if it were to mature and live up to its democratic responsibilities, must abandon its wanton partisanship, a phase in its development sometimes called the "dark ages of American journalism," and move toward providing dispassionate news for the masses.

Another, less becoming, possibility is that the press actually adopted its new moderate approach for economic reasons rather than ethical ones. With the coming of the mass press in the 1830s because of technological advances, for the first time it became evident that the press had great potential as a business. This potential could be realized, however, only if a given newspaper or other medium avoided offending large numbers of its audience. A centrist tone for the press, at least in covering political and social issues, was a more profitable tone.

Whatever their genesis, the rules of journalistic objectivity were designed to prevent the writer from introducing personal values into the news and were intended to serve as a safeguard against ideology. Journalistic objectivity would be best achieved by the news reporter's avoiding the use of strong adjectives, adverbs, value statements, opinion, metaphor, simile, analogy, and so on. In reporting an event, journalists would achieve fairness and balance by using only direct or indirect quotations from all sides of an issue; the assertions of fact would largely be left to stand on their own merits without reportorial comment. The reporter should not interject his or her own opinion, substantiated or not: statements of opinion can come only from others. Background material can be used, of course, but it must come from authoritative sources.

At the first level of analysis, these rules seem to be a reasonable way of going about presenting an unbiased picture of the world to an audience. On closer examination, however, the rules as constituted present some serious problems for news gathering, particularly abroad: the dicta neither accomplish their stated goals nor keep bias out of the news. On the contrary, the rules increase the likelihood that ideology will inform reporting. Certainly, so far as Iran was concerned, the much-vaunted objectivity of the American press did little to present an accurate picture of the forces at work.

In some important ways, the rules have resulted in the ossification of the news-gathering system. Arbitrary rules applied without thought in a bureaucratic setting always produce rigidity. Rigid systems, in turn, are the easiest to predict and therefore manipulate. As in other worldly matters, those in power are the most likely to do the manipulating. Were the rules of journalistic objectivity closer in nature to the law's rules of evidence, perhaps they would be useful. But as they exist, they provide little more than a formula for prefabricated prose, which is to say, cliché-ridden exposition. The problem is that the clichés in the realm of foreign affairs are usually provided by official Washington or its agents.

Journalistic objectivity as it is practiced has come to substitute a passive and reassuringly safe routine for, in the words of Ben Bagdikian, the "disciplines of documentation and critical judgment."[17] In effect, the rules appear to operate on the time-honored American principle that if there are two diametrically opposed claims to truth, the truth must lie somewhere between. This principle, unfortunately, makes no provision for the possibility that one or the other of the claimants, or both, may be lying, misinformed, or merely fantasizing. Only the reporter's personal judgment, based on systematic knowledge of the issue at hand, could make such a determination, but on a routine basis this determination, or at least its inclusion in a story, is disallowed by the dictates of the industry. As they have evolved, the rules of objectivity for journalists have become a substitute for thoughtful analysis.

How this works is revealed in a magazine writer's discussion in the *Columbia Journalism Review* of why he had not used the word "lie" in a piece he had done for the *Atlantic* about the deceptions of President Ronald Reagan:

> My avoidance of the word "lie" was in deference to the rule of journalistic objectivity that says its use implies bias on the reporter's part, *even when the objective facts warrant its use.* But by Webster's definition of the word ("an assertion of something known or believed by the speaker to be untrue; a deliberate misrepresenting of fact with intent to deceive"), I count nine "outright lies" in my article—five by Reagan and four by William French Smith, Edwin Meese, and William Bradford Reynolds (emphasis ours).[18]

The writer concluded that by using such euphemisms as "selective use of information" to describe the president's words, reporters gave the public a distorted view of the president's conduct.

In this respect, journalists are taught to ignore a reality that lawyers forget at their peril: How you use the facts is as important as the facts you have to use. The *interpretation* of demonstrable truth can be more significant than the truth itself. The lawyer, in building a case, is particularly conscious of the importance of emphasis, shading, use of nuance, and so on to produce a cumulative effect that makes some facts stand out to a jury and others fade; some unpleasant truths seem less so and some pieces of obviously damning evidence appear quite reasonable under the circumstances as the prosecutor or defense counsel has *presented* them.

Even here, in the realm of facts, often much of what reporters report, particularly in crisis situations, turns out not to be factual at all, if facts are those things agreed on by reasonable people and not given to dispute. The commercial and workaday constraints of the business, to be sure, cause many of these errors to be made. However, it is ideology at the subconscious level that may make reporters susceptible to believing certain "facts" and not others. The willingness of the American press to assert "factual" claims about the shah's land reform is but one example. In any event, following the rules of objectivity does not prevent these types of errors from being made or repeated.

The problem today with discussions of journalistic objectivity is that the means have come to be mistaken for the desired end. The news industry/profession/craft has come to believe that integrity of the craft rests in how well an arbitrary set of rules are followed. Having followed these rules carefully, journalists assume they must have achieved what was being sought: the truth. Therefore, journalists interpret criticism of their performance as little more than an ideological attack. In this respect, as Gaye Tuchman has observed, news people usually assume that "the critics' accusation that newsworkers are ideological is said to translate into the statement, 'My biases are preferable to yours.'"[19]

At the core of acceptable journalistic practice are two primary elements: deference to established authority, and surface observation. In the first instance, it is thought that by merely accurately reporting what someone in authority says and by attributing it, the reporter's responsibility has been fulfilled; to do more means running the risk of exceeding the limits of reportorial discretion. Despite the news media's folkloric belief that the journalist is the staunch adversary of government, the reporter more usually is forced to ignore one of history's few very clear lessons: Established authority becomes less trustworthy as a source of objective truth in direct relationship to the threat to the authority posed by the truth. This maxim is particularly so in the foreign and defense policy settings, where small power elites are accustomed to operating without fear of contradiction.

Yet in Iran for twenty-five years American reporters turned to the White House, the State Department, defense intellectuals, and members of the shah's regime for their understanding of the White Revolution, land reform, the religious opposition, the 1978 revolution, and so on. It was as if civil rights reporters of the 1960s had turned to, and come to depend only on, Lester Maddox for an assessment of the legitimacy of the motives and complaints of black Americans.

Similarly, by limiting journalists to mere description and enjoining them from *knowledgeable* interpretation or only to interpretations that have been validated by established authority, the press has continued to follow a path abandoned by cultural anthropology and sociology decades ago as one leading to gross distortion. To observe, describe, and—most particularly—interpret without full understanding is most likely to misrepresent. The press's treatment of the Iranian revolution's religious dimension is one example of such a failure.

Under these rules of objectivity, journalism has grown to maturity. The reporter has been denied the powers of informed observation, encouraged to depend on established authority as a source of reality, and prevented from acquiring and cultivating the skills and orientation required to challenge the self-interested view of official Washington. The journalist has been constrained, finally, to believe that to accept contradictions is to be objective, to question them is to be subjective. Yet in the realm of foreign policy, it is only through questioning contradictions and by making them known and blatant that the press can make a significant contribution to the knowledge of the public.

Analysts make a mistake, however, in analyzing press behavior simply in the context of the system's conventions and professional expectations for journalists. Systemic constraints alone do not shape and rule the consciousness of reporters: rearing and socialization perhaps even more than training and professional conditioning are key forces. In this respect, the journalist has usually acquired the dominant world view long before he or she enters journalism.[20] In short, systemic constraints or no, the journalist comes to the subject of U.S. relations with the world from a perspective not remarkably unlike that of the foreign policy elites or of media owners. The canons of journalism do more to keep the perspective intact than to create it.

Most journalists will say they realize that they have beliefs and biases and are subject to the influence of ideology. But to question their work seriously by suggesting that ideology is a factor is to discover quickly that they do not really mean what they say. Journalists in the main also are quick to deny vehemently that their colleagues share an ideological perspective that could be considered a tilt toward liberalism. Denials aside, the clear majority of their number working in the prestige media is liberal. In this discussion, a liberal is a person who, domestically, eschews radical change but is favorably predisposed toward social reforms, and in foreign policy has generally accepted an activist, often interventionist, role for the United States in the name of realpolitik. To be sure, these are gross generalizations and there are many important exceptions. But on balance, the historical record would indicate such a pattern to be the case.

What complicates any discussion of mainstream news media in the United States is the reality that, unlike the personnel in most industries, journalists and first-line decision makers frequently hold values more liberal than the general community, yet the system in which they work is inherently conservative as a social force. Major news organizations are mature, highly capitalized corporations whose main product happens to be perceptions. Ownership in the industry as a whole is among the most concentrated in the United States. The owners and decision makers, therefore, are important members of what journalist and author Sidney Zion, cited in *Harper's* magazine, termed the "League of Gentlemen," his phrase for the establishment. According to Zion, "Even when the press attacks a particular administration, its owners and managers still belong to that League of Gentlemen, and still consider the government to be basically right."[21] A disagreement among friends, in other words, should not be confused with an open breach in the relationship.

Agreeing with Zion about the "League" and its nature, columnist Tom Wicker, an associate editor of the *New York Times,* added in the same issue of *Harper's*: "Sure, someone could write a two-line memo tomorrow to be more skeptical and challenging of established institutions. But they won't do it, not because they don't have the power to do it, but because they don't want to suffer more than the minimal necessary disapproval of the League of Gentlemen."[22]

Journalists are particularly reluctant to admit their liberalism, or at least the possibility that it might inform their reporting, because of criticism from the political right. The mid-1980s in particular marked a resurgence of criticism of the press by the right from such quarters as the Accuracy in Media organization (AIM), which has mounted a sustained attack on what it considers the liberal bias of journalists and on a press that supposedly is antidefense, soft on the Soviet Union, and antinuclear.[23] From this arch-conservative perspective, it is evidence of a liberal bias and insensitivity to the dangers of communism to raise any questions about the right of the United States to impose its will on others, particularly under the highly ideological Reagan presidency.

In particular, recent studies by conservative scholars indicating a liberal and "left-liberal" value system for journalists[24] have elicited ringing and angry retorts from the journalistic establishment. Hinting broadly that the conservative scholarship was not far removed from Spiro Agnew's attack on the liberal press, the *Columbia Journalism Review,* America's most prestigious journal of press criticism, in its response to these empirical studies, based on attitude surveys of a sample of working journalists, made the classic journalistic defense that values do not necessarily dictate journalistic behavior:

> [The authors] tried to show that there was "slippage" from journalists' personal opinions into news stories. . . . The problem with the whole portrait is that it leaves out the most important thing about journalists—their work. Having committed themselves to defining a new class by its political and cultural opinions, and having defined journalists as part of that class . . . [the authors] were then forced to disregard everything about journalists except their personal opinions. But there is little beyond wishful evidence in the study, or elsewhere, that journalists carry their personal opinions over into their work. On the contrary, . . . Lichter and Rothman [the authors] *concede* that "the ability to overcome one's biases is the hallmark of journalistic professionalism" (emphasis ours).[25]

Hodding Carter III, journalist, media critic, and State Department spokesman during the Iranian hostage crisis, has argued a position in stark contrast to the one offered by the *Review*, but for reasons dramatically different from those put forth by the political right. In Carter's view, "The national press as a whole is hopelessly, totally and probably inevitably wedded to the status quo in every way that matters." According to Carter, the editors, publishers, television executives, anchormen, producers, columnists, and reporters whose work gives shape to the national media are "people who have made it in modern America—ostentatiously, gloriously and rewardingly—and they are not about to play Samson in the temple." The evidence that indicates that journalism is liberal or more left-leaning on social and economic issues reminds Carter of "mafiosi who go to mass, reflecting more a tribute to lost virtue than a statement of current commitment." In the view of Carter, "The ideological spread of what is published or broadcast regularly moves from roughly A to E, with A being anchored to the right and E barely making it to center left."[26]

While we happen to agree with Carter's overall conclusion about the relationship of the press to the state, we must disagree with his belief that this is evidence that journalists are not liberal—at least within the American understanding of that term. Moreover, whether merely professed values or practiced ones, the fact remains that the beliefs of journalists working for elite media as expressed in various polls appear to be more liberal than those of the general population. Similarly, without passing judgment on its merit, we would argue that the *Review*'s contention that specific values, say a reporter's feelings about abortion, may not carry over into his or her work in the realm of domestic politics and social issues is irrelevant to a consideration of media behavior in the realm of *foreign policy*. Whatever the ability of a journalist to conquer personal bias on a domestic issue, and we believe that ability may be considerable, it is entirely another matter to assume the absence of effect of a subconscious general world view on a correspondent covering political news— particularly conflict—overseas. The realm of foreign affairs, particularly when perceived U.S. interests are in conflict with those of another nation-state, generally involves eminently familiar and acceptable American policy considerations and values ranged against largely unfamiliar and alien political, economic, and social forces. How are these matters likely to be understood and judged? Against what standards are they likely to be measured? The potential for ideocentrism is obvious.

The charges made by the right about the press and the responses they elicit produce more confusion than clarity about the issues facing the student of the press and foreign policy. First, the complaints by the political right about American foreign policy center on the timidity of Washington and its refusal to apply enough force in confronting Communist expansionism or other threats to U.S. interests. The right's contentions to the contrary, the historical record indicates that rarely since World War II has the United States been reluctant to use its power abroad or to ally itself with dictatorial rulers who seem capable and willing to serve American interests. That the application of American power has not always been successful does not negate the reality and the significance of its use or that the press, generally, up to a point has supported the use of such force as has been exercised. For the right to argue that the United States has been reluctant to use force is to oversimplify the real world and ignore a long string of American involvements abroad, not the least of which were the bloody affairs of Vietnam, Cambodia, and Laos.

The second reality that the right ignores in its criticism of the press and policy is the repeatedly demonstrated fact that at least in the age of nuclear deterrence and superpower rivalry the use of overwhelming force is simply not a practical answer to many international conflicts, whether in East-West or North-South relations; this much the press tends to realize, which earns it the enmity of the unbending right.

Every major study of the values of journalists working for the prominent news organizations which play the greatest role in the foreign policy arena indicate that a majority can be considered "liberal" by any reasonable use of that term.[27] Aside from empirical studies, the studies, biographies, and autobiographies of prominent journalists, ranging from Ben Bradlee's *Conversations with Kennedy*[28] to Ronald Steel's *Walter Lippmann and the American Century,*[29] give testimony to this fact. The attacks from the right, however, obscure a central question: What has it actually meant to be a liberal in the foreign policy setting? What actually are the substantive *strategic* differences in outlook between the liberals and their conservative critics? If the Truman, Kennedy, Johnson, and Carter administrations are examples of the liberal impulse abroad, then the differences cannot be said to be great, particularly if increases in defense spending, the willingness to use force abroad to achieve policy goals, and expedient alliances with status quo rulers are the criteria. In short, at least historically, American liberals were (and are) supportive of U.S. foreign policy during the cold war. The political right's paranoia or misreading of history does not alter this truth.

Lippmann, for instance, may be considered a model of the quintessential journalistic mind at work. According to Steel's brilliant account, Lippmann for most of his life had little problem reconciling his humanistic instincts and commitment to progressive reform with his belief in a world role for the United States and American superiority within the context of the superpower conflict and the cold war. He was reluctant or unwilling to accept the possibility that economic demands or imperial ambitions might play a significant part in explaining American foreign policy, and he was oblivious to the possibility that high public officials could lie about situations in which Americans were losing their lives (Vietnam) until very late in his life. He was, in short, the perfect member of the League of Gentlemen.

While Lippmann often vigorously dissented from orthodoxy and severely criticized the foreign policy establishment, he did so by attacking the problems of control and execution of policy rather than its goals. "The real problem of our foreign policy is not in its objectives,"[30] he wrote in 1952, an opinion he found little cause to revise for almost the rest of his life. Lippmann opposed American alliances with reactionary regimes *in theory*, but he nonetheless ended up supporting such alliances when they were seriously challenged by indigenous Communist movements.[31]

Only after the evidence became irrefutable that the Johnson administration had lied to the public about Vietnam did Lippmann come to oppose American involvement there. Even so, his ever-trusting ideological perspective led him to support a Nixon candidacy in 1968 in the belief that Nixon was authentically interested in ending the war for the United States, not in prevailing. Lippmann saw "a new Nixon, a maturer and mellower man who is no longer clawing his way to the top . . . who has outlived and outgrown the ruthless politics of his early days."[32] The war would continue, of course, for another seven years, a period longer than under any other president, and the Watergate affair, in which more than twenty members of the Nixon administration would be indicted and thirteen would serve time, was yet to transfix the nation.

Because of the professional constraints placed on journalists, to a lesser degree because of commercial ones discussed in the preceding chapter, and most particularly because of their own world view, ideology as we have defined it is more likely, not less likely, to affect reporting about foreign affairs. Precisely because journalists believe they are above and beyond ideology they are most susceptible to its effects. Journalists have been conditioned to believe that by following the narrowly prescribed rules of objectivity they have escaped the embrace of ideology; they are encouraged to believe in a state of innocence that simply does not exist and cannot be achieved under the rules they follow. This belief, genuine and sincere as it may be, prevents the mainstream journalist from moving toward an authentic form of objectivity, which only can begin with recognition of one's own biases. Such a form of objectivity consists of nothing more than striving for authentic autonomy, which is to say acting independently of foreign policy elites and reporting to the public all that is reasonably knowable about a subject at the time.

In journalism, there are two forms of ideology that may be at work: the journalistic system's and the individual's. It is not necessary that the constellation of beliefs of both types be identical, although they often are, but it is always essential that the first be dominant over the second. As we have suggested, individual reporters may differ privately with the dominant ideology, which the media system accepts and serves, but to do so in their work is to become *subjective* by the system's definition, which is unacceptable. On balance, however, the general ideological orientation of the system and the individual correspondent is remarkably similar, except when the reporter comes to question the ideology for varying reasons and under exceptional conditions, as occurred during the latter stages of Vietnam and may be happening again in the mid-1980s in Central America.

The central aspect of America's dominant ideology after World War II is unequivocal acceptance of the legitimacy of the national security state, as Todd Gitlin among others has suggested.[33] As we argued earlier in this chapter, consensus journalism subscribes without reservation to a belief in a national security state made necessary, in Reston's terms, by the "world struggle" between the United States and the Soviet Union. It is a Manichean struggle, in the mainstream view, between freedom and unfreedom, hope and despair, workable capitalism and unworkable communism. It is the ultimate competition, in short, between good and evil. It is ideological to its core—at least for the media. Moreover, widespread acceptance of the idea of the national security state has been coupled with a postwar national ambition to achieve what publisher Henry R. Luce labeled "the American Century," a time when the United States would be dominant and the world would be a better place for it.

As a result, the media have applied a double standard to the United States and its chief adversary, the Soviet Union, in judging everything from interventions to the arms race. Soviet intentions and behavior, in this regard, are consistently portrayed in the darkest possible shades, while American behavior abroad is pictured as a necessary and benign response to Russian perfidy.[34] Caught up in the assumptions of the cold war, the press has tended to see conflict in the world, particularly rebellion in the Third World, only in terms of the East-West paradigm. The press, therefore, engages in a sort of zero-sum journalism: A "loss" to rebellion of a United States client state or market must be a gain for the Soviet Union. Revolution, in this view, is always the result of an imported ideology that has seduced the natives into revolt.

There can be no doubt that the beginnings of the cold war have had everything to do with creating an historically unprecedented (except during time of declared war) willingness by the press to go along with official foreign policy assumptions.[35] The United States has been in a perpetual state of perceived crisis and emergency since 1945. As Robert Karl Manoff has suggested in an important essay, the dawning of the nuclear age created the national security state and locked the news media and the state into permanent embrace:

> By the middle of the 1940s, therefore, the state and the press shared an elective affinity which had allowed the former to fight wars and the latter to report them. The relationship was complex and constant. The key was the problem of loyalty and enthusiasm that mass war [made possible by nuclear weapons] posed for the democratic state. Hiroshima, however, signaled a military revolution, and, hardly less significant, it announced the political transformation the revolution would compel. By the 1960s it would become clear that the bomb had fundamentally altered the relationship between state and civil society around the question of war and peace. This, in turn, was to have significant consequences for the press.[36]

Manoff argues persuasively that American strategy has "become psychologized" or internalized and that anxiety about the possibility of "total warfare" against the homeland has effectively transformed the erstwhile "civil voice" of the press into a "statist" perspective. The statist perspective embraces the viewpoints of permanent Washington, which leads to the journalistic acceptance of its definitions of political situations abroad; journalistic reliance on official sources; and journalistic preoccupation with Washington policy debates and acceptance of the terms in which these debates are couched. By contrast, Manoff defines the journalistic *civil* voice as one with "proud recourse to moral authority, dependence on unmediated expression, respect for individual opinion and independent judgment."[37] In sum, a journalism of deference had replaced an adversary attitude toward the foreign policy and military establishment.

The implications of Manoff's thinking seem reasonable. If the splitting of the atom has radically changed our thinking about the universe, our world, our future, and ourselves, why can't it force us to think differently about our journalism? The psychological burden of total warfare cannot be borne easily or lightly by any institution and certainly not by the press. It follows that a new, far more compliant journalist should result.

There is one other factor in journalism's acceptance of cold-war ideology, however, which is missing from Manoff's compelling analysis, and that is the rise of the corporate state, which has seen a massive merging of private and public interests. Such a corporate state has come about because of, and has benefited largely from, American dominance in the world community, a dominance achieved through industrial, technological, and military strength. Such a state has been built in important ways on a foundation of arms manufacture and defense spending. Few state or local economies, therefore, have not become dependent to varying degrees on either Third World resources and markets, which are often guaranteed by the use of or the threat of use of national power, or continuation of the arms race, or all three. Both state and private sector need what the other has, and traditional lines between the two have become blurred if not entirely erased.

The mass media have been grateful beneficiaries of such a partnership: Big media, big profits, and a big state have not proved economically incompatible. It should not be surprising, then, to discover a predisposition by the press to accept a view of the world similar to its senior partner, the state. This development is, of course, contrary to the expectations held for the press under democratic theory, particularly as it was articulated in the 1700s. Much of the confusion over the role and behavior of the modern press, indeed, is the result of the clash between two-hundred-year-old ethical rhetoric and modern business practice. The framers of the First Amendment could not guess or imagine that the press would someday become profitable. The mythos surrounding the press, in short, was born before the media became big business. Yet the professed values of the American press as taught in civics classes hardly coincide with the business values and practices of the modern corporate state. The result is that the journalistic watchdog, which was to be a check on the excesses of government, rarely leaves the kennel on matters of foreign affairs.

The thrust of our arguments here, obviously, is that the performance of the American news media in covering a quarter of a century of U.S.-Iran relations was more the product of ideology than independent journalistic judgment. Furthermore, the performance of the press in Iran was entirely consistent with its coverage throughout the Third World. The journalism of deference to the national security state too often has meant that what gets covered in the Third World and how it gets covered are dictated almost entirely by assumptions of the dominant ideology. Professional values are not the dominant factor in this regard, nor are specific profit considerations, as is usually argued by media critics.

How this might be so is bound up in the given of cold-war ideology that only the great-power East-West confrontation really matters. The fate of the world rests on the competition between the United States and the Soviet Union, in this view, not the strife between the rich and the poor or between tyranny and aspirations for freedom. The relationship (and tension) between the rich industrialized north and the impoverished developing south are of little consequence. This view was bluntly summed up by former Secretary of State Henry Kissinger, who was once reported to have remarked, "Nothing important can come from the south. History has never been produced in the south. The axis of history starts in Moscow, goes to Bonn, crosses over to Washington, and then goes to Tokyo. What happens in the south is of no importance."[38]

If history is not made in the south, it follows that neither is news. It seems clear from most studies of news flow that the news media generally follow this dictum.[39] The media, to the extent that they both cover and disseminate foreign news, do so by focusing on Western Europe and the Soviets. By and large, the Third World is covered from a paternalistic viewpoint at best and from the viewpoint of social Darwinism at worst.

The approach of the United States to the Third World is beset by several flaws, flaws that find their counterpart in journalistic performance. In writing about American policy in Latin America, Carlos Fuentes, Mexico's fine novelist, has pinpointed some of these defects. What he has had to say applies as much to the U.S. failure, state and journalistic, in Iran and the rest of the Third World as it does to the region of which he writes. According to Fuentes, the United States has failed to "identify change in Latin America in its cultural context," and to "identify nationalism as the bearer of change in Latin America." These failures of identification, Fuentes has written, may be centered in an American world view and ideology which have unique roots:

> The United States, it should be remembered, is the only major power of the West that was born beyond the Middle Ages, modern at birth. As part of the fortress of the Counter-Reformation, Latin America *has had to do constant battle with the past.* We did not acquire freedom of speech, of belief, of enterprise as our birthrights. We have had to

fight desperately for them. The complexity of the cultural struggles underlying Latin America's political and economic struggles has to do with unresolved tensions, sometimes as old as the conflict between pantheism and monotheism; or as recent as the conflict between tradition and modernity (emphasis ours).[40]

As they did in Latin America, policy makers and the press before and during Iran's revolution ignored the country's battle with its past. Because of the prevailing assumptions in the press and its tendency to ignore history, Third World peoples are perceived as being motivated only by material discontent, and their periodic rebellions are not thought to have a moral or political dimension; thus the Third World's complaints are judged to be simply uninteresting and unworthy of our attention. Typically, as a result, unless open rebellion breaks out, Americans have been largely left in the dark about such staunch Third World allies as Nicaragua's Somoza, Chile's Pinochet, and the Philippines' Marcos or are given mythologized pictures of allies such as Chiang Kai-shek, Ngo Dinh Diem, and, of course, the Shah of Iran.

It is perhaps not surprising that the general disdain for the Third World, which is a fundamental aspect of America's dominant ideology and permeates so much official thinking, should be reflected in the performance of journalism, and reflected it is. One indicator of the lack of attention Iran received in the American news media before 1978, for example, can be found in the annual rankings of television news stories. Despite its position as America's most important client state, Third World or otherwise, Iran from 1972 to 1975 did not appear on the list of the twenty most frequently mentioned nations on the three national television networks. South Vietnam, as might be expected, was first, followed by the USSR, Israel, North Vietnam, France, Great Britain, and so on. Half of those nations mentioned, including North and South Vietnam, could be considered Third World countries, but it is clear they owed their place on the list only to dramatic events in which they were involved.[41]

Iran jumped to number five in the rankings for the years 1976–1979, but the increased attention came almost entirely during the 1978–79 revolution.[42] The print media did far better after 1975, quantitatively if not qualitatively, but still focused more on business aspects of the U.S.-Iran relationship than on political forces at work.

When the press did cover Iran, as we have seen in preceding chapters, it did so in ways that created a view of the country and its fortunes that was strikingly similar to the one offered by the shah's regime and by his allies in Washington. In large part, those who successfully led the media to believe in the myths of modernization, the reaction of revolution, and so on had some advantages that are not always available to propagandists. It was possible in the case of Iran for regime apologists to appeal to prejudices, sensibilities, and a world view of the journalistic fraternity that was at once a part of but separate from the statist political perspective and ideology which have been the subject of this chapter. In short ethnocentrism was in the service of ideology. The revolutionary symbolism and idiom of the revolution, for instance, contrasted sharply with the backgrounds and inclinations of American journalists who (1) are nominally Christian and (2) effectively secular.[43] Moreover, a belief in the separation of church and state is deeply rooted in the American cultural and political tradition. It would be absurd to pretend that these factors did not affect the judgment and choice of words of most journalists covering the revolution, or that professionalism or careful attention to the rules of journalistic objectivity could overcome their influence. However, as we argued at the end of chapter 7, ideology is the constant and ethnocentrism is a variable. The same or similar qualities in Iranian revolutionaries which were repugnant to American journalists were ignored or transformed into virtues when the subject at hand was resistance to the Soviets in Afghanistan.

A number of contemporary observers of the press have argued that although ideology may once have played a role in press behavior, the tendency to defer is no more. The lessons of Vietnam, according to this view, have been well learned. A new sensibility prevails among journalists. Too, this argument runs, a generation of journalists who came to maturity during the traumatic years of American involvement in Southeast Asia and during Watergate is well schooled in the pitfalls of the journalism of deference; they will make sure that the state's actions are held to rational account. David Halberstam, the most famous of Vietnam correspondents, has made such a case in an eloquent and passionate argument prompted by events in Central America:

> When I arrived in Vietnam, I was innocent, despite five years in the [U.S.] South and more than a year in the Congo. I believed too much in my own country, the rightness of its cause and the worthiness of its purpose; I believed that high Americans would not lie in a place where young men were dying. I lost that innocence in Vietnam slowly and

painfully. Because of those years I feel different about El Salvador; I think there is nothing to be gained there and a great deal to be lost, that the struggle is about elemental social and economic justice (as perceived by the peasants themselves and not by the U.S. Secretary of State).[44]

There is at least slight evidence that a newer, more tough-minded, less trusting, post-Vietnam sensibility is at work in the American media's coverage of, at least, events in Central America. A striking example of this is *Newsweek*'s running a 1983 cover story with the headline "Central America: The First Casualty," which chronicled the death of Lt. Cmdr. Albert Schaufelberger III, the first American adviser to be killed in El Salvador. No such journalistic announcement accompanied the death of the first adviser to die in Vietnam.[45]

Optimism over coverage of Latin America should be tempered, however, by several qualifications. First, there is no evidence that the post-Vietnam sensibility is at work where American interests are involved elsewhere in the Third World, as the case of Iran made plain. This is particularly so in the Middle East. True, the American press following the invasion of Lebanon by American ally Israel did portray the Palestinian cause in a considerably different and more favorable light than it had in the past. But this change, we must argue, occurred only after a strategic dispute between Israel and the Reagan administration surfaced; moreover, important defections among policy and opinion elites occurred over the invasion which preceded the change in press coverage.[46] And once a policy consensus re-formed, the press returned once again to a generally uncritical view of Israel's behavior in the Middle East.

In similar fashion, press coverage toward Latin America began to change only *after* the foreign policy establishment's consensus broke down and defections from President Reagan's policy became common knowledge. (Arch-conservative critics of journalism's performance in Vietnam have never fully understood that much of the journalistic reporting cited for being hard on U.S. policy was the result of journalistic disagreement over *how* the war was being fought, not over whether it *ought* to be fought; on that there was agreement, until after major elites expressed open disagreement with a military solution for Vietnam and a less trusting attitude by the press began to become clear.)[47] In addition, Latin America presents a special case for North American journalism. First, the trouble spots are in the United States' front yard. Second, probably more American journalists speak Spanish than any other foreign language. Third, Latin American culture does not appear nearly so exotic to people of the United States, if for no other reason than proximity, tourism, and the place "Our Good Neighbors to the South" hold in the curricula of the nation's schools.

Whatever the reasons for somewhat improved coverage of events in the Western Hemisphere—and coverage of the 1983 revolt against Pinochet in Chile was far more balanced than coverage had been of the revolt against Allende—there is little evidence of improvement elsewhere. There has been no real change in the structures of journalism or the economic system that produces it. Journalists continue to exhibit a reflexiveness informed by ideology, reinforced by the commercial imperative, and protected by an unreformed ethical rhetoric. The received or conventional wisdom continues to be confused with an adversary attitude, and journalists continue to place their faith in the rules of objectivity. When confronted with contradictory evidence about the world they cover, journalists still tend to reject the evidence rather than their ideological model. There is no real reason to believe, therefore, that a massively popular revolt against the House of Saud in Saudi Arabia or against Mubarak in Egypt would receive substantively different coverage than the revolution against the shah. In that respect, ideology remains, as much as ever, a factor to account for.

Conclusion

The U.S. press did not "lose" or contribute to the "loss" of Iran. The idea of a superpower "losing" a client state to a popular revolution is a legacy of colonial thinking and has little usefulness in the contemporary analyses of international politics. What the press did contribute to is a monumental failure to understand how Iranians felt about the kind of society in which they lived, a failure that arguably led to disastrous policy choices over a period of twenty-five years.

In this regard the underlying assumption of our work is that the American press, by informing and influencing the general as well as the attentive publics on world events, affects the substance of United States foreign policy. Even though this *affective*—as distinguished from *determining*—impact cannot be denied, at the same time it is too intangible to be easily quantified and too complex to be comprehended in isolation from other sources of influence on policy making.

To be sure, while in office, foreign-policy managers do not openly acknowledge the role played by the media in shaping the domestic environment of foreign policy. After all, in their public position, foreign-policy makers are loath to admit that their decisions are based on anything other than sheer expertise and nonpartisan calculation of what is in the nation's best interest. Such protestations of indifference aside, the memoirs of former officials seem to suggest that the extent and character of media coverage of foreign affairs is an inescapable factor in high-level policy deliberations.

229

It is in the nature of American democracy that foreign policy options under consideration by decision makeɪ౩ often come to reflect in varying degrees the public perception of what is at stake. This is particularly the case when there is partisan debate over policy choices or when there is heightened public sensitivity toward the issues under review. Of course, the former often leads to the latter. But perhaps even more important are those times when a policy choice is *not* in dispute and does not arouse significant public curiosity, as was often the case with Iran from 1953 to 1973. At these times policy making can easily be dominated by special and short-term economic, ideological, strategic, or political concerns, and decisions can be taken which have serious long-term implications for the country without the knowledge of the public at large. In the absence of controversy or public interest, only the press, the Fourth Estate, can question the official position and generate debate on the possible consequences of the policy choice.

We contend that the U.S. policy toward Iran under the shah constituted a clear-cut example of a situation in which, generally, there was little controversy and even less public interest. For the most part, the shah attracted bipartisan support, was spared public controversy until far too late in his rule, and was never subjected to the public scrutiny of, say, the South African regime in the mid-1980s. As we have demonstrated in the preceding chapters, in 1953, 1962–63, 1968, 1973, and 1978 Washington made some crucial choices about Iran with little or no public debate. The American mainstream press must bear a large part of the responsibility for the absence of such debate. Consequently, by 1978 there were more than forty thousand U.S. military and civilian personnel working in Iran, the country had become the largest customer for U.S. weapons, economic ties between the two countries were unprecedented, and the shah was considered one of the two most important strategic allies of the United States in the Third World—all seemingly accomplished without the serious consideration of the American public.

Indeed, a major theme of *All Fall Down: America's Tragic Encounter with Iran,* by Gary Sick, the principal White House adviser on Iran during the Iranian revolution and the hostage crisis, was the unrelieved American ignorance about Iran.[1] The overriding contention in our book is that the U.S. press did very little to relieve either the general or the attentive public of its ignorance about a country that for a quarter of a century was one of the most important client states the United States has ever had. We maintain that the failure of the press to seriously question the wisdom or motivations behind the relationship of the United States and the shah was primarily the result of ignoring the importance of politics in Iran during the period.

We have come to conclude that the ideology and ethnocentrism of news workers seem to have conditioned them to look for politics only in a liberal democratic context. And they tend to confuse their preference for such a politics with the idea of politics itself. This perceptual flaw often leads to a virtual denial of politics in covering Third World affairs because politics in most Third World countries does not have a liberal democratic orientation. Yet to succeed, any attempt to comprehend the character of a nation-state like Iran or the behavior of a leader like the shah (or his successor) must take into account the parameters or the structural and historical limitations of political action within the political culture under study. Such limitations may produce a *style* of politics completely foreign to the Western observer, but it does not render politics nonexistent. Similarly, although repression can force politics underground, it cannot eliminate the will to political participation.

To deny the existence of politics in a given society is to refuse to raise the question of who gets what, when, and how as a result of the existing socioeconomic order and therefore to remain blind to opposition to such a distribution of power and material wealth. The press, deferring to official Washington, assumed that Iranian politics was simply the sum total of the shah's will. Perceived as a benevolent strongman, he was seen to have the capacity to rule with total impunity and to sustain sociopolitical order without serious difficulty. The Iranian military was presumed to be loyal to him, and his technocratic and administrative elites were presumed to be dedicated to his grandiose projects. And the opposition, if mentioned at all in the coverage of Iran, was portrayed as irrelevant to the shah's rule. If he had any serious problem in his modernizing kingdom, we were told, it was because he was trying to do too much too soon for his backward people. From Washington's perspective—and in the view of the mainstream press as well—the shah was, in the words of Henry Kissinger, "that rarest of things, an unconditional ally."

The truth of the matter was that all of the above assumptions were false. The shah was so paranoid about his own officer corps that he felt compelled to personally review individual promotions over the rank of colonel and prohibited his commanders from associating with one another without official permission. Similarly, his upper-echelon civilian elite lived in perpetual fear of his displeasure; they did not dare to give an honest report about the problems of his favored programs or voice criticism of his decisions. As for his political opposition, it was never irrelevant; otherwise the massive activities of the SAVAK would not have been necessary. Economically, Iran was a capitalist society, but its capitalists had no political power and lived in such uncertainty that they were more interested in securing their financial future by sending capital abroad than in making productive investments at home. And so far as the nature of Iran's alliance with the United States was concerned, the shah so distrusted the United States that he kept his terminal cancer a secret from his American friends for fear it might result in Washington's being tempted to replace him immediately. Indeed, the shah died firmly believing that the CIA had been behind the revolution that overthrew him.

Despite the oil income that produced substantial economic growth and integrated Iran into the international market system, the internal politics of Iran remained autocratic and feudal. The shah exercised the kind of power that was total, undivided, monopolistic, and unaccountable. During the last fifteen years of his rule he was almost deified in the daily state propaganda.

It is understandable—if not admirable—that partisan policy makers chose to ignore the feudal politics of Iran in pursuit of various short-term political, military, or economic objectives. But it is inexcusable that the American press should defer to the shortsighted position of official Washington for more than a quarter of a century in a matter of such crucial importance as relations between Iran and the United States. Not even the prestige press during this period elected to pursue sustained investigative journalism on such questions as the rationale behind massive arms sales to Iran; the regime's claims to serving the interests of the Iranian people; the nature of the shah's relationship with his civilian and military elites; the consequences of massive spending on inappropriate technology for the welfare of the society; the internal cohesion (or lack of it) of the Pahlavi regime; and finally, the potential significance of the opposition forces during periodic socioeconomic disruption.

These questions, if seriously pursued, would have produced a portrayal of Iran quite different from the one presented by Washington and reproduced in the mainstream press. Whether belatedly or not and for whatever reasons, mainstream American journalism demonstrated how such questions could be raised, in its coverage of the Philippines during the tumultuous events of 1985–86. But in the case of Iran, it was no wonder that the sudden collapse of the Pahlavi regime came as a total surprise to Washington and the press.

The press, in spite of its vast resources and self-professed sense of responsibility, had no hint that the centerpiece of U.S. geopolitical strategy in the Third World was so hollow that it would collapse in the face of unarmed and largely peaceful challenge. Yet it was not a failure of "intelligence," as many have charged, that kept either official Washington or the press from seeing things clearly in Iran. There was no lack of evidence about the country, its people, or the sources of its discontents. American journalism was certainly capable of transforming the available evidence into insights and undistorted knowledge about Iranian society.

Instead, it was assumed, consciously or otherwise, that Iranians as a people were not capable of rebellion against their rulers; that Iran was the shah, and thus all that mattered in the relations between the United States and Iran was his satisfaction. Logic of this sort, encouraged by foreign policy elites and academic orientalists, led journalists to turn away from the obvious and instead look for outside causes and religious and secular conspiracies to explain the events of the 1978 revolution.

In February of 1979 the Iranian people, for the first time in their modern history, gained control of their own society. It is also the case that the Iranian people then failed to live up to the revolutionary promise of creating a political order based on consensus. Even worse, an enormously popular revolution fell into the familiar historical pattern of devouring its own children and continuing tyranny in a new and intensified form.* It is vitally important, however, that

---

*The question of how a particular faction of the Shi'ite clergy came to establish its hegemonic power in Iran following the revolution is outside the scope of this project. However, given our assumptions about politics in Iran, we should say that implicit in our analysis is the suggestion that the final

these tragic developments not obscure the need for a clearheaded analysis of Iran under the shah and the events that arguably led up to the creation of the so-called Islamic Republic.

In conclusion, our argument is that the press has an important responsibility to bear if the legitimate interests of the United States are to be pursued in future Irans, and future Irans there are certain to be. The foreign policy bureaucracy, as it is now constituted, seems remarkably incapable of the type of understanding demanded by changing conditions in the Third World. It has a clear history of ignoring realities that threaten established policy. This results from a structural resistance to disturbing information and a tendency to suppress such information. American entanglements abroad since World War II should have shown us that this tactic of avoidance merely delays the inevitable confrontation with reality, all the while alienating the people of the country in crisis.

At least in theory, the press has no such structural handicap. Free of *policy restraints,* the press—if it acts independently—is in a much better position to understand political conflict abroad and to transform information into knowledge. The news media have the material and intellectual resources to accomplish this task, but resources alone will not do the job. There must also be a commitment. The press must resist the temptation, for instance, to judge the cultural and political mores of another society; instead, it should concentrate on understanding them. If they are to succeed in this task, journalists must learn to distinguish between prejudice and knowledge. A good place to begin in developing the necessary commitment to authentic understanding and an independent perspective might be the serious consideration by mainstream journalists of the considerable body of scholarship that has been developed by non-status-quo academics, researchers, and journalists.

---

domination of the fundamentalists over the Iranian state and society was neither inevitable nor predictable. We believe various postrevolutionary accounts of events in Iran support this view. Contrary to the view that Iranians somehow seek their own domination, we are convinced that the unprecedented and unexpected appeal of fundamentalism in Iran can only be comprehended as a reaction to the sixty years of pseudodevelopment and dictatorship that preceded it.

Finally, if there is to be any substantive change in the way the press performs in the foreign policy setting, journalists must come to recognize the subtle ways in which ideology in its broadest sense informs what it is they do. Until this recognition is forthcoming, journalists will continue to serve more often as instruments of American foreign policy than as its serious auditors.

Notes

Notes to the Introduction

1. Amos Perlmutter, "Squandering Opportunity in the Gulf," *Wall Street Journal*, 13 October 1983.

2. Martin Walker, *Powers of the Press: Twelve of the World's Influential Newspapers* (London: Pilgrim Press, 1982; paperback ed., New York: Adama Books, 1983), p. 391.

3. See Mansour Farhang, "How the Clergy Gained Power in Iran," in *The Islamic Impulse*, Barbara Stowasser, ed. (Washington, D.C.: Georgetown University Press & Croom Helm, 1987).

4. *Washington Star*, 26 January 1979.

5. Jack Kramer, "If Khomeini Comes to Power in Iran," *Business Week*, 5 February 1979, p. 50.

6. *New York Times*, 17 January 1979.

7. On the composition of the prestige press in the United States and the preeminence of the *New York Times*, see William L. Rivers, *The Opinionmakers* (Boston: Beacon Press, 1967; reprint ed., Beacon, 1970), chap. 2; and Edwin Emery and Michael Emery, *The Press and America: An Interpretive History of the Mass Media*, 5th ed. (Englewood Cliffs, N.J.: Prentice-Hall, 1984), chap. 26; for importance of the *Times* to elite readership, see Carol H. Weiss, "What America's Readers Read," *Public Opinion Quarterly* 38 (1974): 1–22; and Craig H. Grau, "What Publications Are Most Frequently Quoted in *Congressional Record?*" *Journalism Quarterly* 53 (1976): 716–19. On the greater volume of foreign news carried by the *Times*, see Andrew K. Semmel, "Foreign News in Four U.S. Elite Dailies: Some Comparisons," *Journalism Quarterly* 53 (1976): 732–36; and Brantly Womack, "Attention Maps of 10 Major Newspapers," *Journalism Quarterly* 58 (1981): 260–65.

8. In 1958 the Hearst-owned International News Service merged with United Press to form United Press International. Thus references dated before 1958 will refer to United Press (UP) and after 1958 to United Press International (UPI).

9. On the matter of how much information Americans get from television, see, for example, Thomas E. Patterson and Robert D. McClure, *The Unseeing Eye: The Myth of Television Power in National Elections* (New York: G. P. Putnam's Sons, 1976).

10. William C. Adams, ed., *Television Coverage of International Affairs* (Norwood, N.J.: Ablex Publishing Corp., 1982), pp. 3–4.

11. James F. Larson, "International Affairs Coverage on U.S. Network Television," *Journal of Communication* 29 (Spring 1979): 136–47.

12. The best discussion of frame analysis as applied to mass media is by sociologist Gaye Tuchman, *Making News: A Study in the Construction of Reality* (New York: Free Press, 1978). See particularly chap. 9, "News as Constructed Reality." According to Tuchman (p. 3), "News imparts to occurrences their *public character* as it transforms mere happenings into publicly discussable events" (her emphasis). Moreover, she observes (p. 190), "News stories not only lend occurrences their existence as public events, but also impart character to them, for news reports help to shape the public definition of happenings by selectively attributing to them specific details or 'particulars.'" For a more general and theoretical discussion of these matters, see Erving Goffman, *Frame Analysis: An Essay on the Organization of Experience* (Cambridge: Harvard University Press, 1974).

Notes to Chapter One

1. For an examination of how the press covers the Middle East, see Edmund Ghareeb, ed., *Split Vision: The Portrayal of Arabs in the American Media* (Washington: American-Arab Affairs Council, 1983); William C. Adams, ed., *Television Coverage of the Middle East* (Norwood, N.J.: Ablex Publishing Corp., 1981); and Janice Monti Belkaoui, "Images of Arabs and Israelis in the Prestige Press, 1966–1974," *Journalism Quarterly* 57 (Winter 1979). For analysis of stereotypes, see Shelley Slade, "The Image of the Arab in America: Analysis of a Poll on American Attitudes," *Middle East Journal* 35 (Spring 1981); and Michael Suleiman, "National Stereotypes as Weapons in the Arab-Israeli Conflict," *Journal of Palestine Studies* 3 (Spring 1974): 109–21.

2. Bernard C. Cohen, *The Press and Foreign Policy* (Princeton: Princeton University Press, 1963; paperback, 1965).

3. Walter Lippmann, *Public Opinion* (New York: Harcourt, Brace, 1922), quoted in Ronald Steel, *Walter Lippmann and the American Century* (Boston: Little, Brown, 1980), p. 182.

4. Ibid.

5. Ibid.

6. Robert Dallek, *The American Style of Foreign Policy: Cultural Politics and Foreign Affairs* (New York: Alfred A. Knopf, 1982; Mentor, 1983), p. 143.

7. Doris A. Graber, *Processing the News: How People Tame the Information Tide,* Longman Professional Studies in Political Communication and Policy (New York: Longman, 1984), p. 73.

8. James David Barber, *The Pulse of Politics: Electing Presidents in the Media Age* (New York: W. W. Norton, 1980), p. 8.

9. Ibid.

10. Hamilton Jordan, *Crisis: The Last Year of the Carter Presidency* (New York: G. P. Putnam's Sons, 1982), p. 138.

11. Laurence Radway, "The Curse of Free Elections," *Foreign Policy* 40 (Fall 1980): 61–73.

12. Jordan, *Crisis,* p. 364.

13. Ibid., p. 365.

14. Ibid., p. 379.

15. Donald Wilbur, *Riza Shah Pahlavi: The Resurrection and Reconstruction of Iran* (Hicksville, N.Y.: Exposition Press, 1975), p. 175

16. Mohammad Reza Pahlavi, *Answer to History* (Briarcliff Manor, N.Y.: Stein and Day, 1980), p. 13.

17. Ibid., p. 20.

18. Ibid., p. 27.

19. Ibid., p. 20.

20. The authors have seen guest books for the Iranian embassy in Washington and the U.N. ambassador's residence in New York City.

21. The authors wish to thank syndicated columnists Cody Shearer and Maxwell Glen for making a copy of the log available to them.

22. See particularly a two-part column syndicated by Maxwell Glen and Cody Shearer, *Los Angeles Herald-Examiner,* 8 August 1980, and "How Severe Is Corruption in the Press?" *Los Angeles Herald-Examiner,* 9 August 1980. See also Katharine Koch, "The Caviar Caper," *Washington Journalism Review,* October 1980; Claudia Wright, "The Secret of the Shah's Supporters: How Champagne and Caviar Won Kind Words from the Press," *New Statesman,* 9 March 1979, p. 323; R. W. Apple, Jr., New York Times News Service, 18 November 1978; and "Iran: Calm But Not Quiet," *Newsweek,* 27 November 1978, p. 57n. *Newsweek* dealt with the charge that one of its senior editors and chief foreign correspondent, Arnaud de Borchgrave, had received expensive Persian rugs, by discussing it in one of the longest footnotes the authors have ever seen in the newsmagazine. De Borchgrave later left *Newsweek* under less than happy circumstances. In 1985 he became editor of the *Washington Times,* which is owned by the Unification Church

headed by the Reverend Sun Myung Moon. He coauthored an anti-Soviet thriller which had as its theme the successful penetration of the American press by the KGB.

23. Telephone interview by Dorman with Stan Swinton in New York City, 12 October 1980.

24. Maxwell Glen and Cody Shearer, "Top Journalists Took the Shah's Champagne," *Los Angeles Herald-Examiner*, 8 August 1980.

25. Telephone interview by Dorman with Bill Moyers in New York City, 16 October 1980.

26. See William A. Dorman, "Favors Received," *Nation*, 11 October 1980.

27. Glen and Shearer, "Top Journalists Took the Shah's Champagne."

28. Parviz Radji, *In the Service of the Peacock Throne* (London: Hamish Hamilton, 1983), p. 42.

29. Ibid., p. 41.

30. William Sullivan, *Mission to Iran* (New York: W. W. Norton, 1981), pp. 61–79.

31. Mohammad Reza Pahlavi, *Answer to History* (New York: Stein and Day, 1980), p. 146.

32. These categories are those suggested by Gabriel A. Almond, *The American People and Foreign Policy* (New York: Harcourt, Brace, 1950; Frederick A. Praeger, 1960), pp. 139–40.

33. For particularly useful discussions of government use of classification schemes in matters of national security, see David Wise, *The Politics of Lying: Government Deception, Secrecy, and Power* (New York: Random House, Vintage Books, 1973), part 2, and also Thomas M. Franck and Edward Weisband, eds., *Secrecy and Foreign Policy* (New York: Oxford University Press, 1974).

Notes to Chapter Two

1. Nikki R. Keddie, *Roots of Revolution* (New Haven: Yale University Press, 1981), p. 134

2. *New York Times*, 30 April 1951.

3. *New York Times*, 3 June 1951.

4. *New York Times*, 29 November 1951. See also *Times* editorials: 26 September 1952; 3 November 1953.

5. U.S., Department of State, "Steering Group on Preparations for the Talks Between the President and Prime Minister Churchill: Iran," 5 January 1952. Harry S. Truman Library; President's Secretary's Files, p. 2.

6. "A Letter from the Publisher," *Time*, 7 January 1980, p. 3.

7. "Man of the Year," *Time*, 7 January 1952, p. 18.

8. Ibid., p. 20.

9. "Mellow Mossy," *Newsweek*, 12 January 1953, p. 30.

10. Richard W. Cottam, *Nationalism in Iran* (Pittsburgh, Pa.: University of Pittsburgh Press, 1964; reprint, 1979), p. 263.

11. "Man of the Year," *Time*, p. 20.

12. Ibid., p. 21.

13. Keddie, *Roots of Revolution*, p. 133.

14. Ibid.

15. Joe Stork, *Middle East Oil and the Energy Crisis* (New York: Monthly Review Press, 1975), p. 50.

16. *New York Times*, 9 December 1952; see also *Times*, editorial, 17 October 1952.

17. Keddie, *Roots of Revolution*, p. 134. See also, Anthony Sampson, *The Seven Sisters: The Great Oil Companies and the World They Shaped* (New York: Viking Press, 1975; paperback ed. Bantam Books, 1976), p. 144.

18. Stork, *Middle East Oil and the Energy Crisis*, p. 53.

19. Keddie, *Roots of Revolution*, p. 135.

20. Ibid.

21. *New York Times*, 9 December 1952.

22. *New York Times*, 4 September 1952.

23. Ibid.

24. Keddie, *Roots of Revolution*, p. 138.

25. *New York Times*, 9 August 1952. See also editorials, 17 October and 9 December 1952.

26. Ibid.

27. *New York Times*, 4 August 1953.

28. *New York Times*, 17 August 1953.

29. *Washington Post*, 18 August 1953.

30. *Wall Street Journal*, 19 August 1953.

31. Cottam, *Nationalism in Iran*, p. 224.

32. Ibid., p. 223; see also Keddie, *Roots of Revolution*, p. 137; Amin Saikal, *The Rise and Fall of the Shah* (Princeton: Princeton University Press, 1980), p. 44; Barry Rubin, *Paved with Good Intentions: The American Experience and Iran* (New York: Oxford University Press, 1980), pp. 79–83.

33. Cottam, *Nationalism in Iran*, p. 224.

34. Ibid., pp. 216–17.

35. Telephone interview by Dorman with Kennett Love from his home in Long Island, N.Y., 10 July 1984.

36. Ibid.

37. *New York Times*, 22 January 1953; see also 23 January 1953. Clifton Daniel, who wrote these articles, was in Iran for about five weeks in early 1953. His reporting on the Mosaddeq government and on the nationalist movement was fairly evenhanded, and his judgments seemed considered—

with the exception of his treatment of the Tudeh. See, for example, his dispatches, 15–18, 21, 23–25, and 27 January, in which he sums up his impressions of his tour.

38. "World's Eyes on Tehran; Moscow Holds Peace-War Key," *Newsweek*, 9 March 1953, p. 27.

39. Love interview, 10 July 1984.

40. United Press, *Washington Post*, 17 August 1953.

41. United Press, *Christian Science Monitor*, 18 August 1953.

42. United Press, *Washington Post*, 19 August 1953.

43. Associated Press, *Sacramento Bee*, 17 August 1953.

44. The most comprehensive account of the coup has been set forth by the man who ran the operation for the CIA, Kermit Roosevelt, in *Countercoup: The Struggle for the Control of Iran* (New York: McGraw-Hill, 1979). In an unprecedented move in publishing history, the original edition of this book was recalled by the publisher under threat of a libel suit by British Petroleum, which Roosevelt had identified as having suggested the idea of the coup when actually it had been the British Secret Service. A subsequent version of the book was released. For a complete account of the publishing history of the book, see Thomas Powers, "A Book Held Hostage," *Nation*, 12 April 1980, pp. 437–40.

45. Keddie, *Roots of Revolution*, p. 147.

46. For discussion of the agreement, see Saikal, *The Rise and Fall of the Shah*, p. 50; Keddie, *Roots of Revolution*, p. 147; and Sampson, *The Seven Sisters*, p. 157.

47. "Shah Returns in Triumph as Army Kicks Out Mossadegh," *Newsweek*, 31 August 1953, p. 30.

48. "Victory from Exile," *Newsweek*, 31 August 1953, p. 31.

49. Ibid.

50. *New York Times*, 21 August 1953.

51. *Washington Post*, 20 August 1953.

52. *Christian Science Monitor*, 20 August 1953.

53. *New York Times*, 20 August 1953.

54. *New York Times*, 9 August 1953.

55. *New York Times*, 21 August 1953.

56. Ibid. See also, *New York Times*, editorial, 10 November 1953.

57. See *New York Times*, 26 August, 3 and 7 September 1953.

58. *New York Times*, 30 August 1953.

59. See for example, Robert C. Doty, "Now Iran's Big Task Is to Salvage Her Economy," *New York Times*, 30 August 1953, p. E3.

60. Richard and Gladys Harkness, "The Mysterious Doings of the CIA," *Saturday Evening Post*, 30 October, 6 and 12 November 1954.

61. Roosevelt, *Countercoup: The Struggle for the Control of Iran*. Also see Andrew Tully, *C.I.A.: The Inside Story* (New York: William Morrow,

1962; paperback ed. Crest Books, 1963), chap. 7; and David Wise and Thomas B. Ross, *The Invisible Government* (New York: Random House, 1964).

62. Love interview, 10 July 1984.

63. Ibid.

64. Ibid.

65. Kennett Love, "The American Role in the Pahlevi Restoration: On 19 August 1953," unpublished manuscript, p. 1. All excerpts from this paper are quoted with the permission of Kennett Love.

66. "New York Times Covers and Aids 1953 C.I.A. Coup in Iran," *CounterSpy* 4 (September–October 1980); see also Jonathan Kwitny, *Endless Enemies* (New York: Congdon and Weed, 1984). In 1984 Love sued Kwitny and John Kelly, editor of *CounterSpy,* for copyright infringement and libel.

67. Kennett Love, "The American Role in the Pahlevi Restoration: On 19 August 1953," p. 1.

68. Ibid., p. 41.

69. Ibid., p. 1.

70. Love interview, 10 July 1984.

71. Love, "The American Role in the Pahlevi Restoration: On 19 August 1953," pp. 1–2.

72. Love interview, 10 July 1984.

73. Love, "The American Role in the Pahlevi Restoration: On 19 August 1953," p. 2.

74. Ibid., p. 31.

75. Love interview, 10 July 1984.

76. Love, "The American Role in the Pahlevi Restoration: On 19 August 1953," p. 32.

77. Love interview, 10 July 1984.

78. *CounterSpy,* p. 4.

79. Love, "The American Role in the Pahlevi Restoration: On 19 August 1953," p. 3.

80. Ibid., p. 5.

81. Love interview, 10 July 1984.

82. Ibid.

83. Ibid.

84. Ibid.

85. Ibid.

86. Ibid.

87. Telephone interview by Dorman with Prof. Richard Cottam from his home in Pittsburgh, Pa., 18 January 1985.

88. "Allen Dulles of the Silent Service," *New York Times* Sunday Magazine, 29 March 1953.

89. "Allen Dulles and the CIA," *Time,* 3 August 1953.

90. Letter from Kennett Love (K. L.) to Emanuel R. Freedman (E. R. F.), Tehran to New York City, 10 February 1954.

91. Letter from E. R. F. to K. L., NYC to Cairo, 30 June 1954.

92. Ibid.

93. Letter from K. L. to E. R. F., Cyprus to NYC, 26 July 1954.

94. Letter from K. L. to E. R. F., Tehran to NYC, 11 September 1954.

95. Letter from E. R. F. to K. L., NYC to Tehran, 14 September 1954.

96. Letter from K. L. to E. R. F., Tehran to NYC, 20 October 1954.

97. Cable from E. R. F. to K. L., NYC to Tehran, 20 October 1954.

98. Letter from K. L. to E. R. F., Tehran to NYC, 20 October 1954.

99. Letter from K. L. to E. R. F., Tehran to NYC, 1 September 1954.

100. Cottam interview, 18 January 1985.

101. Letter from K. L. to E. R. F., Cyprus to NYC, 26 July 1954.

102. Letter from K. L. to E. R. F., Tehran to NYC, 1 September 1954.

103. Letter from K. L. to E. R. F., Tehran to NYC, 9 September 1954.

104. Letter from K. L. to William A. Dorman, Long Island to Sacramento, 29 July 1986.

105. Letter from K. L. to W. A. D., Long Island to Sacramento, 8 January 1985.

106. Cottam, *Nationalism in Iran*, p. 2.

107. Ibid.

Notes to Chapter Three

1. *Christian Science Monitor*, 5 August 1954.

2. *Washington Post*, 6 August 1954.

3. *New York Times*, 6 February 1954.

4. *New York Times*, 8 August 1954.

5. A. Kessel, "Iran's Fabulous Oil and Some Popular Fables," *Nation*, 11 September 1954, pp. 209–12.

6. For a discussion of the nature of the "Royal Dictatorship," see chap. 7 in Nikki R. Keddie, *Roots of Revolution* (New Haven: Yale University Press, 1981).

7. *New York Times*, 3, 7, and 11 March 1954.

8. *New York Times*, 7 March 1954.

9. Ibid.

10. *New York Times*, 11 March 1954.

11. Letter from Kennett Love (K. L.) to Emanuel R. Freedman (E. R. F.), Tehran to New York City, 10 February 1954.

12. Ibid.

13. Ibid.

14. Letter from K. L. to E. R. F., Cairo to NYC, 8 August 1954.

15. Richard W. Cottam, *Nationalism in Iran* (Pittsburgh, Pa.: University of Pittsburgh Press, 1979), p. 288.

16. *New York Times*, editorial, 15 December 1954.

17. See, for example: "The Bold Shah," *Time*, 18 April 1955, p. 42; "The Soldier's Place," *Newsweek*, 18 April 1955, p. 47; *New York Times*, 28 May 1957; *New York Times*, 6, 12, 15, and 30 May 1961; "Guns and/or Butter," *Newsweek*, 30 July 1962, p. 37; editorials, *New York Times*, 26 July 1962 and 19 July 1962; *New York Times*, 20 July 1962; and *Washington Post*, 19 July 1962.

18. Cottam, *Nationalism in Iran*, p. 288.

19. Keddie, *Roots of Revolution*, p. 144.

20. *New York Times*, 28 July 1954.

21. *Christian Science Monitor*, 18 April 1960; for a discussion of the Iranian people and their feelings toward the monarchy, see Cottam, *Nationalism in Iran*, p. 330.

22. "Atlantic World Report on Iran," *Atlantic*, 1 April 1955, pp. 14–18.

23. Ibid., p. 14.

24. Ibid.

25. Ibid.

26. Keddie, *Roots of Revolution*, p. 148.

27. Sam Pope Brewer, "Iran Is Reported Subversion Free," *New York Times*, 2 December 1956, p. 31.

28. Ibid.

29. Sam Pope Brewer, "Unrest Viewed as Threat in Iran," *New York Times*, 2 January 1978, p. 5.

30. *New York Times*, 28 January 1958.

31. *New York Times*, 25 February 1958.

32. *New York Times*, 27 October 1958.

33. See *New York Times*, 29 October, 5 and 6 November, 1958.

34. Richard Dudman, "The Free World: For Example, Iran," *New Republic*, 25 March 1957, p. 8.

35. "The Shah's Gamble," *Time*, 8 December 1958, p. 25.

36. "The Big Noise," *Time*, 27 April 1959, p. 24.

37. Barry Rubin, *Paved with Good Intentions: The American Experience and Iran* (New York: Oxford University Press, 1980), pp. 91–110, passim.

38. Ibid., p. 97.

39. Ibid., p. 102.

40. Mohammed Reza Shah Pahlavi, *Mission for My Country* (London: Hutchinson, 1961), p. 314.

41. Ibid.

42. See, for instance, Amin Saikal, *The Rise and Fall of the Shah* (Princeton: Princeton University Press, 1980), part 1, chap. 2, pp. 46–79.

43. Ibid., p. 47.
44. Ibid., pp. 47–48.
45. Ibid., pp. 51–54 passim.
46. Michael M. J. Fischer, *Iran: From Religious Dispute to Revolution*, Harvard Studies in Cultural Anthropology, no. 3 (Cambridge: Harvard University Press, 1980), p. 187.
47. Cottam, *Nationalism in Iran*, p. 299. In his memoirs, *Answer to History* (New York: Stein and Day, 1980), pp. 23–24, the shah explains how he was pressured by President Kennedy to appoint Ali Amini as his prime minister. He writes, "I remember so well my first meetings with the Kennedys at the White House: Jacqueline Kennedy spoke of Amini's wonderful flashing eyes and how much she hoped I would name him Prime Minister. Eventually, I gave Amini the job."
48. Saikal, *Rise and Fall of the Shah*, pp. 75–76.
49. See Richard Cottam, *Nationalism in Iran*, p. 296.
50. For a discussion of the shah's version of a two-party system, see Cottam, *Nationalism in Iran*, p. 290; Keddie, *Roots of Revolution*, p. 150; and Saikal, *Rise and Fall of the Shah*, p. 63.
51. *New York Times*, 28 August 1960.
52. "The Shah's Dilemmas," *Newsweek*, 12 September 1960, p. 51.
53. "Reformer in Shako," *Time*, 12 September 1960, p. 31.
54. Ibid.
55. Ibid., p. 37.
56. "Iran's Ex-Strong Man," *New York Times*, 30 August 1960.
57. *New York Times*, 4 September 1960, IV, p. 4.
58. *Christian Science Monitor*, 13 May 1961.
59. *New York Times*, editorial, 10 November 1961.
60. *New York Times*, 9 August 1961.
61. *New York Times*, 22 July 1961.
62. *New York Times*, editorial, 10 April 1962.
63. *Washington Post*, 12 April 1962.
64. *New York Times*, 6 November 1961.
65. *New York Times*, 24 November 1961.
66. Harrison E. Salisbury, "Iran Report: Change Sweeps a Feudal Land," *New York Times*, 4 December 1961, p. 1 and p. 10.
67. Ibid., p. 10.
68. Ibid.
69. *Christian Science Monitor*, 11 October 1962.
70. *Christian Science Monitor*, 29 September 1962.
71. *Christian Science Monitor*, 26 January 1962.
72. *Christian Science Monitor*, 10 September 1962.
73. *Washington Post*, 23 December 1984.

Notes to Chapter Four

1. *New York Times,* 30 August 1962.
2. Barrington Moore, Jr., *Social Origins of Dictatorship and Democracy* (Boston: Beacon Press, 1966), p. 485.
3. Farhad Kazemi, *Poverty and Revolution in Iran: The Migrant Poor, Urban Marginality, and Politics* (New York: New York University Press, 1985). Preface.
4. Ibid., p. 32.
5. Ibid., p. 41.
6. Ibid.
7. Ibid., pp. 41–42.
8. Ibid., p. 44.
9. Ibid., p. 52.
10. Richard W. Cottam, *Nationalism in Iran* (Pittsburgh, Pa.: University of Pittsburgh Press, 1979), p. 297.
11. Ibid., p. 306. See also Nikki R. Keddie, *Roots of Revolution* (New Haven: Yale University Press, 1981), p. 156.
12. *New York Times,* 23 January 1963.
13. Ibid.
14. *New York Times,* editorial, 7 February 1963.
15. *Christian Science Monitor,* 4 March 1963.
16. Ibid.
17. "A Future to Outshine Ancient Glories," *Life,* 31 May 1963, pp. 52–62.
18. Jay Walz, "Iran's Shah Leads a White Revolution," *New York Times,* Sunday Magazine, 27 October 1963, p. 23.
19. *New York Times,* 10 June 1964.
20. Ibid.
21. "Here He Is Again," *Nation,* 8 June 1964, pp. 565–66.
22. Cottam, *Nationalism in Iran,* p. 307.
23. *New York Times,* 28 January 1963.
24. "Legal Revolution," *U.S. News & World Report,* 11 February 1963, p. 16.
25. Cottam, *Nationalism in Iran,* p. 307n.
26. *New York Times,* 15 September 1963.
27. *New York Times,* editorial, 20 September 1963.
28. Keddie, *Roots of Revolution,* p. 4.
29. *Christian Science Monitor,* 26 January 1963.
30. Cottam, *Nationalism in Iran,* pp. 306–7.
31. *Christian Science Monitor,* editorial, 28 May 1963.
32. Cottam, *Nationalism in Iran,* p. 307.

248   NOTES TO PAGES 95–105

33. "Iran: Progress at a Price," *Time*, 14 June 1963, p. 35.

34. *Washington Post*, 6 June 1963.

35. *New York Times*, 6 June 1963.

36. "Iran: Rioting for Islam," *New Republic*, 29 June 1963, p. 10.

37. John Fischer, "The Editor's Easy Chair: The Shah and His Exasperating Subjects," *Harper's Magazine*, April 1965, p. 24. For a similar liberal treatment of the White Revolution, see H. B. Bloomer, "Iran: Remolding a Nation Nearer to the Heart's Desire," *Reporter*, 16 January 1964, pp. 32–36.

38. Ibid., p. 32.

39. *New York Times*, editorial, 10 June 1963.

40. Ibid.

41. Such attention as was paid to Iranian student protests in the United States usually took the form of a "shirt-tail" paragraph or two following a news story. See, for example, *New York Times*, 9 June 1963.

42. "Iran: Progress at a Price," *Time*, 14 June 1963, p. 35.

43. Michael M. J. Fischer, *Iran: From Religious Dispute to Revolution*, Harvard Studies in Cultural Anthropology, no. 3 (Cambridge: Harvard University Press, 1980), p. 188. See also Keddie, *Roots of Revolution*, p. 158. For estimates of casualty figures, see Fischer, p. 124; Cottam, *Nationalism in Iran*, p. 308; Barry Rubin, *Paved with Good Intentions: The American Experience and Iran* (New York: Oxford University Press, 1980), p. 109; and Keddie, p. 158.

44. *Christian Science Monitor*, 15 January 1962.

45. *Christian Science Monitor*, 4 March 1963.

46. "Atlantic Report: Iran," *Atlantic*, 19 May 1954, pp. 14–18.

47. *Los Angeles Times*, 21 December 1975.

48. Keddie, *Roots of Revolution*, p. 149.

49. Eric J. Hooglund, *Land and Revolution in Iran, 1960–1980*, Modern Middle East Series, vol. 7 (Austin: University of Texas Press, 1982), p. 40.

50. Ibid., p. 43.

51. Ibid.

52. Ibid., chap. 7. See also Amin Saikal, *The Rise and Fall of the Shah* (Princeton: Princeton University Press, 1980), p. 85.

53. See Azar Tabari, "Land, Politics, and Capital Accumulation," a review-essay, *MERIP*, March–April 1983, pp. 26–30; Nikki R. Keddie, *Roots of Revolution*, p. 160.

54. Hooglund, *Land and Revolution in Iran*, p. xv.

55. Ibid., p. 53.

56. Ibid., p. 22.

57. *Sacramento Bee*, 28 August 1978.

58. Hooglund, *Land and Revolution in Iran*, p. 88.

59. Ibid., p. 90.

60. Ann T. Schulz, "Iran's New Industrial State," *Current History*, January 1977, p. 18.

61. Hooglund, *Land and Revolution in Iran*, p. 109.
62. Ibid., p. 115.
63. Ibid., pp. 115, 119.
64. Ibid., p. 121.
65. Keddie, *Roots of Revolution*, p. :67.
66. Hooglund, *Land and Revolution in Iran*, p. 148.
67. *Christian Science Monitor*, 6 August 1963.
68. *Christian Science Monitor*, 13 August 1963.
69. *Christian Science Monitor*, 16 March 1964.
70. *Christian Science Monitor*, 26 July 1965.
71. James A. Bill, "Iranian Land Reform Has Nettles," *Christian Science Monitor*, 22 July 1968. This article drew a lengthy Telex of protest from Iran's Washington press counselor, Kambiz Yazdan-Panah, on 7 August 1968, which Bertram B. Johansson, assistant overseas news editor, sent to Professor Bill with a covering letter describing the embassy's response as a "diatribe." According to Bill, Johansson was one of the reasons why the *Monitor*'s coverage was better than average during the 1960s.
72. Telephone interview by Dorman with Prof. James Bill, University of Texas, from his home in Austin, 5 July 1985.
73. *Los Angeles Times*, 23 March 1975.
74. "Iran's Race for Riches," *Newsweek*, 24 March 1975, p. 38.
75. *Wall Street Journal*, 20 November 1975.
76. *New York Times*, 17 July 1970.
77. Keddie, *Roots of Revolution*, p. 163.
78. Ibid., p. 166.
79. Richard Falk, professor of international law, Princeton University, in conversation, Sacramento, Calif., March 1982.
80. Saikal, *Rise and Fall of the Shah*, p. 187.
81. Hooglund, *Land and Revolution in Iran*, p. 135.
82. Saikal, *Rise and Fall of the Shah*, p. 186.
83. *New York Times*, 30 January 1965.
84. Ibid.
85. See Keddie, *Roots of Revolution*, pp. 157–58.
86. Shahrough Akhavi, *Religion and Politics in Contemporary Iran: Clergy State Relations in the Pahlavi Period* (Albany: State University of New York Press, 1980), pp. 93, 97–103 passim. See also Cottam, *Nationalism in Iran*, p. 308, 13n.
87. Ann K. S. Lambton, *The Persian Land Reform: 1962–1966* (London: Clarendon Press Oxford, 1969), p. 112.
88. For actual clergy ownership of lands, see Akhavi, *Religion and Politics in Contemporary Iran*, pp. 95–96.
89. Keddie, *Roots of Revolution*, pp. 289n, 290n.
90. For a discussion of the nature of *vaqf*, see Hooglund, *Land and Revolution in Iran*, pp. 12–13.

91. Ibid., p. 63, 80–81.
92. Lambton, *Persian Land Reform*, p. 240.
93. Fischer, *Iran: From Religious Dispute to Revolution*, pp. 114, 117.
94. Akhavi, *Religion and Politics in Contemporary Iran*, pp. 132, 134, 142.
95. Saikal, *Rise and Fall of the Shah*, p. 188.
96. Rubin, *Paved with Good Intentions*, p. 112.
97. *New York Times*, 25 September 1967.
98. *New York Times*, 17 July 1970.

Notes to Chapter Five

1. "Proud as a Peacock," *Time*, 31 March 1967, p. 28. See also, "Revolution from the Throne," *Time*, 6 October 1967, pp. 32–34.
2. See *Washington Post*, 27 October 1967; "Royal Revolution in Iran," *Reader's Digest*, October 1967, pp. 127–31; *Christian Science Monitor*, 17 October 1967.
3. *New York Times*, 27 October 1967.
4. Ibid. See also *New York Times*, 29 October 1967, IV, p. 4.
5. "Iran: A King Crowns Himself and His Queen," *Newsweek*, 6 November 1967, pp. 44–47.
6. "In Iran—A Crown Well Earned," *Life*, 10 November 1967, pp. 28–29.
7. "Iran's Shah Crowns Himself and His Empress," *National Geographic*, March 1968, pp. 300–21.
8. *New York Times*, 25 October 1971.
9. *New York Times*, 19 October 1971.
10. *New York Times*, 12 October 1971.
11. See Sally Quinn, "Splendor in the Dust," *Washington Post*, 13 October 1971, p. B1.
12. *New York Times*, 15 October 1971.
13. *New York Times*, 13 October 1971; for similar examples, see *New York Times*, 21 June; 27 July; 27 and 29 September; 2, 3, 5, 14, 16, and 21 October—all 1971.
14. *New York Times*, 19 October 1971.
15. *New York Times*, 12 October 1971.
16. "Iran: Model Middle Eastern State," *Holiday*, September 1971, pp. 44–45 +.
17. "Iran's Birthday Party," *Newsweek*, 25 October 1971, pp. 58–59.
18. "Iran: The Show of Shows," *Time*, 25 October 1971, pp. 32–33.
19. "Party at Persepolis," *Life*, 15 October 1971, pp. 34–36; and "The Shah's Princely Party," *Life*, 29 October 1971, pp. 22–30.

20. Nikki R. Keddie, *Roots of Revolution* (New Haven: Yale University Press, 1981), p. 180.

21. *New York Times,* editorial, 12 October 1971.

22. Ibid.

23. *New York Times,* editorial, 24 November 1967.

24. *New York Times,* 18 March 1968.

25. *New York Times,* 28 April 1968.

26. *New York Times,* 9 December 1968.

27. *New York Times,* 3 May 1970.

28. "A Welcome for Capitalists," *Time,* 25 May 1970, p. 94.

29. *New York Times,* 26 November 1970.

30. *Christian Science Monitor,* 15 October 1971.

31. See, for example, ibid.

32. *New York Times,* 11 December 1965.

33. *New York Times,* 11 February 1972.

34. Ibid.

35. Ibid.

36. *New York Times,* 21 September 1972.

37. *New York Times,* editorial, 28 October 1967.

38. *Washington Post,* 6 March 1967.

39. See for example, M. Tehranian, "Politics of Anti-Americanism," *Nation,* 24 October 1966, pp. 415–18. Article deals with how the shah used anti-American propaganda when it suited his purposes for international political reasons.

40. *Christian Science Monitor,* 15 February 1964.

41. *Christian Science Monitor,* 6 March 1972.

42. *Christian Science Monitor,* 2 June 1965.

43. Ibid.

44. *Christian Science Monitor,* 7 June 1965.

45. *Christian Science Monitor,* editorial, 28 October 1967.

46. *Christian Science Monitor,* 1 December 1971.

47. *Christian Science Monitor,* editorial, 2 June 1972.

48. Anthony Sampson, *The Arms Bazaar: From Lebanon to Lockheed* (New York: Viking Press, 1977), p. 252.

49. *New York Times,* 25 July 1971.

50. Ibid.

51. Barry Rubin, *Paved with Good Intentions: The American Experience and Iran* (New York: Oxford University Press, 1980), p. 128. See also Amin Saikal, *The Rise and Fall of the Shah* (Princeton: Princeton University Press, 1980), chap. 2.

52. Ibid., p. 116.

53. Quoted in Fred J. Cook, "The Billion Dollar Mystery: A Documented Thriller Involving American Foreign Aid, the Shah of Iran, A Desert

Chieftain, Swiss Banks, Tapped Wires, Secret Diplomacy and Some Celebrated Americans," *Nation*, 12 April 1965, p. 381.

54. Fred Halliday, *Arabia Without Sultans* (London: Penguin Books, 1975), pp. 364–66; see also Richard Cottam, *Nationalism in Iran* (Pittsburgh, Pa.: University of Pittsburgh Press, 1979), pp. 338–39.

55. Mark A. Bruzonsky, ed., *The Middle East: U.S. Policy, Israel, Oil and the Arabs*, 3d ed. (Washington: Congressional Quarterly, 1977), p. 82.

56. Amin Saikal, *The Rise and Fall of the Shah*, p. 155.

57. Anthony Sampson, *The Arms Bazaar*, p. 252.

58. Ibid., p. 246.

Notes to Chapter Six

1. As quoted in Amin Saikal, *The Rise and Fall of the Shah* (Princeton: Princeton University Press, 1980), p. 128. For a discussion of Iran and price increases during the embargo, see Saikal, chap. 4; Robert Graham, *Iran: The Illusion of Power* (London: Croom Helm, 1978), chap. 5; Robert Sherrill, *The Oil Follies*, (Garden City, N.Y.: Anchor Press, 1983), chap. 4; Joe Stork, *Middle East Oil and the Energy Crisis* (New York: Monthly Review Press, 1975), chap. 9; and Barry Rubin, *Paved with Good Intentions: The American Experience and Iran* (New York: Oxford University Press, 1980), chap. 5.

2. Barry Rubin, *Paved with Good Intentions*, p. 130. See also, Saikal, *Rise and Fall of the Shah*, chap. 2.

3. See Henry Kissinger, *White House Years* (Boston: Little, Brown, 1979), p. 1264.

4. *New York Times*, 22 February 1973.

5. Ibid.

6. *New York Times*, 22 July 1973.

7. *New York Times*, editorial, 24 July 1973.

8. Ibid.

9. *New York Times*, 10 February 1975.

10. *Washington Post*, editorial, 25 January 1975.

11. *Washington Post*, editorial, 13 February 1976.

12. *Washington Post*, editorial, 5 August 1976.

13. *Los Angeles Times*, editorial, 6 August 1976.

14. *Wall Street Journal*, 8 May 1973.

15. *Christian Science Monitor*, 25 January 1974.

16. *New York Times*, 12 May 1974.

17. *New York Times* Sunday Magazine, 26 May 1974, Sec. VI, p. 9.

18. *Christian Science Monitor*, 6 September 1974.

19. *Washington Post*, editorial, 30 December 1974.

20. *New York Times*, 3 June 1974.

21. For an example of coverage of Iran's increasing deficit, see *New York Times*, 9 December 1975, p. 59.

22. As quoted in Barry Rubin, *Paved with Good Intentions*, p. 143.

23. Ibid., p. 144.

24. For a survey of 1978–80 use in the news of academic opinion on Iran, see Patricia J. Higgins, "Anthropologists and Issues of Public Concern: The Iran Crisis," *Human Organization*, Summer 1984, pp. 132–45.

25. Robert Graham, *Iran: The Illusion of Power*, pp. 83–84.

26. Ibid., p. 87.

27. Ibid., p. 86.

28. Ibid., p. 87.

29. Ibid., p. 89.

30. Ibid., p. 9.

31. David Holden, "Shah of Shahs, Shah of Dreams," *New York Times Sunday Magazine*, 26 May 1974, Sec. VI, p. 37.

32. "Iran's Race for Riches," *Newsweek*, 24 March 1975, p. 38.

33. *New York Times*, 5 March 1975.

34. *Los Angeles Times*, editorial, 9 March 1975.

35. *New York Times*, 15 March 1975.

36. *Christian Science Monitor*, 19 May 1975.

37. *Los Angeles Times*, 7 February 1979, part II, p. 1.

38. *New York Times*, 16 March 1975.

39. *New York Times*, 4 January 1975.

40. Jane W. Jacqz, ed., *Iran: Past, Present and Future* (New York: Aspen Institute for Humanistic Studies, 1976), preface.

41. William A. Dorman, "Respectability Conferred: Did the Aspen Institute 'Front' for the Shah?" *Nation*, 20 June 1981, pp. 750–53. Telephone interviews were conducted with Joseph E. Slater, president of Aspen Institute, New York City, December 1980; Charles W. Yost, former U.S. ambassador to the United Nations and Aspen/Iran Program Coordinator, Washington, D.C., October 1980; Moselle Kimbler, assistant to the coordinator, Washington, D.C., October 1980.

42. So listed in various Aspen Institute publications during the 1970s.

43. Jacqz, *Iran: Past, Present and Future*, p. 463n.

44. For some representative examples of how the American press portrayed the Shah's decision to establish the Rastakhiz party, see *Washington Post*, *Los Angeles Times*, and *New York Times*, all 3 March 1975.

45. C. L. Sulzberger, "The Consequences of Growth," *New York Times*, 16 March 1975.

46. Ibid.

47. *New York Times*, 13 May 1975.

48. *Washington Post*, 24 June 1975.

49. *New York Times*, 13 May 1975.

50. *New York Times*, 11 June 1975.

51. *New York Times*, 9 December 1975.

52. *Washington Post*, 11 August 1975.

53. For examples of news treatment of increasing violence in Iran in 1976–77, see *New York Times*, 17, 21, and 23 May 1976; *Christian Science Monitor*, 18 May, 30 August 1976; *Washington Post*, 11 and 12 May 1977.

54. *New York Times*, 4 July 1973.

55. *New York Times*, 3 February 1974.

56. *New York Times*, 30 September 1974.

57. *Amnesty International Annual Reports: 1974–75* (London: Amnesty International Publications, 1975), p. 8. According to Amnesty's secretary general, Martin Ennals, "The Shah of Iran retains his benevolent image despite the highest rate of death penalties in the world, no valid system of civilian courts, and a history of torture which is beyond belief." See also *New York Times*, 29 February 1976, 29 November 1976, and 24 June 1977; and *Washington Post*, 29 May 1976. For a discussion of the Pahlavi regime's repression of lawyers, writers, and other professionals, see Michael M. J. Fischer, *Iran: From Religious Dispute to Revolution*, Harvard Studies in Cultural Anthropology, no. 3 (Cambridge: Harvard University Press, 1980), p. 192; and Shahrough Akhavi, *Religion and Politics in Contemporary Iran: Clergy State Relations in the Pahlavi Period* (Albany: State University of New York Press, 1980), pp. 159–60.

58. *New York Times*, 30 May 1976.

59. *Washington Post* and *New York Times*, 29 May 1976.

60. See Reza Bahareni, "Torture in Iran," *New York Times*, 21 April 1976. For reviews of Bahareni's book, *The Crowned Cannibals* (New York: Random House, Vintage Books, 1977), see *New York Times*, 17 and 20 June 1977; and *Washington Post*, 4 September 1977. The *Post* review is by Richard T. Sale, whose series for the *Post* on Iran is discussed in this chapter. He was highly critical of Bahareni's book.

61. See *New York Times*, 29 May 1976, p. 2; and *Washington Post*, 9 June 1976, p. A23.

62. See *New York Times*, 9 September 1976, p. 89.

63. See *Washington Post*, 8 November 1976, p. A23; *New York Times*, 10 November 1976, p. 9; and 17 December 1976, p. 1.

64. *New York Times*, 2 January 1977; see also, *New York Times*, 15 May 1977, p. 1; and *Washington Post*, 14 May 1977, p. 1.

65. *Christian Science Monitor*, 3 March 1977.

66. *New York Times*, 4 March 1975.

67. *New York Times*, 2 August 1975.

68. John B. Oakes, *New York Times*, 30 September 1975.

69. See *Los Angeles Times*, 20 January 1975. This was the only mention of the London *Times* article that we found in our sample.

70. See Jack Anderson and Les Whitten columns in *Washington Post,* 29 May 1976, p. B11; 26 October 1976, p. B15; 29 October 1976, p. D15; and 4 November 1976, p. DC 11.

71. *Washington Post,* 9 May 1977, p. 1; and 10 May 1977, p. 1.

72. "60 Minutes," March 2, 1980.

73. *Washington Post,* 24 June 1975.

74. *New York Times,* editorial, 17 November 1977.

75. Lewis Simons, "Shah of Iran Keeps Iron Hand on Nation," *Washington Post* news service, published in *Los Angeles Times,* 2 June 1974, Part I, p. 8.

76. Samuel P. Huntington, "Revolution and Political Order," in *Revolutions: Theoretical, Comparative, and Historical Studies,* Jack A. Goldstone, ed. (New York: Harcourt Brace Jovanovich, 1986), pp. 39–40.

77. Richard T. Sale, *Washington Post,* 8 through 13 May 1977.

78. Frances FitzGerald, "Giving the Shah Anything He Wants," *Harper's,* November 1974, pp. 249–55. See also a reply from M. Falsafi and rejoinder by the author, *Harper's,* January 1975, pp. 250–99.

Notes to Chapter Seven

1. For a U.S. policy maker's view, from inside the Carter administration, of this intelligence failure, see Gary Sick, *All Fall Down: America's Tragic Encounter with Iran* (New York: Random House, 1985), chap. 5.

2. *Washington Post,* editorial, 12 September 1978.

3. "The Press Plays Catch-Up in Iran," *Time,* 29 January 1979, p. 74.

4. Michael M. J. Fischer, *Iran: From Religious Dispute to Revolution,* Harvard Studies in Cultural Anthropology, no. 3 (Cambridge: Harvard University Press, 1980), p. 190.

5. *Sacramento Bee,* 27 November 1978.

6. Telephone interview by Dorman with Prof. Thomas M. Ricks, Georgetown University, member of editorial group, RIPEH [The Review of Iranian Political Economy and History], March 1982.

7. Eric Rouleau, "Khomeini's Iran," *Foreign Affairs* 59 (Fall 1980): 1.

8. *Sacramento Bee,* 9 October 1978.

9. *Sacramento Union,* 27 November 1978.

10. Nikki R. Keddie, *Roots of Revolution* (New Haven: Yale University Press, 1981), p. 177.

11. *Seattle Post-Intelligencer,* 14 August 1978.

12. *Sacramento Bee,* 4 September 1978.

13. *Le Monde,* 6 May 1978.

14. "Trouble in Moslem World: The Hard-Liners," *U.S. News & World Report,* 26 June 1978, p. 35.

15. *Wall Street Journal,* 15 August 1978.

16. "The Shah vs. the Shi'ites," *Time*, 5 June 1978, p. 39.

17. Elaine Sciolino, "I Cry For Them," *Newsweek*, 6 November 1978, p. 80.

18. *New York Times*, 1 February 1979.

19. *Los Angeles Times*, 26 January 1979.

20. *Sacramento Union*, 12 February 1979.

21. Frances FitzGerald, "The Shah Discovers His People," *New Times* 11 (11 December 1978): 9.

22. "The Shah vs. the Shi'ites," *Time*, 5 June 1978, p. 39.

23. For a discussion of the titles adopted by the "Pahlavi dynasty," see William H. Forbis, *Fall of the Peacock Throne* (New York: Harper & Row, 1980), p. 44.

24. *Washington Post*, editorial, 8 November 1978.

25. Meg Greenfield, "Islam and Us," *Newsweek*, 26 March 1979, p. 116.

26. *Sacramento Bee*, 11 September 1978.

27. *Sacramento Bee*, 6 September 1978.

28. "Iran at the Brink," *Newsweek*, 18 December 1978, p. 40.

29. Ibid.

30. "Hard Choices in Tehran," *Time*, 25 December 1978, p. 32.

31. "The Weekend of Crisis," *Time*, 18 December 1978, p. 32.

32. For an extended analysis of the meaning of the martyrdom of Husayn and of Muharram, see Fischer, *Iran: From Religious Dispute to Revolution*, 5.

33. *Washington Post*, 20 January 1978.

34. See also *Washington Post*, 11 January 1978; 7 April 1978.

35. See, for example, *Washington Post*, 4 March 1978.

36. *Washington Post*, 2 April 1978.

37. *Washington Post*, 26 May 1978; see also, 5 March 1978.

38. *Washington Post*, 6 November 1978.

39. *New York Times*, 4 December 1979.

40. "The Shah's Divided Land," *Time*, 18 September 1978, p. 32.

41. For a discussion of Shariati, see Keddie, *Roots of Revolution*, pp. 215–25.

42. Edward W. Said, *Covering Islam: How the Media and the Experts Determine How We See the Rest of the World* (New York: Pantheon Books, 1981), pp. 7–8.

43. "The Darker Forces of Islam," *Washington Post*, 5 January 1979. An interesting counterpoint to the news media's general approach to Islam as a political force was published in *Newsweek* on 1 January 1979 in the form of a two-page look at Catholicism as a source of opposition to Communism in Eastern Europe. In "The Church Defiant," Paul Martin sketched a largely sympathetic view of religious sources of discontent behind the Iron Curtain, as his lead testified:

When news reached the Polish village of Opole Stare that a countryman had been elected Pope, the simple folk responded with an eloquent gesture: they built a church. Overnight, two steeples rose over the rusted tin roof of a brick-and-weatherboard cottage. Thousands of Roman Catholics crowded the streets to dedicate the humble—and illegal—Church of the Blessed Maximilian.

44. Stephen S. Rosenfeld, "Breaking the Link With Modernity," *Washington Post,* 5 January 1979.

45. Ibid.

46. See Keddie, *Roots of Revolution,* pp. 157–58.

47. For a discussion of conservative clergy and their attitudes and actions toward women, see Azar Tabari, "The Role of the Clergy in Modern Iranian Politics," in Nikki R. Keddie, ed., *Religion and Politics in Iran* (New Haven: Yale University Press, 1983); and Keddie, *Roots of Revolution,* pp. 179–80 and 240–41.

48. For a discussion of women and women's issues in the revolution, see Farah Azari, ed., *Women of Iran: The Conflict with Fundamentalist Islam* (London: Ithaca Press, 1983), and Azar Tabari and Nahid Yeganeh, eds., *In the Shahdow of Islam: The Women's Movement in Iran* (London: Zed Press, 1982).

49. Keddie, *Roots of Revolution,* pp. 179–80.

50. Oriana Fallaci, "Shah of Iran: Visions, Wives, Oil 'Curse'," *Los Angeles Times,* 30 December 1973, Part VI, p. 1.

51. Walter Lippman and Charles Merz, "A Test of the News," *New Republic,* 4 August 1920, p. 3.

52. Louis Harris, "Americans Favor Military Government in Iran," ABC News–Harris Survey, 30 January 1979.

Notes to Chapter Eight

1. Bernard C. Cohen, *The Press and Foreign Policy* (Princeton: Princeton University Press, 1963; Princeton paperback ed., 1965), pp. 124–27.

2. Ibid., p. 125.

3. Ibid.

4. Ibid., p. 127.

5. Peter M. Sandman, David M. Rubin, and David B. Sachsman, *Media: An Introductory Analysis of American Mass Communications* (Englewood Cliffs, N.J.: Prentice-Hall, 1972), p. 404. Most journalism texts do not mention foreign news at all, and this particular text was among the most thoughtful available at the time.

6. Ibid.

7. Ibid., pp. 404–5.

8. For a widely praised criticism of television in this vein, see Fred W. Friendly, *Due to Circumstances Beyond Our Control* (New York: Random House, 1967), particularly chap. 10.

9. See, for example, Theodore Edward Kruglak, *The Foreign Correspondents: A Study of the Men and Women Reporting for the American Information Media in Western Europe* (Geneva: Librairie E. Droz, 1955; Greenwood Press, 1974), pp. 116–21.

10. See, particularly, Lee Brown, *The Reluctant Reformation: On Criticizing the Press in America* (New York: David McKay, 1974), chap. 2.

11. James Reston, *The Artillery of the Press: Its Influence on American Foreign Policy* [published for the Council on Foreign Relations] (New York: Harper & Row, 1967), p. 5.

12. Lawrence W. Lichty, "Video versus Print," *Wilson Quarterly,* Special Issue, 1982, p. 55.

13. Ibid.

14. Mort Rosenblum, *Coups and Earthquakes: Reporting the World for America* (New York: Harper & Row, 1979), p. 8.

15. Leo Bogart, "Newspapers in Transition," *Wilson Quarterly,* Special Issue, 1982, p. 64.

16. Leo Bogart, "The Great Reader Interest in International News," *The Bulletin* [of the American Society of Newspaper Editors], October 1983, p. 15.

17. Mort Rosenblum, *Coups and Earthquakes,* p. 9.

18. Theodore Edward Kruglak, *Foreign Correspondents,* p. 72.

19. Ibid., chap. 1.

20. Marna Perry, "Foreign Correspondents Are Staging a Comeback," *presstime* [published by American Newspaper Publishers Association], April 1980, p. 18.

21. Mort Rosenblum, *Coups and Earthquakes,* pp. 29–31.

22. Ibid., pp. 29–30.

23. Ibid. An even more recent study by Jim Dunlop, "In America's Interest: Some U.S. Media are Expanding Their Foreign Coverage," *Topic* [published by the World Press Institute], June 1983, pp. 10–13, shows the totals holding relatively steady, with the major gain registered by the *Post,* which had added four foreign correspondents to its roster.

24. Gary M. Hook, "How It's Done," *APME News* [publication of the Associated Press], March 1983, p. 4.

25. Mort Rosenblum, *Coups and Earthquakes,* p. 29.

26. Ibid.

27. Ibid., p. 31.

28. Stephen Hess, "The Golden Triangle: Press Relations at the White House, State Department and Department of Defense," paper presented at War, Peace and News Media Conference, New York University, 19 March 1983.

29. Mort Rosenblum, *Coups and Earthquakes,* p. 9.

30. Ibid., p. 167.

31. Marna Perry, "Foreign Correspondents Are Staging a Comeback," p. 18.

32. Ibid.

33. Timothy Crouse, *The Boys on the Bus* (New York: Random House, 1973).

34. *Washington Post,* 12 November 1975.

35. Thomas Griffith, "Playing Catch-Up in Iran," *Time,* 29 January 1979, p. 74.

36. Todd Gitlin, *The Whole World Is Watching* (Berkeley and Los Angeles: University of California Press, 1980), p. 98.

37. Ze'ev Chafets, *Double Vision: How the Press Distorts America's View of the Middle East* (New York: William Morrow, 1985), p. 36.

38. Edward Said, *Covering Islam: How the Media and the Experts Determine How We See the Rest of the World* (New York: Pantheon Books, 1981), pp. 101–2. Said's book deals with how the press covers Islam in general and the Iranian hostage crisis in particular. The book had its genesis in two earlier Said articles: "Iran and the Press: Whose Holy War?" *Columbia Journalism Review,* March–April 1980, pp. 23–33; and "Hiding Islam: Why the American Press Misses the Story in Iran," *Harper's,* January 1981, pp. 25–32.

39. Ibid., p. 102.

40. Flora Lewis, "A Day in the Life," *Esquire,* May 1980, p. 87.

41. Ibid., p. 88.

42. Ibid.

43. Ben H. Bagdikian, *The Media Monopoly* (Boston: Beacon Press, 1983), p. 4.

44. Ibid., p. 5.

45. Ibid., p. 37.

Notes to Chapter Nine

1. John Tebbel, *The Media in America* (New York: Thomas Y. Crowell, 1974), p. viii.

2. L. John Martin and Anju Grover Chaudhary, "Goals and Roles of Media Systems," in Martin and Chaudhary, eds., *Comparative Mass Media Systems,* Longman Series in Public Communication (New York: Longman, 1983), p. 8. For further discussion of differences in assumptions about press systems, see John C. Merrill, "The Global Perspective," in J. C. Merrill, ed., *Global Journalism,* Longman Series in Public Communication (New York: Longman, 1983, Part I.

3. Martin and Chaudhary, "Goals and Roles of Media Systems," p. 8.

4. Ibid., p. 46.

5. Ibid., p. 50.

6. Ibid., p. 8.

7. For a study of how correspondents view the question of ideology, see Frederick T. C. Yu and John Lutter, "The Foreign Correspondent and His Work," *Columbia Journalism Review* 3 (Spring 1964), p. 10.

8. "How Safe a Bet Is Iran?" *Newsweek*, 21 May 1973, p. 41.

9. Gaye Tuchman, *Making News: A Study in the Construction of Reality* (New York: Free Press, 1978), p. 179. For an excellent discussion of these matters, see also Tuchman, chap. 8, and Michael Gurevitch, Tony Bennett, James Curran, and Janet Woollacott, eds., *Culture, Society, and the Media* (London: Methuen, 1982), particularly Stuart Hall, "The Rediscovery of 'Ideology': Return of the Repressed in Media Studies," pp. 56–90.

10. How the two are sometimes confused can be seen in the conclusion reached by Stephen Hess in his study "The Golden Triangle: Press Relations at the White House, State Department and Department of Defense," paper presented at War, Peace and News Media Conference, New York University, 19 March 1983, p. 5. According to Hess:

> Despite surveys that show mainstream reporters do not agree with the policy thrust of Ronald Reagan (or other conservative presidents), my year of press-room eavesdropping (more important than any interviewing) convinced me that *ideology* is not an overt factor in serious reporting. Indeed, little of what reporters say to each other, day after day, has anything to do with policy, unlike, for example, the "small talk" in faculty common rooms (emphasis ours).

11. For a provocative analysis of the press and Watergate which challenges the conventional wisdom, see Edward J. Epstein, *Between Fact and Fiction* (New York: Random House, Vintage Books, 1975), pp. 19–32.

12. "60 Minutes" on CBS, 2 March 1980.

13. James Reston, *The Artillery of the Press: Its Influence on American Foreign Policy* [published for the Council on Foreign Relations] (New York: Harper & Row, 1967), pp. vii–viii.

14. Gay Talese, *The Kingdom and the Power* (New York: World, 1969; Bantam Books, 1970), p. 5.

15. Carey McWilliams, *The Education of Carey McWilliams* (New York: Simon and Schuster, 1979), p. 229.

16. The *Columbia Journalism Review* is an excellent source for varied case studies and critiques of how the press covers the Third World. See also, William A. Dorman, "Peripheral Vision: U.S. Journalism and the Third World," *World Policy*, Summer 1986.

17. Ben Bagdikian, *The Media Monopoly* (Boston: Beacon Press, 1983), p. ix.

18. James N. Miller, "Lies" [letter to the editor], *Columbia Journalism Review*, May–June 1985, p. 72.

19. Tuchman, *Making News*, p. 178.

20. For an analysis of the social backgrounds and conditioning of foreign correspondents, see the excellent study by John Crothers Pollock, *The Politics of Crisis Reporting: Learning to Be a Foreign Correspondent* (New York: Praeger, 1981).

21. "Can the Press Tell the Truth?" *Harper's*, January 1985, pp. 48–50.

22. Ibid.

23. For a treatment of the political right's assault on the news media, see Walter Schneir and Miriam Schneir, "Beyond Westmoreland: The Right's Attack on the Press," *Nation*, 30 March 1985, pp. 361–67.

24. See Stanley Rothman and S. Robert Lichter, "Media and Business Elites: Two Classes in Conflict," *Public Interest*, Fall 1982, pp. 117–25; and Linda Lichter, S. Robert Lichter, and Stanley Rothman, "The Once and Future Journalists," *Washington Journalism Review*, December 1982, pp. 26–27. See also S. Robert Lichter, "America and the Third World: A Survey of Leading Media and Business Leaders," in William C. Adams, ed., *Television Coverage of International Affairs* (Norwood, N.J.: Ablex Publishing Corp., 1982.) pp. 67–78. For a critique of the methodology and conclusions reached by Rothman et al., see Herbert J. Gans, "Are U.S. Journalists Dangerously Liberal?" *Columbia Journalism Review*, November–December 1985, pp. 29–33.

25. "Comment," *Columbia Journalism Review*, May–June 1983, p. 23. For a more approving assessment of the same studies, see Charles B. Seib [former ombudsman for the *Washington Post*,], "Meet the Media Elite," *presstime*, March 1982, pp. 26–27.

26. Hodding Carter III, *Wall Street Journal*, 16 August 1984.

27. For example, see John W. C. Johnstone, Edward J. Slawski, and William W. Bowman, *The News People: A Sociological Portrait of American Journalists and Their Work* (Urbana: University of Illinois Press, 1976), p. 93; Stephen Hess, *The Washington Reporters* (Washington, D.C.: The Brookings Institution, 1981), pp. 87–88; and Leo C. Rosten, *The Washington Correspondents* (New York: Harcourt Brace, 1937; reprint ed., Arno Press, 1974). For a description of how State Department and Pentagon reporters go about their tasks, see Stephen Hess, *The Government/Press Connection: Press Officers and Their Offices* (Washington, D.C.: The Brookings Institution, 1984).

28. Benjamin C. Bradlee, *Conversations With Kennedy* (New York: W. W. Norton, 1975; reprint ed., Pocket Books, 1976).

29. Ronald Steel, *Walter Lippmann and the American Century* (Boston: Little, Brown, 1980).

30. Ibid., pp. 486–87.

31. Ibid., p. 488.

32. Ibid., p. 589.

33. Todd Gitlin, *The Whole World Is Watching: Mass Media in the Mak-*

ing and Unmaking of the New Left (Berkeley and Los Angeles: University of California Press, 1980), p. 271.

34. For development of this theme, see W. A. Dorman, "Seeing Russia Through Red Tinted Glasses," *Bulletin of the Atomic Scientists,* February 1985, pp. 18–22.

35. James Aronson, in his *The Press and the Cold War* (Indianapolis: Bobbs-Merrill, 1970), makes a persuasive argument that the beginning of the cold war for the press should date to 1917, not 1946.

36. Robert Karl Manoff, "Covering the Bomb: The Nuclear Story and the News," *Working Papers,* Summer 1983, pp. 19–27. This is a reworked version of a paper he delivered at the War, Peace and News Media Conference at New York University, 19 March 1983.

37. For further consideration of the press and the national security state, see W. A. Dorman, "Media: Playing the Government's Game," *Bulletin of the Atomic Scientists,* 40th Anniversary Issue, August 1985, pp. 118–24.

38. Seymour M. Hersh, "The Price of Power: Kissinger, Nixon and Chile," *Atlantic Monthly,* December 1982, p. 35.

39. See for example "International Information: A New Order?" [special section] *Journal of Communication* 29 (Spring 1979); Anthony Smith, *The Geopolitics of Information: How Western Culture Dominates the World* (London: Faber & Faber, 1980), chap. 3; and Jeremy Tunstall, *The Media Are American: Anglo-American Media in the World* (London: Constable, 1977).

40. Carlos Fuentes, "Latin America: 'Let Us Work It Out Ourselves'," *Los Angeles Times,* 19 June 1983, Part IV, p. 2.

41. William C. Adams, ed., *Television Coverage of International Affairs* (Norwood, N.J.: Ablex Publishing Corp., 1982), p. 31.

42. Ibid., p. 32.

43. For a social profile of journalists which includes consideration of their religious orientation, see Stanly Rothman and S. Robert Lichter, "Media and Business Elites: Two Classes in Conflict?" *Public Interest,* Fall 1982, p. 121. The most comprehensive study of the social profile of American journalists is contained in John W. C. Johnstone, Edward J. Slawski, and William W. Bowman, *The New People: A Sociological Portrait of American Journalists and Their Work* (Urbana: University of Illinois Press, 1976), see especially chaps. 2 and 3.

44. David Halberstam, "The Press in Vietnam and El Salvador," *Wall Street Journal,* 23 February 1982.

45. "Central America: The First Casualty," *Newsweek,* 6 June 1983, cover. This observation was made to the authors by Kazem Attaram.

46. See William A. Dorman and Mansour Farhang, "The U.S. Press and Lebanon," *SAIS Review* 3 (Winter–Spring 1983): 65–81.

47. For a discussion of the relationship of dissenting elites to press cov-

erage and coverage of Vietnam in general, see Daniel C. Hallin, *The "Uncensored War": The Media and Vietnam* (New York: Oxford University Press, 1986). This is the most persuasive argument we have seen against the case that the media were opposed to the Vietnam War.

Notes to the Conclusion

1. Gary Sick, *All Fall Down: America's Tragic Encounter with Iran* (New York: Random House, 1985).

Index

226; and agriculture, 85–86; and feudal politics, 87–88; and oil, 87; and
political instability, 88, 148–50, 164,
167; resistance to, 3, 4, 5, 85, 89,
93, 111, 142, 148, 159, 176, 179;
and Shi'ite movement, 172, 175, 176;
and sociopolitical order, 84–85, 94,
149; and Westernization, 71, 111,
114, 142, 172. *See also* Press, U.S.:
coverage of shah's modernization programs; Pahlavi, Mohammad Reza
Shah: reforms of; White Revolution
Moon, Reverend Sun Myung, 240n22
Moore, Barrington, Jr., 84
Morris, Joe Alex, 169
Mosaddeq, Mohammad, 31–62, 67, 71,
74; and nationalism, 64, 72, 94; overthrow of, 30, 41–57, 60, 62, 63, 64–
65, 123, 162, 209; plebiscite of, 68,
92; and U.S. press, 31–62, 66, 67,
69, 78, 92, 124–25, 175–76, 241n37
Mossad, 70
Movement for the Liberation of Iran,
171
Moyers, Bill, 25
Mussolini, Benito, 42

Nasser, 77
Nategh, Homa, 177
Nation, 65, 91, 124, 158, 210
National Front Movement, 31–33, 43,
94–95, 107, 123, 154
National Geographic, 117
Nationalism, 31–35, 37, 43, 49, 64, 72,
164
New Iran Party, 124
New Republic, 73, 96
Newsweek, 7, 45, 108, 138, 165, 167,
239n22; and Central America, 227;
first interview with Khomaini in, 160;
on Mosaddeq, 37, 47–48; readership
of, 190; and revolution of 1978, 166,
167; on shah, 76, 117, 119, 204
New York Review of Books, 26
New York Times, 7, 50–62, 66–69; and
arms deals, 133, 134; bureau in Tehran, 154; columnists of, 123, 187;
editorial welcome to shah (1954), 69;
foreign correspondents of, 44, 46,
191, 192, 193, 195, 196, 197, 207;
on human rights abuses, 123, 145,
147; and invasion of Cuba, 210; on

Iran, 71–72, 77, 78–80, 81, 108,
114, 143; on Khomaini, 6, 160; on
Mosaddeq, 35, 40, 41–42, 48–49,
65, 66, 67; and 1978 revolution, 163,
166, 169, 170, 172; on SAVAK, 144;
on shah, 48, 66, 67, 70, 76, 82, 89–
90, 93, 97, 110, 117, 118, 119–20,
122–23, 137; on Tudeh party, 45; and
U.S. change of policy, 127; and U.S.-
Iran trade agreement, 139
Ngo Dinh Diem, 225
Nicaragua, 99–100, 156, 210, 211, 225
Nixon, Richard, 71, 125, 128, 133,
135, 208, 220
Nixon Doctrine, 125, 126–30, 132
North Atlantic Treaty Organization
(NATO), 74, 75, 198

Oakes, John B., 145
Oil: access to, 36, 38, 39, 47, 64, 126,
129; and arms, 129; boycott of Iranian, 40, 43; companies, consortium
of, 47, 65–66; crisis of 1973, 11,
109, 131, 132, 133, 135, 153, 169;
Iranian control of, 41; nationalization
of, 31–35, 38, 39–40, 41; revenues
from, 39, 73, 86, 108, 109, 114,
137, 166, 169, 232; and U.S. companies, 47, 65
Oman, 128–29
OPEC, 30, 132, 133, 138

Pace, Eric, 114, 142–143, 144
Pahlavi, Mohammad Reza Shah, 1;
compared with Khomaini, 5–6; coronation of, 116, 117; cultural festivals
of, 117–20; as dictator, 43–44, 63–
64, 66, 67, 87, 99, 123, 131, 142–
43, 144, 147, 148, 161, 164, 232;
distrust of U.S., 27, 232; Five-Year
Plan of, 71; and Israel, 129; and military, 231–32; military spending of,
82, 128, 129, 131, 132, 232; *Mission
for My Country*, 142; and Mosaddeq,
32, 34, 42, 46, 47; and national plebiscite, 91–93; and oil crisis, 132; and
one-party system, 141–43; opponents
of, 4–5, 6, 95–96, 98, 99, 124, 232;
overthrow of, 27, 162, 163, 181; and
Pahlavi dyansty, 30, 51, 162; power
of, 70, 87, 152, 154, 162, 232; public relations of, 81, 83, 91, 113, 120,

Designer: Betty Gee
Compositor: Graphic Composition, Inc.
Text: 10 / 12 Times Roman
Display: Goudy Bold
Printer: Maple-Vail Book Mfg. Group
Binder: Maple-Vail Book Mfg. Group